Industrialisation
and Culture
1830–1914

Industrialisation and Culture
1830-1914

edited by
Christopher Harvie, *Lecturer in History*
Graham Martin, *Reader in Literature*
Aaron Scharf, *Professor in Art History*
at the Open University

published by
Macmillan *for*
The Open University Press

First published 1970 by
MACMILLAN AND CO LTD
London and Basingstoke
Associated companies in New York Toronto
Dublin Melbourne Johannesburg and Madras

SBN 333 11702 6 (hard cover)

Printed in Great Britain by
ROBERT MACLEHOSE AND CO LTD
The University Press, Glasgow

Contents

Part Two

10 Contents

P   Literature (contd.)

Introduction

This book was conceived as a collection of readings to be used in association with the correspondence material and radio and television broadcasts of the last eight units of the foundation course in the Humanities at the Open University. The rationale of this 'extended case study' is best given in the brief introduction which Graham Martin, chairman of the working group, drafted:

The purpose of this block of units is to explore selected aspects of the complex and deep-seated changes in British society that resulted from the process known as 'industrialisation'. This process may seem, at first sight, a simple affair, having principally to do with the appearance of the familiar industrial 'landscape', with its factories, mills, coalmines, and associated ports and railways. But there was much more to it than that. Generally, we can say that industrialisation disrupted traditional patterns of social life. It made available a new richness of individual experience in some directions but in others it imposed new constraints, some of them more tyrannical than any that had existed in the past.

Physically, it liberated man by overcoming the barrier of distance, by cheapening commodities, and by diversifying social experiences. Politically, it helped to release him from the encumbrance of prescriptive privilege and traditional inequality. Philosophically, it was accompanied by a change in man's ways of thinking of himself, a change from the idea of man as a child of God to man as a child of nature, no less an object for scientific investigation than other natural phenomena.

But it also produced widespread misery from the living conditions and economic exploitation suffered, especially by its first victims, the labouring poor, or, as they came to be known, the working class. And there were more subtle effects. Contemporary thinkers maintained that it promoted a commercial spirit which damaged the quality of personal and social relationships, encouraged a competitive self-interest, depreciated the life of the feelings and the values of art, and seriously disturbed the balance between man and the world of nature. Yet, paradoxically, by stimulating this debate, it also created a keener awareness and a fuller understanding of the values that it threatened.

It is because industrialisation affected human life in these deeper, less obvious ways that we have entitled the block 'Industrialisation and Culture'. In this context, the term 'culture' means 'the intellectual and artistic activities of a society', and the full nature of historical change can only be understood by giving them adequate attention.

The first two units examine the 'industrialising' of an activity — transport in this case — and its implications in social and personal terms. The third unit discusses the debate between the proponents and critics of industrial change. The fourth unit is devoted to some philosophical consequences of the application of the methods of the natural sciences to the study of man and his mind. The fifth and sixth deal with industry and art: the implications for the artist of new techniques and materials, the relationship of the arts and public taste, and the role of the artist as a critic of society. The last two units concentrate on D. H. Lawrence's novel 'The Rainbow', in its reflection of some social changes brought about by industrialisation, and of Lawrence's critical view of these changes.

In its layout 'Industrialisation and Culture' corresponds roughly to the progression, history—social criticism and philosophy—art—literature. The editors divided their labour appropriately: Christopher Harvie dealt with the first two sections, Aaron Scharf with the third, and Graham Martin with the fourth, although there was a great deal of cross-discipline collaboration in each.

Three factors have, broadly speaking, governed the choice of extracts: possible use within the structure of the correspondence units, as material for exercises and assignments; value as illustrations of aspects of the age; and, especially in the first section, the desire to indicate something of the variety of types of source material available to the historian.

Techniques of presenting the extracts have varied. Where the range of subjects covered is considerable, as in the first section, separate and extended introductions have been written to each extract. Where the documents relate more closely to one another in subject-matter, the introductions to specific extracts have been abbreviated and lengthier introductions to groups of extracts substituted. Extracts are given a letter and number identification which relates to their position in each section – e.g. D2 refers to the 'Dictionary of National Biography' article on Sir William Fairbairn, the second extract in the 'Enterprise' section – which should provide a simple system of reference. Suggestions for further reading have been given where appropriate.

Finally the editors would like to thank all the members of the foundation course team of the Arts Faculty for their help and encouragement in this project. Particular thanks must go to Godfrey Vesey, who selected the extracts for the philosophy section, to Arthur Marwick for much helpful advice about the arrangement of the first section, and to the Dean, John Ferguson, for his enthusiasm and understanding. Not to speak, of course, of our secretaries, who turned chaos into order.

Christopher Harvie
Graham Martin
Aaron Scharf

Acknowledgements

Grateful acknowledgement is made to the following sources for material used in this book:

Edward Arnold (Publishers) Ltd for extract from E. M. Forster's 'Howards End'; Balliol ollege, Oxford, for extract from T. H. Green's 'Green Papers'; Mrs Dorothy Cheston Bennett and Methuen & Co. Ltd for extract from 'Clayhanger' by Arnold Bennett; the Bodleian Library, Oxford, for 'Bryce Papers E. 30', Robinson Ellis to James Bryce, 1 July 1860; 'Modern English Biography', reprinted by permission of the publishers, Frank Cass & Co. Ltd, London, 1965; Chatto & Windus Ltd for extract from 'Vision and Design' by Roger Fry, and for extract from 'Art' by Clive Bell; J. M. Dent & Sons Ltd for extract from 'The Heart of Darkness' by Joseph Conrad; the London School of Economics and Political Science for extract from 'My Apprenticeship' by Beatrice Webb; J. P. Mayer for translation from Alexis de Tocqueville, 'Notes on England' (Faber, 1957); Laurence Pollinger Ltd for extract from D. H. Lawrence, 'Twilight in Italy'; the Society of Authors for extract from 'Major Barbara', Act 3, by George Bernard Shaw; the estate of H. G. Wells for extracts from 'The War of the Worlds' and 'Tono Bungay' by H. G. Wells. The publishers have been unable to trace the copyright-holders of some extracts, but will be pleased to make the necessary arrangement at the first opportunity.

Part One

Section A

The Mechanical Age

The Mechanical Age

Thomas Carlyle (1795–1881)

A 1

Were we required to characterise this age of ours by any single epithet, we should be tempted to call it, not an Heroical, Devotional, Philosophical, or Moral Age, but, above all others, the Mechanical Age. It is the Age of Machinery, in every outward and inward sense of that word; the age which, with its whole undivided might, forwards, teaches and practises the great art of adapting means to ends. Nothing is now done directly, or by hand; all is by rule and calculated contrivance. For the simplest operation some helps and accompaniments, some cunning abbreviating process is in readiness. Our old modes of exertion are all discredited, and thrown aside. On every hand, the living artisan is driven from his workshop, to make room for a speedier, inanimate one. The shuttle drops from the fingers of the weaver, and falls into iron fingers that ply it faster. The sailor furls his sail, and lays down his oar; and bids a strong, unwearied servant, on vaporous wings, bear him through the waters. Men have crossed oceans by steam; the Birmingham Fire-king has visited the fabulous East; and the genius of the Cape, were there any Camoens now to sing it, has again been alarmed, and with far stranger thunders than Gama's. There is no end to machinery. Even the horse is stripped of his harness, and finds a fleet fire-horse yoked in his stead. Nay, we have an artist that hatches chickens by steam; the very brood-hen is to be superseded! For all earthly, and for some unearthly purposes, we have machines and mechanic furtherances; for mincing our cabbages; for casting us into magnetic sleep. We remove mountains, and make seas our smooth highway; nothing can resist us. We war with rude Nature; and, by our resistless engines, come off always victorious, and loaded with spoils.

What wonderful accessions have thus been made, and are still making, to the physical power of mankind; how much better fed, clothed, lodged and, in all outward respects, accommodated men now are, or might be, by a given quantity of labour, is a grateful reflection which forces itself on every one. What changes, too, this addition of power is introducing into the Social System; how wealth has more and more increased, and at the same time gathered itself more and more into masses, strangely altering the old relations, and increasing the distance between the rich and the poor, will be a question for Political Economists, and a much more complex and important one than any they have yet engaged with.

But leaving these matters for the present, let us observe how the mechanical genius of our time has diffused itself into quite other provinces. Not the external and physical alone is now managed by machinery, but the internal and spiritual also. Here too nothing follows its spontaneous course, nothing is left to be accomplished by old natural methods. Everything has its cunningly devised implements, its preëstablished apparatus; it is not done by hand, but by machinery. Thus we have machines for Education: Lancastrian machines; Hamiltonian machines; monitors, maps and emblems. Instruction, that mysterious communing of Wisdom with Ignorance, is no longer an indefinable tentative process, requiring a study of individual aptitudes, and a perpetual variation of means and methods, to attain the same end; but a secure, universal, straightforward business, to be conducted in the gross, by proper mechanism, with such intellect as comes to hand. Then, we have Religious machines, of all imaginable varieties; the Bible-Society, professing a far higher and heavenly structure, is found, on inquiry, to be altogether an earthly contrivance: supported by collection of moneys, by fomenting of vanities, by puffing, intrigue and chicane; a machine for converting the Heathen. It is the same in all other departments. Has any man, or any society of men, a truth to speak, a piece of spiritual work to do; they can nowise proceed at once and with the mere natural organs, but must first call a public meeting, appoint committees, issue prospectuses, eat a public dinner; in a word, construct or borrow machinery, wherewith to speak it and do it. Without machinery they were hopeless, helpless; a colony of Hindoo weavers squatting in the heart of Lancashire. Mark, too, how every machine must have its moving power, in some of the great currents of society; every little sect among us, Unitarians, Utilitarians, Anabaptists, Phrenologists, must have its Periodical, its monthly or quarterly Magazine; — hanging out, like its windmill, into the *popularis aura*, to grind meal for the society.

With individuals, in like manner, natural strength avails little. No individual now hopes to accomplish the poorest enterprise single-handed and without mechanical aids; he must make interest with some existing corporation, and till his field with their oxen. In these days, more emphatically than ever, 'to live, signifies to unite with a party, or to make one.' Philosophy, Science, Art, Literature, all depend on machinery. No Newton, by silent meditation, now discovers the system of the world from the falling of an apple; but some quite other than Newton stands in his Museum, his Scientific Institution, and behind whole batteries of retorts, digesters and galvanic piles imperatively 'interrogates Nature,' — who, however, shows no haste to answer. In defect of Raphaels, and Angelos, and Mozarts, we have Royal Academies of Painting, Sculpture, Music; whereby the languishing spirit of Art may be strengthened, as by the more generous diet of a Public Kitchen. Literature, too, has its Paternoster-row mechanism, its Trade-dinners, its Editorial conclaves, and huge subterranean, puffing bellows; so that books are not only printed, but, in a great measure, written and sold, by machinery.

National culture, spiritual benefit of all sorts, is under the same management. No Queen Christina, in these times, needs to send for her Descartes; no King Frederick for his Voltaire, and painfully nourish him with pensions and flattery: any sovereign of taste, who wishes to enlighten his people, has only to impose a new tax, and with the proceeds establish Philosophic Institutes. Hence the Royal and Imperial Societies, the Bibliothèques, Glyptothèques, Technothèques, which front us in all capital cities; like so many well-finished hives, to which it is expected the stray agencies of Wisdom will swarm of their own accord, and hive and make honey. In like manner, among ourselves, when it is thought that religion is declining, we have only to vote half-a-million's worth of bricks and mortar, and build new churches. In

Ireland it seems they have gone still farther, having actually established a 'Penny-a-week Purgatory Society'! Thus does the Genius of Mechanism stand by to help us in all difficulties and emergencies, and with his iron back bears all our burdens.

These things, which we state lightly enough here, are yet of deep import, and indicate a mighty change in our whole manner of existence. For the same habit regulates not our modes of action alone, but our modes of thought and feeling. Men are grown mechanical in head and in heart, as well as in hand. They have lost faith in individual endeavour, and in natural force, of any kind. Not for internal perfection, but for external combinations and arrangements, for institutions, constitutions — for Mechanism of one sort or other, do they hope and struggle. Their whole efforts, attachments, opinions, turn on mechanism, and are of a mechanical character.

From Thomas Carlyle, 'Signs of the Times', 1829.

Notes

'Birmingham Fire-king': Matthew Boulton and James Watt had their famous works for building steam engines at Birmingham from the 1770s on. 'The genius of the Cape' refers to Luis Vaz de Camoens'(1524-80) epic 'Lusiads' which described, in heroic manner, Vasco da Gama's discovery of the sea route to India via the Cape of Good Hope. 'Lancastrian and Hamiltonian machines': Joseph Lancaster and James Hamilton were educational reformers active in the first decades of the nineteenth century. Lancaster promoted the system of instruction by 'monitors' or pupil-teachers, enabling a single master to direct, by almost military methods, a large class, and Hamilton advocated language learning by observation of actual speech, not by attendance to rigid rules.

'The Bible Society' was an evangelical group founded in 1804 to 'encourage a wider circulation of the Holy Scriptures without note or comment'. 'Unitarians, Utilitarians, Anabaptists, Phrenologists': The Unitarian, as distinct from the Trinitarian, believes in the divinity of God alone; the sect was strong among provincial and industrial leaders at the end of the eighteenth century and the beginning of the nineteenth. Utilitarians believed in the submission of all doctrines to Jeremy Bentham's test: do they promote 'the greatest happiness of the greatest number'? Anabaptism (anachronistic at this time) refers to a Reformation sect which combined belief in adult baptism with quasi-socialist doctrines. Phrenology was a pseudo-science popular among intellectuals of the eighteenth and early nineteenth centuries who argued that the brain, and consequently the human mind, could be analysed through an examination of the structure of the skull.

Popularis aura: from Latin, the public ear. 'Paternoster row mechanism' was a reference to the organisation of journalism. Paternoster Row adjoins Fleet Street. 'Bibliothèques, Glyptothèques, Technothèques' are hybrid words out of Greek by French, signifying libraries, museums of sculpture and of technology.

See also H 7, H 8, H 9.

The Industry of Newcastle

William Bell Scott (1811–90)

A 2

'In the NINETEENTH CENTURY, the Northunbrians
show the World what can be done with IRON and COAL.'
(A mural in Wallington Hall Northumberland.)

Section B

The Face of the Country

A Midland Journey
George Eliot (1819–80)

'George Eliot' was the nom de plume of Mary Ann Evans, the daughter of a Warwickshire land agent, who passed her most impressionable years while the country was agitated by the politics of the first Reform Act and had the temper of its life changed by the first railways. Both are reflected in this extract from 'Felix Holt', a novel written at the time of the second Reform Act of 1867. The impression given is initially of contrast between pleasant rural and unpleasant urban society, but closer reading reveals that, to Eliot's eyes, the charm of the villages masked a society which was stupid, credulous and occasionally vicious; and although the new industrialism appeared to promote dirt and sensual indulgence, it could also respond to its problems in a way of which the old order had never been capable. Even a convinced enemy of capitalist industry like Engels was able to write in the 1840s that 'The English worker today is no longer an Englishman of the old school. He no longer resembles his capitalist neighbour in being a mere machine for making money. His capacity for feeling has developed.'

But where Eliot saw the transition from rural to industrial life as a matter of decision on the part of the individual, Engels saw it simply as the work of the economic system. Eliot assumed that people lived in industrial towns because they wanted to; Engels argued that they had no choice in the matter. Eliot's remedies — she actually used the name 'Felix Holt' in writing an address to working men in the year the novel was published — were therefore essentially contributions towards the ordering of industrial society; workers should develop self-reliance, and spend their high wages on books and their time in the library rather than in the pub.

B 1

Five-and-thirty years ago the glory had not yet departed from the old coach-roads: the great roadside inns were still brilliant with well-polished tankards, the smiling glances of pretty barmaids, and the repartees of jocose ostlers; the mail still announced itself by the merry notes of the horn; the hedge-cutter or the rick-thatcher might still know the exact hour by the unfailing yet otherwise meteoric apparition of the pea-green Tally-ho or the yellow Independent; and elderly gentlemen in pony-chaises, quartering nervously to make way for the rolling swinging swiftness, had not ceased to remark that times were finely changed since they used to see the pack-horses and hear the tinkling of their bells on this very highway.

In those days there were pocket boroughs, a Birmingham unrepresented in Parliament and compelled to make strong representations out of it, unrepealed corn-laws, three-and-sixpenny letters, a brawny and many-breeding pauperism, and other departed evils; but there were some pleasant things too, which have also departed. *Non omnia grandior aetas quae jugiamus habet*, says the wise goddess: you have not the best of it in all things, O youngsters! the elderly man has his enviable memories, and not the least of them is the memory of a long journey in mid-spring or autumn on the outside of a stage-coach. Posterity may be shot, like a bullet through a tube, by atmospheric pressure from Winchester to Newcastle: that is a fine result to have among our hopes; but the slow old-fashioned way of getting from one end of our country to the other is the better thing to have in the memory. The tube-journey can never lend much to picture and narrative; it is as barren as an exclamatory O! Whereas the happy outside passenger seated on the box from the dawn to the gloaming gathered enough stories of English life, enough of English labours in town and country, enough aspects of earth and sky, to make episodes for a modern Odyssey. Suppose only that his journey took him through that central plain, watered at one extremity by the Avon, at the other by the Trent. As the morning silvered the meadows with their long lines of bushy willows marking the watercourses, or burnished the golden corn-ricks clustered near the long roofs of some midland homestead, he saw the full-uddered cows driven from their pasture to the early milking. Perhaps it was the shepherd, head-servant of the farm, who drove them, his sheep-dog following with a heedless unofficial air as of a beadle in undress. The shepherd with a slow and slouching walk, timed by the walk of grazing beasts, moved aside, as if unwillingly, throwing out a monosyllabic hint to his cattle; his glance, accustomed to rest on things very near the earth, seemed to lift itself with difficulty to the coachman. Mail or stage coach for him belonged to that mysterious distant system of things called 'Gover'ment,' which, whatever it might be, was no business of his, any more than the most out-lying nebula or the coal-sacks of the southern hemisphere: his solar system was the parish; the master's temper and the casualties of lambing-time were his region of storms. He cut his bread and bacon with his pocket-knife, and felt no bitterness except in the matter of pauper labourers and the bad-luck that sent contrarious seasons and the sheep-rot. He and his cows were soon left behind, and the homestead too, with its pond overhung by elder-trees, its untidy kitchen-garden and cone-shaped yew-tree arbour. But everywhere the bushy hedgerows wasted the land with their straggling beauty, shrouded the grassy borders of the pastures with catkined hazels, and tossed their long blackberry branches on the corn-fields. Perhaps they were white with May, or starred with pale pink dogroses; perhaps the urchins were already nutting amongst them, or gathering the plenteous crabs. It was worth the journey only to see those hedgerows, the liberal homes of unmarketable beauty — of the purple-blossomed ruby-berried night-shade, of the wild convolvulus climbing and spreading in tendrilled strength till it made a great curtain of pale-green hearts and white trumpets, of the many tubed honey-suckle which, in its most delicate fragrance, hid a charm more subtle and penetrating than beauty. Even if it were winter the hedgerows showed their coral, the scarlet haws, the deep-crimson hips, with lingering brown leaves to make a resting-place for the jewels of the hoar-frost. Such hedgerows were often as tall as the labourers' cottages dotted along the lanes, or clustered into a small hamlet, their little dingy windows telling, like thick-filmed eyes, of nothing but the darkness within. The passenger on the coach-box, bowled along above such a hamlet, saw chiefly the roofs of it: probably it turned its back on the road, and seemed to lie away from everything but its own patch of earth and sky, away from the parish church by long fields and green lanes, away from all intercourse except that of tramps. If its face could be seen, it was most likely dirty; but the dirt was Protestant dirt, and the big, bold, gin-breathing tramps were Protestant tramps. There was no sign of superstition near, no crucifix or image to indicate a misguided reverence: the inhabitants were probably so free from superstition that they were in much less awe of the parson than of the overseer. Yet they were saved from the excesses of Protestantism by not knowing how to read, and by the absence of handlooms and mines to be the pioneers of Dissent: they were kept safely in the *via media* of indifference, and could have registered themselves in the census by a big black mark as members of the Church of England.

But there were trim cheerful villages too, with a neat or handsome parsonage and grey church set in the midst; there was the pleasant tinkle of the blacksmith's anvil, the patient cart-horses waiting at his door; the basket-maker peeling his willow wands in the sunshine; the wheelwright putting the last touch to a blue cart with red wheels; here and there a cottage with bright transparent windows showing pots full of blooming balsams or geraniums, and little gardens in front all double daisies or dark wallflowers; at the well, clean and comely women carrying yoked buckets, and towards the free school small Britons dawdling on, and handling their marbles in the pockets of unpatched corduroys adorned with brass buttons. The land around was rich and marly, great corn-stacks stood in the rick-yards — for the rick-burners had not found their way hither; the homesteads were those of rich farmers who paid no rent, or had the rare advantage of a lease, and could afford to keep their corn till prices had risen. The coach would be sure to overtake some of them on their way to their outlying fields or to the market-town, sitting heavily on their well-groomed horses, or weighing down one side of an olive-green gig. They probably thought of the coach with some contempt, as an accommodation for people who had not their own gigs, or who, wanting to travel to London and such distant places, belonged to the trading and less solid part of the nation. The passenger on the box could see that this was the district of protuberant optimists, sure that old England was the best of all possible countries, and that if there were any facts which had not fallen under their own observation, they were facts not worth observing: the district of clean little market-towns without manufactures, of fat livings, an aristocratic clergy, and low poor-rates. But as the day wore on the scene would change: the land would begin to be blackened with coal-pits, the rattle of handlooms to be heard in hamlets and villages. Here were powerful men walking queerly with knees bent outward from squatting in the mine, going home to throw themselves down in their blackened flannel and sleep through the daylight, then rise and spend much of their high wages at the ale-house with their fellows of the Benefit Club; here the pale eager faces of handloom-weavers, men and women, haggard from sitting up late at night to finish the week's work, hardly begun till the Wednesday. Everywhere the cottages and the small children were dirty, for the languid mothers gave their strength to the loom; pious Dissenting women, perhaps, who took life patiently, and thought that salvation depended chiefly on predestination, and not at all on cleanliness. The gables of Dissenting chapels now made a visible sign of religion, and of a meeting-place to counterbalance the ale-house, even in the hamlets; but if a couple of old termagants were seen tearing each other's caps, it was a safe conclusion that, if they had not received the sacraments of the Church, they had not at least given into schismatic rites, and were free from the errors of Voluntaryism. The breath of the manufacturing town, which made a cloudy day and a red gloom by night on the horizon, diffused itself over all the surrounding country, filling the air with eager unrest. Here was a population not convinced that old England was as good as possible; here were multitudinous men and women aware that their religion was not exactly the religion of their rulers, who might therefore be better than they were, and who, if better, might alter many things which now made the world perhaps more painful than it need be, and certainly more sinful. Yet there were the grey steeples too, and the churchyards, with their grassy mounds and venerable headstones, sleeping in the sunlight; there were broad fields and homesteads, and fine old woods covering a rising ground, or stretching far by the roadside, allowing only peeps at the park and mansion which they shut in from the working-day world. In these midland districts the traveller passed rapidly from one phase of English life to another; after looking down on a village dingy with coal-dust, noisy with the shaking of looms, he might skirt a parish all of fields, high hedges, and deep-rutted lanes; after the coach had rattled over the pavement of a manufacturing town, the scene of riots and trades-union meetings, it would take him in another ten minutes into a rural region, where the neighbourhood of the town was only felt in the advantages of a near market for corn, cheese, and hay, and where men with a considerable banking account were accustomed to say that 'they never meddled with politics themselves.' The busy scenes of the shuttle and the wheel, of the roaring furnace, of the shaft and the pulley, seemed to make but crowded nests in the midst of the large-spaced, slow-moving life of homesteads and far-away cottages and oak-sheltered parks. Looking at the dwellings scattered amongst the woody flats and the ploughed uplands, under the low grey sky which overhung them with an unchanging stillness as if Time itself were pausing, it was easy for the traveller to conceive that town and country had no pulse in common, except where the handlooms made a far-reaching straggling fringe about the great centres of manufacture; that till the agitation about the Catholics in '29, rural Englishmen had hardly known more of Catholics than of the fossil mammals; and that their notion of Reform was a confused combination of rick-burners, trades-unions, Nottingham riots, and in general whatever required the calling-out of the yeomanry. It was still easier to see that, for the most part, they resisted the rotation of crops and stood by their fallows: and the coachman would perhaps tell how in one parish an innovating farmer, who talked of Sir Humphrey Davy, had been fairly driven out by popular dislike, as if he had been a confounded Radical; and how, the parson having one Sunday preached from the words, 'Break up your fallow-ground,' the people thought he had made the text out of his own head, otherwise it would never have come 'so pat' on a matter of business; but when they found it in the Bible at home, some said it was an argument for fallows (else why should the Bible mention fallows?), but a few of the weaker sort were shaken, and thought it was an argument that fallows should be done away with, else the Bible would have said, 'Let your fallows lie;' and the next morning the parson had a stroke of apoplexy, which, as coincident with a dispute about fallows, so set the parish against the innovating farmer and the rotation of crops, that he could stand his ground no longer, and transferred his lease.

The coachman was an excellent travelling companion and commentator on the landscape: he could tell the names of sites and persons, and explain the meaning of groups, as well as the shade of Virgil in a more memorable journey; he had as many stories about parishes, and the men and women in them, as the Wanderer in the 'Excursion', only his style was different. His view of life had originally been genial, and such as became a man who was well warmed within and without, and held a position of easy, undisputed authority; but the recent initiation of Railways had embittered him: he now, as in a perpetual vision, saw the ruined country strewn with shattered limbs, and regarded Mr Huskisson's death as a proof of God's anger against Stephenson. 'Why, every inn on the road would be shut up!' and at that word the coachman looked before him with the blank gaze of one who had driven his coach to the outermost edge of the universe, and saw his leaders plunging into the abyss. Still he would soon relapse from the high prophetic strain to the familiar one of narrative. He knew whose the land was wherever he drove; what noblemen had half-ruined themselves by gambling; who made handsome returns of rent; and who was at daggers-drawn with his eldest son. He perhaps remembered the fathers of actual baronets, and knew stories of their extravagant or stingy housekeeping; whom they had married, whom they had horsewhipped, whether they were particular about preserving their game, and whether they had had much to do with canal companies. About any actual landed proprietor he could also tell whether he was a Reformer or an Anti-Reformer. That was a distinction which had 'turned up' in latter times, and along with it the paradox, very puzzling to the coachman's mind, that there were men of old family and large estate who voted for the Bill. He did not grapple with the paradox; he let it pass, with all the discreetness of an experienced theologian or learned scholiast, preferring to point his whip at some object which could raise no questions.

From George Eliot, 'Felix Holt, the Radical', 1867, chap. 1.

Notes

'Dissenting' and 'Voluntaryism' are synonyms for Nonconformist worship. 'Agitation about the Catholics' refers to the controversy and Protestant panic which accompanied the granting of civil rights to British Catholics in 1829. 'Rick-burners, trades-unions, Nottingham riots' refer to the social unrest of the period around 1830, although the 'Unions' which promoted the Reform cause were political rather than industrial organisations. Nottingham Castle was sacked by a radical mob on 12 October 1831. 'The Wanderer in the "Excursion"' refers to Wordsworth's poem of 1814. Mr Huskisson, a former Chancellor of the Exchequer, was killed by a locomotive on the opening day of the Liverpool and Manchester Railway, 1830.

Further Reading

Raymond Williams, 'Culture and Society', 1958, chap. 5.

See also G 1, 95, P4.

Under the Viaduct

Gustave Doré (1833–83)

B 2

'Here civilisation makes its miracles, and civilised man is turned back into a savage.' Over 100,000 people were displaced from their homes in London alone as a result of railway building, and many were crowded even closer in the centres of cities because they could not afford to travel to work on the railways which had evicted them.

The French artist Gustave Doré became a major artistic institution in Britain through the wide circulation of engravings of his works and his illustrated editions of popular writings. Some of his work is pretentious technically but imaginative, and occasionally his sombre images of squalor leave a profound, sulphurous impression.

B 2.

From Gustave Doré and Blanchard Jerrold, 'London', 1872.

Manchester

Alexis de Tocqueville (1805–59)

Manchester in a sense asked for the rough treatment it got from two notable foreign visitors, Tocqueville and Friedrich Engels. 'We are called the Manchester party, and our policy is the Manchester policy, and this building, I suppose, is the school room of the Manchester school', John Bright was to say in 1851, speaking, obviously enough, in the Free Trade Hall, and extolling, obviously enough, the virtues of 'laissez-faire'. With its satellites, Stockport, Salford, Oldham, Manchester was the most impressive example of urban expansion up to the mid-century, and in its dependence on factory industry and its persistent identification, through Cobden, Bright and the Anti-Corn-Law League, with the gospel of the market economy, the city demanded attention as a portent of the new age. As such it naturally attracted the attention and the criticism of less committed observers like Alexis de Tocqueville, a French aristocrat whose faith in the stability of the old regime had been shattered by the Revolution of 1830 and who then explored the social and political background of the new forces making for democracy in America and Britain. But where Engels in his 'Condition of the Working Class in England' (1844) saw urban squalor as the act of the exploiting bourgeoisie, Tocqueville blamed this on the absence of a tradition of governmental intervention. 1835 in fact saw Manchester given its first Corporation under the terms of the Municipal Reform Act, but essentially all this did was to deprive little local oligarchies of the rich pickings of old privileges. It was not until after the public health agitation of the 1840s that local government began to assume the shape we recognise today.

B 3

2 July 1835

An undulating plain, or rather a collection of little hills. Below the hills a narrow river (the Irwell), which flows slowly to the Irish sea. Two streams (the Meddlock and the Irk) wind through the uneven ground and after a thousand bends, flow into the river. Three canals made by man unite their tranquil, lazy waters at the same point. On this watery land, which nature and art have contributed to keep damp, are scattered palaces and hovels. Everything in the exterior appearance of the city attests the individual powers of man; nothing the directing power of society. At every turn human liberty shows its capricious creative force. There is no trace of the slow continuous action of government.

Thirty or forty factories rise on the tops of the hills I have just described. Their six stories tower up; their huge enclosures give notice from afar of the centralisation of industry. The wretched dwellings of the poor are scattered haphazard around them. Round them stretches land uncultivated but without the charm of rustic nature, and still without the amenities of a town. The soil has been taken away, scratched and torn up in a thousand places, but it is not yet covered with the habitations of men. The land is given over to industry's use. The roads which connect the still-disjointed limbs of the great city, show, like the rest, every sign of hurried and unfinished work; the incidental activity of a population bent on gain, which seeks to amass gold so as to have everything else all at once, and, in the interval, mistrusts all the niceties of life. Some of these roads are paved, but most of them are full of ruts and puddles into which foot or carriage wheel sinks deep. Heaps of dung, rubble from buildings, putrid, stagnant pools are found here and there among the houses and over the bumpy, pitted surfaces of the public places. No trace of surveyor's rod or spirit level. Amid this noisome labyrinth, this great sombre stretch of brickwork, from time to time one is astonished at the sight of fine stone buildings with Corinthian columns. It might be a medieval town with the marvels of the nineteenth century in the middle of it. But who could describe the interiors of these quarters set apart, home of vice and poverty, which surround the huge palaces of industry and clasp them in their hideous folds. On ground below the level of the river and overshadowed on every side by immense workshops, stretches marshy land which widely spaced ditches can neither drain nor cleanse. Narrow, twisting roads lead down to it. They are lined with one-story houses whose ill-fitting planks and broken windows show them up, even from a distance, as the last refuge a man might find between poverty and death. None-the-less the wretched people living in them can still inspire jealousy of their fellow-beings. Below some of their miserable dwellings is a row of cellars to which a sunken corridor leads. Twelve to fifteen human beings are crowded pell-mell into each of these damp, repulsive holes.

The fetid, muddy waters, stained with a thousand colours by the factories they pass, of one of the streams I mentioned before, wander slowly round this refuge of poverty. They are nowhere kept in place by quays: houses are built haphazard on their banks. Often from the top of one of their steep banks one sees an attempt at a road opening out through the debris of earth, and the foundations of some houses or the debris of others. It is the Styx of this new Hades. Look up and all around this place and you will see the huge palaces of industry. You will hear the noise of furnaces, the whistle of steam. These vast structures keep air and light out of the human habitations which they dominate; they envelope them in perpetual fog; here is the slave, there the master; there is the wealth of some, here the poverty of most; there the organised efforts of thousands produce, to the profit of one man, what society has not yet learnt to give. Here the weakness of the individual seems more feeble and helpless even than in the middle of a wilderness.

A sort of black smoke covers the city. The sun seen through it is a disc without rays. Under this half-daylight 300,000 human beings are ceaselessly at work. A thousand noises disturb this dark, damp labyrinth, but they are not at all the ordinary sounds one hears in great cities.

The footsteps of a busy crowd, the crunching wheels of machinery, the shriek of steam from boilers, the regular beat of the looms, the heavy rumble of carts, those are the noises from which you can never escape in the sombre half-light of these streets. You will never hear the clatter of hoofs as the rich man drives back home or out on expeditions of pleasure. Never the gay shouts of people amusing themselves, or music heralding a holiday. You will never see smart folk strolling at leisure in the streets, or going out on innocent pleasure parties in the surrounding country. Crowds are ever hurrying this way and that in the Manchester streets, but their footsteps are brisk, their looks preoccupied, and their appearance sombre and harsh. . . .

From this foul drain the greatest stream of human industry flows out to fertilise the whole world. From this filthy sewer pure gold flows. Here humanity attains its most complete development and its most brutish; here civilisation makes its miracles, and civilised man is turned back almost into a savage.

> Alexis de Tocqueville, 'Journeys to England and Ireland', trans. G. Lawrence and K. P. Mayer, ed. J. P. Mayer, 1958, pp. 105-8.

Further Reading

Friedrich Engels, 'The Condition of the Working Class in England', 1844, new ed. with introduction by E. J. Hobsbawm, 1969, pp. 57-108.
Asa Briggs, 'John Bright and the Creed of Reform', in 'Victorian People', 1954
Asa Briggs, 'Manchester', in Victorian Cities', 1963.

See also G 4, J 2, P 4.

Section C

Machinery

The Steam Engine

Erasmus Darwin (1731–1802)

Erasmus Darwin, grandfather of Charles, was a Midlands doctor and dilettante whose friends included the brilliant circle of industrialists, scientists and philosophers who met as the Birmingham Lunar Society. The group included James Watt, Josiah Wedgwood the pottery manufacturer, and Joseph Priestley, scientist and political radical, and was eager to explore advances in technology, economics and political ideas. They constituted a provincial radical intelligentsia but in a sense they were not yet fully committed to the industrial system. They did not have to devote all their energies to keeping their place in the struggle of the market and could afford to let their minds range speculatively over a great variety of topics. Darwin's little hymn to the steam engine is typical of this frame of mind. The machine is intriguing and ingenious; it has yet to become obsessive.

C 1

> Nymphs! you erewhile on simmering cauldrons play'd,
> And call'd delighted SAVERY to your aid;
> Bade round the youth explosive STEAM aspire
> In gathering clouds, and urged the wave with fire;
> Bade with cold streams the quick expansion stop,
> And sunk the immense of vapour to a drop. —
> Press'd by the ponderous air the Piston falls
> Resistless, sliding through its iron walls;
> Quick moves the balanced beam, of giant birth,
> Wields his large limbs, and nodding shakes the earth.

The Giant-Power from earth's remotest caves
Lifts with strong arm her dark reluctant waves;
Each caverned rock, and hidden den explores,
Drags her dark coals, and digs her shining ores. —
Next, in close cells of ribbed oak confined,
Gale after gale, he crowds the struggling wind;
The imprisoned storms through brazen nostrils roar,
Fan the white flame, and fuse the sparkling ore.
Here high in air the rising stream he pours
To clay-built cisterns, or to lead-lined towers;
Fresh through a thousand pipes the wave distils,
And thirsty cities drink the exhuberant rills. —
There the vast mill-stone with inebriate whirl
On trembling floors his forceful fingers twirl.
While flashing teeth the golden harvests grind,
Feasts without blood! and nourish human-kind.

Soon shall thy arm UNCONQUER'D STEAM! afar
Drag the slow barge, or drive the rapid car;
Or on wide-waving wings expanded bear
The flying chariot through the fields of air.
— Fair crews triumphant, leaning from above,
Shall wave their fluttering kerchiefs as they move;
Or warrior-bands alarm the gaping crowd,
And armies shrink beneath the shadowy cloud.

From 'The Botanic Garden', 1791, pp. 26-30.

Note

Thomas Savery demonstrated a pumping engine to the Royal Society in 1699 which used condensing steam to create a vacuum in the way illustrated by the poem. With modifications, this became the 'atmospheric' engine, the first practical steam engine.

Further Reading

Brian Simon, 'Studies in the History of Education', 1960, chap. 1.
L. T. C. Rolt, 'James Watt', 1962, Chaps. 3, 8.

An Experiment on a Bird in an Air-pump

Joseph Wright of Derby (1734–97)

C 2

From the painting of 1769 in the Tate Gallery.

Wright of Derby painted most of the members of the Lunar Society and interested himself in their scientific and industrial activities. His painting captures the mixture of apprehension and excitement among those involved in the experiment. His friends must have reacted in a similar way to the practical application of their own inventions and ideas.

The New Machine
Isambard Kingdom Brunel (1806–59)

Brunel was never slow to make the impressive statement when his less self-confident contemporaries treated their projects more gingerly. His memoranda on the Great Western Railway which provided the rationale for the 7-ft gauge — 'It seemed to me that the whole machine was too small for the work to be done, and that it required that the parts should be on a scale commensurate with the mass and the velocity to be obtained' — and his instructions to the captain of the 'Great Eastern', his last great project, betray the fascination which the process of adaptation to mechanisation on the grand scale had for an engineer of genius. Nevertheless, we are left in no doubt that the machine is no longer a novelty to be admired, but a fixture for man to come to terms with.

C 3

I have come to the conclusion which you will no doubt readily acquiesce in, that our first practical mechanical success, upon which so much of our financial success hangs (although others might reap the benefit even of our failure in the first instance), will depend mainly upon the skilful management in our earliest voyages of the machine we are about to set afloat; but I have also come to the conclusion, the correctness of which may not be so immediately apparent to you, that this machine, though nominally a ship, not only admits of, but requires, a totally different management from that which may have successfully navigated ordinary ships, and that most of the habits, feelings, and sensations, amounting to instinct, possessed by a good sailor, and the peculiar power of skilful adaptation of expedients to emergencies, which constitute the merits of a first-rate sailor, have to be put aside for a time rather than applied in the first instance to make a successful commander of the vessel. . . .

Ships are navigated with far too reckless a confidence in the mere personal instinct and skill of those in command, and in their ability to get out of a scrape in time. Methodical systems and mechanical means of ensuring accuracy are far too much neglected, or rather have not kept pace at all with the great improvements in speed and the power of locomotion which science has introduced, whether in the construction of steam vessels or even of sailing ships, and which the advance of the day now calls for. . . .

What I most dread is the confidence of our commander resulting from his previous experience preventing his appreciating the peculiarities of the case, and applying that greatly increased amount of method and system which is essential to change that, which is now rendered only highly probable by the skill of man, into mechanical certainty. The man who takes charge of such a machine, in which is embarked so large a capital, must have a mind capable of setting aside, without forgetting, all his previous experience and habits, and must be prepared to commence as an observer of new facts, and seize rapidly the results. A man of sense and observation, with a good mechanical head, and with decision and courage, would succeed without much previous nautical knowledge; but, unquestionably, a man familiar with all that is going on around would be much more competent, provided he does not allow his habits derived from former experience to induce him to neglect any of the new means of information in his power, to all which his former knowledge should be made subservient.

The exact course to be taken by such a vessel must be determined upon and laid down upon the charts after a due consideration of all the circumstances which can possibly affect the time occupied in the voyage between any two points, and particularly by examining and considering well all the information which scientific observers have collected and recorded as to the currents, probabilities of fogs, or of ice, and other impediments, the chances of meeting vessels, which must be avoided as much as possible, the average direction of prevailing winds. . . . The business of the commander would be, therefore, to adhere rigidly to the exact course previously deliberately determined upon, and not to be tempted to deviate except slightly, and even then only according to rules which he shall have previously laid down for himself. . . .

Finally, the commander's attention must be devoted exclusively to the general management of the whole system under his control, and his attention must not be diverted by frivolous pursuits and unimportant occupations. I believe that even in the present large steamers much advantage would result from relieving the captain from all care of the passengers and cargo; . . . while the commander is of course supreme over every department, he should not be embarrassed by undertaking any one, still less should he have his mind occupied with the troublesome and frivolous concerns of a vast hotel, nor should he be hampered by the necessity of attending to the hours and the forms of a large society. . . .

The result of all these general views is, that the command of this ship must be considered to consist mainly in the superintending and keeping up in a high state of order the perfect working of a highly methodical pre-arranged system, by means of which the ship is to be made to go like a piece of very accurate machinery, precisely in the course which has been pre-arranged, and precisely at the speed, and with the consumption of power, which has been ascertained to be the highest attainable with the requisite economy; and there must be a proper establishment of assistants, competent to control each department of this system. . . .

That the principles thus laid down as to following exactly a prescribed and predetermined course, and as to regulating exactly the consumption of power and consequently of fuel, and the keeping up a system of what may be termed scientific observation for the purpose of ensuring this regularity, I submit should be rigidly enforced; and the commander should be required to adopt these principles as the guide of his conduct, and to use the measures that are placed at his disposal for working this machine in the manner and with the precision pointed out.

Isambard Kingdom Brunel, 'Memorandum on the Management of the Great Ship' from 'The Life of Isambard Kingdom Brunel, Civil Engineer', by Isambard Brunel, 1870, pp. 324-35.

Further Reading

L. T. C. Rolt, 'Isambard Kingdom Brunel', 1957, chaps. 13, 14.

See also K 1.

Inside The Mill

C 4

A MULE SPINNER, OPERATED BY ONE HAND, CARRYING 3,000 SPINDLES, DOING THE WORK OF 3,000 GIRLS.

The interior of a textile mill in the 1830s. Notice the unguarded machinery.

Ground in the Mill

Henry Morley (1822–94)

Nothing can be easier than to make a case. . . . against any particular system, by pointing out with emphatic caricature its inevitable miscarriages and by pointing out nothing else. Those who so address us may assume a tone of philanthropy, and for ever exult that they are not so unfeeling as other men are; but the real tendency of their exhortations is to make men dissatisfied with their inevitable condition, and what is worse, to make them fancy that its irremediable evils can be remedied. . . .

Thus Walter Bagehot, banker, political scientist and editor of 'The Economist', condemned the 'sentimental radicalism' of Charles Dickens and his followers in 1858. Henry Morley, a London journalist, literary critic, and pioneer of adult education, who wrote regularly for Dickens's 'Household Words', would take himself right into Bagehot's line of fire with this gruesome indictment of the machine and its managers. Assuming that Morley's brief was to criticise insufficient safety precautions in factories, he goes on to attack the manufacturers' greed and to depict the machine itself as a merciless automaton which punishes those not prepared to come to terms with it. Bagehot, whom Kitson Clark has described as a 'liberal realist', considered that such criticism, by simply screaming about inhumanity, did not do justice to the complex problems politicians were faced with in ordering a sophisticated industrial society. Too often, however, his arguments amount to a dismissal of the misfortunes of factory children, sweated labourers and the like as the inevitable fate of the minority who must be sacrificed for the general good. On the other hand, Bagehot was right in alleging that the 'sentimental school' could offer no prescription for the ills they diagnosed, and no logical critique of the society which produced them. Such a task was left to Marx and Engels, who assimilated humanitarian criticism to a lucid if dogmatic economic analysis.

C 5

'It is good when it happens,' say the children, – 'that we die before our time.' Poetry may be right or wrong in making little operatives who are ignorant of cowslips say anything like that. We mean here to speak prose. There are many ways of dying. Perhaps it is not good when a factory girl, who has not the whole spirit of play spun out of her for want of meadows, gambols upon bags of wool, a little too near the exposed machinery that is to work it up, and is immediately seized, and punished by the merciless machine that digs its shaft into her pinafore and hoists her up, tears out her left arm at the shoulder joint, breaks her right arm, and beats her on the head. No, that is not good; but it is not a case in point, the girl lives and may be one of those who think that it would have been good for her if she had died before her time.

She had her chance of dying, and she lost it. Possibly it was better for the boy whom his stern master, the machine, caught as he stood on a stool wickedly looking out of window at the sunlight and the flying clouds. These were no business of his, and he was fully punished when the machine he served caught him by one arm and whirled him round and round till he was thrown down dead. There is no lack of such warnings to idle boys and girls. What right has a gamesome youth to display levity before the supreme engine. 'Watch me do a trick!' cried such a youth to his fellow, and put his arm familiarly within the arm of the great iron-hearted chief. '*I'll* show you a trick,' gnashed the pitiless monster. A coil of strap fastened his arm to the shaft, and round he went. His leg was cut off, and fell into the room, his arm was broken in three or four places, his ankle was broken, his head was battered; he was not released alive.

Why do we talk about such horrible things? Because they exist, and their existence should be clearly known. Because there have occurred during the last three years, more than a hundred such deaths, and more than ten thousand (indeed, nearly twelve thousand) such accidents in our factories, and they are all, or nearly all, preventible.

These few thousands of catastrophes are the results of the administrative kindness so abundant in this country. They are all the fruits of mercy. A man was lime-washing the ceiling of an engine-room; he was seized by a horizontal shaft and killed immediately. A boy was brushing the dust from such a ceiling, before whitewashing: he had a cloth over his head to keep the dirt from falling on him; by that cloth the engine seized and held him to administer a chastisement with rods of iron. A youth while talking thoughtlessly took hold of a strop that hung over the shaft: his hand was wrenched off at the wrist. A man climbed to the top of his machine to put the strap on the drum: he wore a smock which the shaft caught; both his arms were then torn out of the shoulder-joints, both legs were broken, and his head was severely bruised: in the end, of course, he died. What he suffered was all suffered in mercy. He was rent asunder, not perhaps for his own good; but, as a sacrifice to the commercial prosperity of Great Britain. There are few amongst us — even among the masters who share most largely in that prosperity — who are willing, we will hope and believe, to pay such a price as all this blood for any good or any gain that can accrue to them.

These accidents have arisen in the manner following. By the Factory Act, passed in the seventh year of Her Majesty's reign, it was enacted, among other things, that all parts of the mill-gearing in a factory should be securely fenced. There were no buts and ifs in the Act itself; these were allowed to step in and limit its powers of preventing accidents out of a merciful respect, not for the blood of the operatives, but for the gold of the mill-owners. It was strongly represented that to fence those parts of machinery that were higher than the heads of workmen — more than seven feet above the ground — would be to incur an expense wholly unnecessary. Kind-hearted interpreters of the law, therefore, agreed with mill-owners that seven feet of fencing should be held sufficient. The result of this accommodation — taking only the accounts of the last three years — has been to credit mercy with some pounds and shillings in the books of English manufacturers; we cannot say how many, but we hope they are enough to balance the account against mercy made out on behalf of the English factory workers thus: — Mercy debtor to justice, of poor men, women and children, one hundred and six lives, one hundred and forty-two hands or arms, one thousand two hundred and eighty-seven (or, in bulk, how many bushels of) fingers, for the breaking of one thousand three hundred and forty bones, for five hundred and fifty-nine damaged heads, and for eight thousand two hundred and eighty-two miscellaneous injuries. It remains to be settled how much cash saved to the purses of the manufacturers is a satisfactory and proper off-set to this expenditure of life and limb and this crushing of bone in the persons of their work-people.

Henry Morley, 'Ground in the Mill',
from 'Household Words', 22 April 1854.

Further Reading

G. Kitson Clark, 'The Making of Victorian England', 1962, pp.49-51.

See also F 7, F 8, P 6.

A Threat to Wreck a Threshing Machine, c. 1830–1
'Captain Swing'

C 6

The installation of machinery was strenuously resisted by those whose labour, and consequent livelihood, it threatened to make redundant. Hence the breaking of power-looms by hand-loom operatives and the farm labourer's hostility to the horse-powered threshing machine which he saw depriving him of his winter work. 'Captain Swing' became the farm-worker's equivalent of the mythical power-loom wrecker 'General Ludd' when anger against the threshing machines fanned the riots which flared in the southern countryside in 1830 and 1831 and were severely put down by the Government.

See also F 1, F 2.

Sir

This is to acquaint you
that if your thrashing Ma-
-chines are not destroyed by
you directly we shall com-
-mence our Labours

signed on behalf
of the whole
Swing

C 6   *A "Swing" letter. From E. J. Hobsbawm and G. Rude, 'Captain Swing', 1969.*

Threshing By Steam

C 7

'The primum mobile of this little world' – a steam thresher at work on an English farm in the 1860s.

See also P 7.

The Elegance of the Machine

C 8

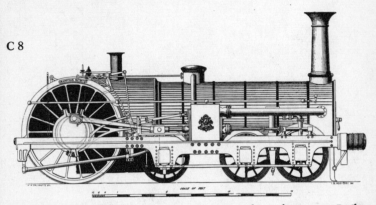

Crampton's patent express engine, London and North Western Railway Company, from p. 50 of the Official Catalogue to the Great Exhibition, 1851.

C 9

The paddle steamer 'Columba', built in 1878 by J. and G. Thompson of Govan.

Section D

Enterprise

The Industries of the Monklands

'And yet a great deal of money is made here', said a local businessman to Alexis de Tocqueville when the latter was regretting Manchester. The criticisms launched at the ugliness — as distinct from the squalor — of industrial Britain were the reactions of a minority to a phenomenon which was accepted, and even enthused over, by the majority of their fellow-citizens, like the writer of this entry in the 'Ordnance Gazetteer' on the industries of the coal and ironfields of the Monklands, south-east of Glasgow.

The 'Ordnance Gazetteers' (10 volumes for England and Wales, 6 for Scotland) are a useful source for research into local and industrial history. In Scotland they succeeded the 'Statistical Accounts' of the 1790s and 1830s which were compiled by parish ministers to give a more extended account of the economy, history, geology, social and religious life of the country, parish by parish. Unfortunately there was no parallel to this in England save in the occasional productions of the 'statistical societies' which were a feature of provincial life.

The fact that this sort of sophisticated statistical information came from Scotland illustrates the rapidity with which the Scots adapted to industrialisation. The Scots educational system, which produced the writers of the 'Accounts', encouraged an interest in economics and social science which the classical and mathematical specialisations of Oxford and Cambridge did not.

D 1

Old Monkland

The parish is chiefly remarkable for its working of coal and iron. In an account of it published before the beginning of the 19th century, one reads: 'This parish abounds with coal; and what a benefit it is for

Glasgow and its environs to be so amply provided with this necessary article! There are computed to be a greater number of colliers here than in any other parish in Scotland.' The progress in the coal-trade since the period alluded to has been almost magical; and as scarcely a year passes without new pits being sunk, while the old ones continue in vigorous operation, it would seem that scarcely any limits can be set to the vast aggregate production. . . .

Still more than to its coal, however, is the parish of Old Monkland, in recent times, indebted to its ironstone and ironworks. . . . The introduction of the hot air blast (1828), the increasing demand for iron for railway and other purposes, but, above all, the abundant possession of the most valuable of all the iron metals — the blackband - which contains so much coal as nearly to burn itself — are the main causes which have contributed to the almost unparalleled advance of Old Monkland in population and prosperity. To the burning of ironstone were added, in 1830 and the following years, works and machinery for the manufacture of malleable iron; and these have already risen to compare with the pig-iron works, in the proportion of about 30 to 100 in the yearly value of their produce. Everywhere are heard the rattling of machinery, the sonorous stroke of mighty hammers, and the hissing and clanking of the steam-engine; and the flames which perpetually belch from the craters of its numerous furnaces, and for miles around light up the country on the darkest nights, have not inappropriately earned for Old Monkland the title of the 'Land of Fire.' Fortunes have here been realised in the iron trade with a rapidity only equalled by the sudden and princely gains of the adventurers who sailed with Pizarro to Peru. It is understood, for example, that the profits of a single establishment in this line during the year 1840 were nearly £60,000; while little more than twenty years before the co-partners of this company were earning their bread by the sweat of their brow, in following the agricultural vocation of their fathers. . . .

Several kinds of sandstone, and several varieties of trap, within the parish, are in great request for local building purposes, and have been largely quarried. The facilities of communication by road, railway, and canal are remarkably great, having been multiplied and ramified in proportion to the large and rapidly increasing demands of the district for heavy traffic.

Pop. (1801) 4006, (1831) 9580, (1841) 19,675, (1861) 29,543, (1871) 34,073, (1881) 37,323, (1891) 44,616.

From 'The Ordnance Gazetteer of Scotland',
1896, vol. v, pp. 47-8.

See also E 2.

Sir William Fairbairn (1789–1874)

William Fairbairn was a 'self-made man' of the sort idealised by Samuel Smiles, but his father, a small farmer, must have been wealthy enough to pay the costs of his apprenticeship to an engine-wright. From then on his rise must have been largely that of a scarce and therefore costly specialist in an economy which had a growing need of his services. According to Professor Checkland, he and his friend and fellow-Scot James Nasmyth 'were the arch-types of their generation of engineers, heading large concerns built by their own efforts, yielding high wages and good conditions of work, utterly impatient of the attempts of trade unionists to interfere with their operations'. In his scientific work, too, he reflected the absorption of his generation in the proof of practical application rather than in research of a more fundamental and therefore more abstract nature.

The 'Dictionary of National Biography' to 'supply full, accurate and concise biographies of all noteworthy inhabitants of the British Islands and the Colonies (exclusive of living persons) from the earliest historical period to the present time' was projected by the publisher George Smith and Leslie Stephen in 1882. Sixty-three volumes were produced, in an alphabetical order, between then and 1900, containing notices of 29,120 men and women (12,608 from the nineteenth century). Since then supplements issued decade by decade have considerably increased this number. With its chronological and bibliographical information on its subjects, it remains despite its age, a valuable research tool.

D 2

FAIRBAIRN, Sir WILLIAM (1789–1874), engineer, was born at Kelso, Roxburghshire, on 19 Feb. 1789. His father, Andrew Fairbairn, was a farm-servant and an expert ploughman; had been impressed during the American war, and on returning to Scotland married the daughter of a Jedburgh tradesman, named Henderson, by whom he had five children. Mrs Fairbairn, though a delicate woman, was a good housewife, and till 1804 spun and manufactured all the clothes of the family. William learnt his letters from one 'bowed Johnnie Ker,' and acquired a little arithmetic and elementary knowledge at the parish school. His father farmed three hundred acres for a time under Lord Seaforth with the assistance of the elder children, while William had to take care of his delicate brother, Peter. To save the trouble of carrying the child he constructed a 'wagon' with a few simple tools, and then took to building boats and little mills. He afterwards had a little plain schooling at Mullochy, under a Mr Donald Fraser, and then learnt book-keeping under an uncle who kept a school at Galashiels. When fourteen years old he joined his family at Kelso, where they had been settled by the father, who was managing a farm near Knaresborough. William got employment at 3s. a week, until he was laid up by an accident, upon a bridge then being built by Rennie.

Towards the end of 1803 the elder Fairbairn moved with his family to a farm near Newcastle-on-Tyne belonging to the Percy Main colliery. William was employed in the colliery, and on 24 March 1804 was apprenticed to John Robinson, a millwright. He spent his leisure in reading, three days in the week being systematically allotted to mathematical studies and the others to general literature. He also applied his mechanical ingenuity to the construction of an orrery. Being appointed to the care of the engines at the colliery he got more time for reading, and became a member of the Shields library. Here he became a friend of George Stephenson. At the end of his apprenticeship, in March 1811, he obtained employment as a millwright at Newcastle, and afterwards in the construction of some works at Bedlington, where he met his future wife. The works being finished, he sailed for London in December 1811 with a fellow-workman named Hogg. They obtained employment after some difficulties. A clergyman named Hall introduced Fairbairn to the Society of Arts and to Tilloch, the founder of 'Tilloch's Philosophical Magazine,' and employed him in the construction of a steam-engine for digging. The machine failed after absorbing some of Fairbairn's savings. He made something by a sausage-machine, and set out for Bath and Dublin, where by October 1813 he had finished a nail machine, and then went to Manchester. Soon afterwards he married Dorothy, youngest daughter of John Mar, a Kelso burgess. He was employed by a master with whom in 1817 he had some disagreement about a new Blackfriars bridge at Manchester, and thereupon set up in partnership with an old shopmate, James Lillie. They soon acquired a good reputation by providing the machinery for a cotton-mill, and their business rapidly increased. In 1824 Fairbairn went to Zurich to erect two water-mills. By an ingenious contrivance he surmounted the difficulties due to the irregular supply of water, and constructed wheels which worked regularly whatever the height of the river. By 1830 Fairbairn and Lillie had a clear balance of near £40,000, and were able besides to increase their works so as to employ three hundred hands.

Fairbairn became a member of the Institution of Civil Engineers in 1830. He now began to investigate the properties of iron boats with a special view to improving the system of canal traction. His partner was not favourable to the experiments which he undertook for the Forth and Clyde Company. The publication of his results brought him the thanks of the institution, and the company employed him to construct a light iron passage-boat called the Lord Dundas, which ran for two years between Port Dundas, Glasgow, and Port Eglintoun, Edinburgh.

Fairbairn and Lillie lost much at this time in a speculation for starting a cotton-mill, which crippled their resources as millwrights and led to a dissolution of the partnership, Lillie setting up in opposition to Fairbairn. Fairbairn now devoted his energies to ship-building. He first built his ships in sections at Manchester, but in 1835 decided to take works at Millwall, Poplar, in partnership with an old pupil, Andrew Murray. He was supported by government and the East India Company, but found the strain too great and abandoned the Millwall establishment, where two thousand hands were employed. At Manchester he undertook many engineering schemes, experimented on the properties of iron, and, to meet a strike of his workmen, introduced the riveting machine, which has made a revolution in the manufacture of boilers. He took great interest in questions connected with boilers, and founded an association for the prevention of boiler explosions.

In 1839 he inspected the government works at Constantinople, and was decorated by the sultan, who also gave him a firman to be 'chief fabricator' of machinery for the Turkish government in England. He was consulted in 1840 upon the drainage of the Haarlem lake. In 1841 he gave advice to the English government upon the prevention of accidents by machinery. In 1842 he took out a patent (17 July, No. 9409) for improvements in the construction of iron ships, which proved too troublesome for general application. He read a paper on the prevention of smoke before the British Association at York in 1844. When Stephenson designed the tubular bridge at the Menai Straits he consulted Fairbairn, who made many experiments, and was ultimately appointed to superintend the construction of the bridge 'in conjunction with' Stephenson. The tube was successfully raised in April 1848. Misunderstandings having arisen as to Fairbairn's precise position, he gave up his appointment, and in 1849 published 'An Account of the Construction of the Britannia and Conway Tubular Bridges, with a complete History of their Progress,' containing his own account of the affair. In October 1846 he took out a patent for the new principle of wrought-iron girders he had devised for the bridge, although Stephenson shared in the patent. He stated in 1870 that he had built and designed nearly a thousand bridges. In 1849-50 he submitted plans, which, however, were not adopted, for a bridge over the Rhine at Cologne. Fairbairn made many investigations into the properties of the earth's crust in conjunction with William Hopkins, the Cambridge mathematician, and was a high authority upon all mechanical and engineering problems.

Fairbairn caught a chill, from which he never recovered, at the opening of the new buildings of Owens College in 1870. He died 18 Aug. 1874 at the house of his son-in-law, Mr Bateman of Moor Park, Surrey. He was buried at Prestwick, Northumberland.

Fairbairn had seven sons and two daughters by his wife. He declined a knighthood in 1861, but accepted a baronetage in 1869. In 1840 he bought the Polygon, Ardwick, near Manchester, where he lived till his death, and received many distinguished visitors. He spoke often and well at the British Association and similar meetings. He served as juror in the London exhibitions of 1851 and 1862, and at the Paris exhibition of

1855. In 1855 he was made a member of the Legion of Honour, and he was a foreign member of the Institute of France. He received the gold medal of the Royal Society in 1860, and was president of the British Association in 1861. He received the honorary LL.D. degree of Edinburgh in 1860 and of Cambridge in 1862. He was president of the Institution of Mechanical Engineers in 1854, and of the Manchester Literary and Philosophical Society from 1855 to 1860. A full list of his numerous contributions to the 'Transactions of the Royal Society' and the proceedings of many scientific and learned bodies is given in the life by Mr Pole.

[Life of Sir W. Fairbairn, partly written by himself, edited and completed by W. Pole, 1877; Account of the Construction of the Britannia and Conway Bridges, 1849; Smiles' George and Robert Stephenson, and Industrial Biography; Iron, its History, Properties, &c.; Fortunes made in Business; various papers contributed by Fairbairn to the proceedings of scientific societies.] J. B.—Y. [James Burnley].

Article in vol. xviii of the original edition of the 'Dictionary of National Biography', published in 1889-90.

Further Reading

S. G. Checkland, 'The Rise of Industrial Society in England', 1964, chap. 4.

Thomas Brassey at Work

Sir Arthur Helps (1813–75)

That the biography of the greatest of all British railway contractors was written by the Clerk to the Privy Council, with a dedication to the Queen, tells us something of the stature of the man who by his death had built railways throughout the world and whose activities were almost those of an ambassador. Brassey (1805-70) was a Cheshire landowner's son who started his career on the Grand Junction Railway, built to connect the Liverpool and Manchester and London and Birmingham railways in 1837, and in the next thirty-three years was to carry through some ninety construction schemes. He had the reputation of being a humane and fair-minded employer in an industry in which the business morals of the builders and operators of the railways were not always above criticism, and in which the lives of the navvies were objects of scandal and concern to the districts on which they descended. Helps himself had taken some part in the Christian Socialism of Kingsley and Maurice in 1848, and the emphasis in the book on Brassey's virtues as employer, not just on business success, probably stems from the governing classes' renewing interest in labour relations with the extension of the franchise in 1867 and the legalisation of the unions between 1871 and 1875.

D 3

When Mr Brassey took any contract, he let out portions of the work to sub-contractors. His way of dealing with them was this: he generally furnished all the materials, and all the plant. I find him on one occasion ordering as many as 2400 waggons from Messrs Ransome & May. He also provided the horses. The sub-contractors contracted for the manual labour alone. . . . I find that the sub-contracts varied from £5000 to £25,000; and that the number of men employed upon them would be from one to three hundred — the former being more common than the latter. . . .

Mr Brassey's mode of dealing with the sub-contractors was of an unusual kind, and such as could not have been adopted except by a man who had great experience of all kinds of manual work, and who was also a very just man. They did not exactly contract with him, but he appointed to them their work, telling them what price he should give for it. All the evidence I have before me shows that they were content to take the work at his price, and that they never questioned his accuracy.

. . . Frequently the work appointed to the sub-contractor turned out to be of a more difficult nature than had been anticipated. He however could not desist from the work on that account, nor make any appeal in unity to his employer. He would wait until the time when Mr Brassey should come round to visit the works. This was generally . . . once or twice a month.

He came, walking along the line as usual, with a number of followers. . . . If a cutting, taken to be clay, turned out after a very short time to be rock, . . . he looked round, counted the number of waggons at the work, scanned the cutting, and took stock of the nature of the stuff. 'This is very hard', said he to the sub-contractor. 'Yes, it is a pretty deal harder than I bargained for' . . . 'What is your price for this cutting?' 'So much a yard, sir' . . . 'If you say your price is so much, it is quite clear that you do not do it for that. I am glad that you have persevered with it, but I shall not alter your price; it must remain as it is, but the rock must be measured for you twice; will that do for you?'

'Yes, very well indeed, and I am very much obliged to you, sir.'

If he came down to look at a line of railway, he would walk over it, look at the crops of the country, and regard easy works as beneath his notice: he never looked at them; but if there was a difficult point, as he could see by the section, then there was something to look at, and he would go and always put his thumb on the sore place. . . . He economized his time and brought his experience and judgement to bear where they were useful. He applied to engineering, that peculiar quality of concentration which is equally necessary in all other walks of life, in order to achieve success.

... one of these visits of inspection would often 'cost Mr Brassey a thousand pounds', and as he went along the line in these inspections he remembered even the navvies, and saluted them by their names.

From 'The Life and Labours of Mr Brassey', 1872, pp. 47-50, 125.

Further Reading

Jack Simmons, 'The Railways of Britain', Routledge, 1962.
Michael Robbins, 'The Railway Age', Penguin, 1966, chaps. 3, 4, 8.
Terry Coleman, 'The Railway Navvies', Penguin, 1968.

See also F 5, H 9.

Section E

Communications

The Liverpool and Manchester Railway

The publication of a prospectus advertising the intention to promote a company was the first stage in railway construction. A provisional committee would then have a Bill introduced in Parliament to create a company empowered to purchase land and contract for the construction of the line, and permitted to raise the necessary funds by issuing shares. In the case of the Liverpool and Manchester, the first line to be worked throughout by locomotives, the prospectus had to be something of a manifesto as well. Notice the 'Manchester School' economics and also the relatively local nature of the market to be catered for. The attention given to passenger traffic is also limited. In fact, half the line's revenue was to come from this, and it was speed in passenger rather than freight transit that was to influence the promotion of most of the early railways. It is also interesting to note that Henry Booth, one of the scheme's main promoters, was the uncle of Charles Booth the social investigator, and that Edward Pease, secretary to the Fabian Society and close associate of the Webbs, came from the Quaker family which built the Stockton and Darlington. The provincial commercial entrepreneurs were not invariably as dedicated to the pursuit of profits as their critics made out, and when the energy and originality of the provincial intellect was harnessed to a genuine social concern, its contribution would be very effective.

E 1

The Committee of the Liverpool and Manchester Railroad Company think it right to state, concisely, the grounds upon which they rest their claims to public encouragement and support.

The importance, to a commercial state, of a safe and cheap mode of transit for merchandise from one part of the country to another, will be readily acknowledged. This was the plea, upon the first introduction of canals: it was for the public advantage; and although the new mode of conveyance interfered with existing and inferior modes, and was opposed to the feelings and prejudices of landholders, the great principle of the public good prevailed, and experience has justified the decision.

It is upon the same principle that railroads are now proposed to be established; as a means of conveyance manifestly superior to existing modes: possessing moreover this recommendation, in addition to what could have been claimed in favour of canals, namely, that the railroad scheme holds out to the public not only a cheaper, but far more expeditious conveyance than any yet established.

In deciding upon the proposed route, the Committee have been anxious, at considerable inconvenience and expense, to select a line which may not only be eligible . . . but may be as little objectionable as possible with reference to individual and local interest. The ground has been surveyed by eminent engineers, and the estimated expense of a railroad, upon the most improved construction, including the charge for locomotive engines to be employed on the line, is £400,000, which sum it is proposed to raise in 4,000 shares of £100 each.

The total quantity of merchandise passing between Liverpool and Manchester is estimated, by the lowest computation, at 1,000 tons per day. The bulk of this merchandise is transported either by the Duke of Bridgwater's Canal or the 'Mersey and Irwell Navigation'. By both of these conveyances goods must pass up the river Mersey, a distance of 16 or 18 miles, subject to serious delays from contrary winds and not infrequently to actual loss or damage from tempestuous weather. The average length of passage, by these conveyances, including the customary detention on the wharfs, may be taken at 36 hours. . . . The average charge upon merchandise for the last 14 years has been about 15s. a ton.

By the projected railroad, the transit of merchandise between Liverpool and Manchester will be effected in 4 or 5 hours, and the charge to the merchant will be reduced at least one-third. Here, then, will be accomplished an immense pecuniary saving to the public, over and above what is perhaps still more important, *the economy of time*. . . . It will afford stimulus to the productive industry of the country; it will give a new impulse to the powers of accumulation, the value and importance of which can be fully understood only by those who are aware how seriously commerce may be impeded by petty restrictions, and how commercial enterprise is encouraged and promoted by an adherance to the principles of fair competition and free trade.

The Committee are aware that it will not immediately be understood by the public how the proprietors of a railroad, requiring an invested capital of £400,000, can afford to carry goods at so great a reduction upon the charge of the present water companies. . . . It is not that the water companies have not been able to carry goods on more reasonable terms, but that, strong in the enjoyment of their monopoly, they have not thought it proper to do so. . . . IT IS COMPETITION THAT IS WANTED. . . .

But it is not altogether on account of the exorbitant charges of the water-carriers that a railroad is desirable. The present canal establishments are inadequate to . . . the regular and punctual conveyance of goods at all periods and seasons. In summer time there is frequently a deficiency of water, obliging boats to go only half-loaded, while, in winter, they are sometimes locked up with frosts, for weeks together. . . .

In addition to the transport of goods between Liverpool and Manchester, an important branch of revenue may be expected to result to the proprietors of the projected road, from the conveyance of coals from the rich mines in the vicinity of St Helens. . . . These coals at present pass along the Sankey Canal, and down the Mersey to Liverpool, a distance of about 30 miles. By the railway the distance will be shortened to one half, and the charge for transit very materially reduced.

Amongst the widely-diffused benefits to be expected from the proposed railroad, must especially be enumerated, no inconsiderable advance in the commercial prosperity of Ireland. The latent energies of that country, her capabilities as a manufacturing power, will be developed by being brought into easy contact and communication with the manufacturing districts of this Kingdom; whilst every article of her agricultural industry will experience an increased demand, from the cheapness and facility with which it will be introduced into the prosperous counties of Lancaster and York. In the present state of trade and of commercial enterprise dispatch is no less essential than economy. Merchandise is frequently brought across the Atlantic from New York to Liverpool in 21 days; while, owing to the various causes of delay above enumerated, goods have in some instances been longer on their passage from Liverpool to Manchester.

The immediate and prominent advantages to be derived from the proposed railroad are, increased facilities to the general operations of commerce, arising out of that punctuality and dispatch which will attend the transit of merchandise between Liverpool and Manchester, as well as immense pecuniary saving to the trading community. . . . Moreover, as a cheap and expeditious means of conveyance for travellers, the railway holds out the fair prospect of a public accommodation, the magnitude and importance of which cannot be immediately ascertained. . . .

From T. Baines, 'History of Liverpool', 1852, pp. 601-3.

Further Reading

Jack Simmons, 'The Railways of Britain', chaps. 1, 2.
Michael Robbins, 'The Railway Age', chaps. 1-4, 8-10.
L. T. C. Rolt, 'George and Robert Stephenson', Longmans, 1960, chaps. 5, 6, 9.

See also G 6.

The Coming Railway Age

'The Scotsman'

When a collaborator of George Stephenson read 'The Scotsman's' glowing forecast of the benefits of the locomotive-worked railway on 22 December 1824, he dismissed as nonsense the idea of a train travelling at over ten miles an hour. Yet by the time of the death of the editor, Charles Maclaren (1782-1866), all his forecasts had come to pass. Railways had been of central importance in the war which unified Italy in 1859—60, many of them built by Thomas Brassey, and in the American Civil War; and long-distance travel throughout Europe had become commonplace. The idea of 'improvement' associated with the railway and other examples of mechanisation conformed to the political and economic ideologies associated with the Edinburgh of the Enlightenment — of Adam Smith and Dugald Stewart, which Thomas Love Peacock satirised in the person of Mac Quedy in 'Crotchet Castle', 1830. Maclaren, a farmer's son who made good as a geologist and as editor of the 'Encyclopaedia Britannica', founded in Edinburgh in 1768, started 'The Scotsman' in 1817 as a major organ of Whig—Liberal reform in Scotland. He was fairly typical of the 'Modern Athenian', and shows the sort of mind which adapted to and mastered the new technologies. The Enlightenment did not confine itself to Scotland: future Liberal politicians and administrators like Lord Brougham, Lord John Russell and Sir James Kay-Shuttleworth attended Edinburgh University, the Liberal 'Edinburgh Review' and the conservative 'Quarterly Review' dominated the British periodical press for half a century, and University College, London — the first major extension of higher education in England — owed its foundation in 1828 substantially to Edinburgh graduates.

E 2

When the steam-coach is brought fully into use, practice will teach us many things respecting it, of which theory leaves us ignorant. With the facilities for rapid motion which it will afford, however, there is nothing very extravagant in expecting to see the present extreme rate of travelling (ten miles per hour) doubled. We shall then be carried at the rate of 400 miles per day, with all the ease we now enjoy in a steam boat, but without the annoyance of sea-sickness, or the danger of being burned or drowned. It is impossible to anticipate the effects of such an extended facility of communications, when generally introduced. From Calais to Paris, or Constantinople for instance, would be but a journey of five days; and the tour of Europe might be accomplished in a shorter time, than our grandfathers took to travel to London and back again. The Americans, with their characteristic ardour for improvement, are now collecting information about railways and locomotive machines in England; and to them these investigations will prove of inestimable value. It is pleasing indeed to think, that at the moment when the gigantic Republics of the new world are starting into existence, the inventive genius of man is creating new moral and mechanical powers to cement and bind their vast and distant members together and to give the human race the benefits of a more extended and perfect civilisation.

Nor ought we to overlook the additional security which an opulent and highly improved country will in future derive from the facility of its internal means of communication. Were a foreign enemy, for instance, to invade England, 500 steam-wagons could convey 50,000 armed men in one day to the point assailed; and within one week it would be easy, by the same means, to collect half a million at one spot, all quite fresh and fit for action. We cannot scan the future march of improvement; and it would be rash to say that even a higher velocity than 20 miles an hour may not be found applicable. Tiberius travelled 200 miles in two days, and this was reckoned an extraordinary effort. But in our times a shopkeeper or mechanic travels twice as fast as the Roman Emperor, and 20 years hence he may travel with a speed that would leave the fleetest courser behind. Such a new power of locomotion cannot be introduced without working a vast change in the state of society. With so great a facility and celerity of communication, the provincial towns of an empire would become so many suburbs of the metropolis — or rather the effect would be similar to that of collecting the whole inhabitants into one city. Commodities, inventions, discoveries, opinions, would circulate with a rapidity hitherto unknown, and above all, the intercourse of man with man, nation with nation, province with province, would be prodigiously increased.

From 'The Scotsman', 22 December, 1825.

Further Reading

Michael Robbins, 'The Railway Age', chaps. 6, 12, 14.
T. C. Smout, 'A History of the Scottish People', chap. 19.
Brian Simon, 'Studies in the History of Education, 1780-1870', chap. 2.

See also D 3, F 7, H 9.

To Brighton and Back for Three and Sixpence

Charles Rossiter (d. 1891)

Every painting, the Victorians thought, should tell a story or point an improving moral, in the sensible belief that one effective way of coping with vast and continuing social and economic changes was to concentrate on the minutiae of individuals' relationships. The new developments in mass-transport gave them plenty of scope for this, and they did not fail to take advantage of them, with paintings like W. P. Frith's 'Paddington Station' and Ford Madox Brown's 'The Last of England'.

Apart from its narrative side, Rossiter's painting shows the discomfort third-class railway passengers had to endure before, in the 1870s, they were discovered to be a profitable source of revenue. A penny a mile may seem little enough today, but it meant about a shilling a mile to the Victorians. Hence the 'shabby-genteel' aspect of the passengers. Working-class excursionists, and working-class resorts like Blackpool, did not come on the scene until the 1880s.

E 3

Painting of 1859 in the City Art Gallery, Birmingham.

The Investments of Professor and Mrs T. H. Green

Thomas Hill Green (1836-82), a clergyman's son, was Professor of Moral Philosophy at Oxford and a prominent temperance and educational reformer. In 1869 he married Charlotte Symonds, the daughter of a Bristol doctor. The portfolio of their investments shows how the propertied intelligentsia of the country, university and literary men, kept their money, in secure low-yield railway shares. There is still a hint of local interest in the North Country investments of Green and the West Country companies in which his wife's father must have invested, but twenty years later the portfolio would include more overseas bonds like those of the Victorian railways. The Greens were typical sleeping partners in the vast joint-stock enterprises of the second half of the century.

E4

Schedule of Property held by Trustees of the Marriage Settlement of Mr and Mrs T. H. Green

1. Settled by T. H. Green

Amount	Description	Income	Cash
£2000	Manchester Sheffield and Lincolnshire Railway 4% £90		£2078
£644	Midland Railway 6%	£38.12.9	£877.1.10
£1100	Great Western and London and North Western Joint 6%	£66	£1500
£1220	Midland Railway Preference 4.5%	£57.4.9	£1294.6.3
£700	North Eastern Railway 5%	£35	£735
		£280.17.6	£6484.8.1

2. Settled by Mrs T. H. Green

Amount	Description	Income	Cash
£1500	Bristol Docks Bonds 4%	£60	£1500
£2500	Great Western Railway Consols 5%	£125	£2797. 4.6
£1400	Victoria Government Railway Bonds 6%	£84	£1552. 5.0
£660	Monmouth Railway 5%	£32	£714. 3.0
£700	North Eastern Railway 4%	£28	£646. 6.6
£1000	Cornwall Railways	£45	£1011. 7.6
£49.15.6	Consols	£1. 9.11	£45.17.2
£1452.18.10	Consols	£43.11. 8	£1343.19.5
£1167.16.3	3½%s	£35. 0. 8	£1080. 4.6
£300	Rhymney Railway 5%	£15	£300
		£469. 2. 3	£10991. 7.7

Income tax deducted at 10%

From the Green Papers, Balliol College, Oxford.

Further Reading
Michael Robbins, 'The Railway Age', chaps. 9, 10.

The Grand Hotel, Scarborough, c. 1860
Cuthbert Brodrick, Architect

E 5

If you are for public life at our Great Pavilionstone Hotel, you walk into that establishment as if it were your club; and find ready for you, your news-room, dining-room, smoking-room, billiard-room, music-room, public breakfast, public dinner twice a-day (one plain, one gorgeous), hot baths and cold baths.

If you want to be bored, there are plenty of bores always ready for you, and from Saturday to Monday in particular, you can be bored, (if you like it) through and through. Should you want to be private at our

Great Pavilionstone Hotel, say but the word, look at the list of charges, choose your floor, name your figure — there you are, established in your castle, by the day, week, month or year. . . . Are you going across the Alps, and would you like to air your Italian at our Great Pavilionstone Hotel? Talk to the Manager — always conversational, accomplished, and polite. Do you want to be aided, abetted, comforted, or advised, at our Great Pavilionstone Hotel? Send for the good landlord, and he is your friend. . . .

You shall find all the nations of the earth, and all the styles of shaving and not shaving, hair cutting and hair letting alone, for ever flowing through our hotel. Couriers you shall see by hundreds; fat leathern bags for five-franc pieces, closing with violent snaps, like discharges of fire-arms, by thousands; more luggage in a morning than, fifty years ago, all Europe saw in a week.

So Dickens described the new railway hotel at Folkestone, one of a multitude which were to rear themselves throughout Europe on mountains, by golf-courses, in spas and above all on the sea coast. They became the passenger equivalent of the freight warehouse, the joint-stock palaces of the middle class who set out to absorb, with the aid of Thomas Cook's travel agency and Murray's or Baedeker's guides, the culture of the Continent.

The Journeys of James Bryce

James Bryce (1838-1922) was the son of a Glasgow schoolmaster who rose to become Professor of Law at Oxford, Liberal Cabinet Minister and Britain's most famous ambassador to the U.S.A. He was also a formidable traveller, and managed to visit practically every area of the globe except the polar regions and Indonesia, a tribute less to his energy, remarkable though that was, than to the expansion of the world communications network. A result of this was his interest in foreign politics; like many who saw improved communications promoting international co-operation, he devoted much time to fostering movements for arbitration between nations, the protection of minorities, and the restraining of national rivalries.

E 6

1870 Goes the Northern Circuit. Appointed Regius Professor of Civil Law at Oxford. First visit to United States with A. V. Dicey. New York, Newport, Boston, Cornell, Niagara, the White Mountains, Philadelphia, Washington.

1871 Bar work, teaching at Oxford, journalism. Visit to Switzerland and the Rhine with C. P. Ilbert and Miss Ilbert and with his sisters May and Katherine.

1872 Visits Iceland with C. P. Ilbert and Aeneas Mackay.

1873 Climbs in Pyrenees with C. P. Ilbert.

1874 Stands unsuccessfully as Liberal candidate for the Wick Burghs. Visits Portugal on legal business for Messrs Carver of Manchester. Visits Oporto, Lisbon, Coimbra, Busaco, and travels in the mountains.

1875 Again visits Portugal on legal business – travels through Spain, visiting Santander, Burgos, Valladolid, Avila, El Escorial, Madrid, Toledo, Córdova, Granada da Seville, Málaga, Cádiz, Gibraltar.

1876 Travels in the Caucasus and Armenia with Aeneas Mackay and ascends Ararat. First visit to Constantinople.

1877 Publishes 'Trade Marks, Registration Act and Trade Mark Law', 'Transcaucasia and Ararat' published. Death of his father Dr James Bryce.

1878 Prominent member of the Eastern Question Committee. Journey to the Carpathians with Leslie Stephen.

1879 Elected to the Alpine Club. Working on the Eastern Question Campaign. Holiday in Norway, Denmark and Finland.

From H. A. L. Fisher, 'James Bryce', 1927, ii, 314.

Section F

Transition

A Farm Sale near Reigate

William Cobbett (1762–1835)

Riding through southern England in the 1820s William Cobbett, sometime Tory pamphleteer against the 'Horrid Barbarity' of the French Revolution, now popular tribune, observed and commented volubly on the new social relationships induced by industrialisation and the adoption of the values of commerce. The fund-holders and stock-jobbers he assaulted played a considerable part in providing the capital for industrial investment out of income derived from interest on loans they made to the Government. The Government in its turn covered this by taxes which tended to be disproportionately sever on the poorer classes. Cobbett's politics were a jumble of eccentric prejudice and humane perception. Seen from today, his clash with Macaulay in the Commons over the emancipation of the Jews does not show him in a pleasant light, his panacea of straw-bonnet weaving seems absurd, and the rural commonwealth to which he looked back a myth, but he sensed accurately the change in men's relationships from those of obligation and custom to those determined by cash payment. Both his defects and his strengths proved persistent in radical social criticism throughout the century.

F 1

Reigate, Thursday Evening
20th October, 1825

Having done my business at Hartswood to-day about eleven o'clock, I went to a *sale* at a farm, which the farmer is quitting. Here I had a view of what has long been going on all over the country. The farm, which belongs to *Christ's Hospital,* has been held by a man of the name of Charington, in whose family the lease has been, I hear, a great number of years. The house is hidden by trees. It stands in the Weald of Surrey, close by the *River Mole,* which is here a mere rivulet, though just below this house the rivulet supplies the very prettiest flour-mill I ever saw in my life.

Every thing about this farm-house was formerly the scene of *plain manners* and *plentiful living.* Oak clothes-chests, oak bedsteads, oak chests of drawers, and oak tables to eat on, long, strong, and well supplied with joint stools. Some of the things were many hundreds of years old. But all appeared to be in a state of decay and nearly of *disuse.* There appeared to have been hardly any *family* in that house, where formerly there were in all probability, from ten to fifteen men, boys, and maids and, which was the worst of all, there was a *parlour!* Aye, and a *carpet* and *bell-pull* too! One end of the front of this once plain and substantial house had been moulded into a *'parlour;'* and there was the mahogany table, and the fine chairs, and the fine glass, and all as bare-faced upstart as any stock-jobber in the kingdom can boast of. And, there were the decanters, the glasses, the 'dinner-set' of crockery ware, and all just in the true stock-jobber style. And I dare say it has been *'Squire* Charington and the *Miss* Charingtons; and not plain Master Charington, and his son Hodge, and his daughter Betty Charington, all of whom this accursed system has, in all likelihood, transmuted into a species of mock gentlefolks, while it has ground the labourers down into real slaves. Why do not farmers now *feed* and *lodge* their work-people, as they did formerly? Because they cannot keep them *upon so little* as they give them in wages. This is the real cause of the change. There needs no more to prove that the lot of the working classes has become worse than it formerly was. This fact alone is quite sufficient to settle this point. All the world knows, that a number of people, boarded in the same house, and at the same table, can, with as good food, be boarded much cheaper than those persons divided into twos, threes, or fours, can be boarded. This is a well-known truth: therefore, if the farmer now shuts his pantry against his labourers, and pays them wholly in money, is it not clear, that he does it because he thereby gives them a living *cheaper* to him; that is to say, a *worse* living than formerly? Mind he has a *house* for them; a kitchen for them to sit in, bed rooms for them to sleep in, tables, and stools, and benches, of everlasting duration. All these he has; all these *cost him nothing;* and yet so much does he gain by pinching them in wages that he lets all these things remain as of no use, rather than feed labourers in the house. Judge, then, of the *change* that has taken place in the condition of these labourers! And, be astonished, if you can, at the *pauperism* and the *crimes* that now disgrace this once happy and moral England.

The land produces, on an average, what it always produced, but, there is a new distribution of the produce. This 'Squire Charington's father used, I dare say, to sit at the head of the oak-table along with his men, say grace to them, and cut up the meat and the pudding. He might take a cup of *strong beer* to himself, when they had none; but, that was pretty nearly all the difference in their manner of living. So that *all* lived well. But, the 'Squire had many *wine-decanters* and *wine-glasses* and 'a *dinner set*', and a '*breakfast set*,' and '*desert knives*,' and these evidently imply carryings on and a consumption that must of necessity have greatly robbed the long oak table if it had remained fully tenanted. That long table could not share in the work of the decanters and the dinner set. Therefore, it became almost untenanted; the labourers retreated to hovels, called cottages; and, instead of board and lodging, they got money; so little of it as to enable the employer to drink wine; but, then, that he might not reduce them to *quite starvation*, they were enabled to come to him, in the *king's name*, and demand food *as paupers*. And, now, mind, that which a man receives in the *king's name*, he knows well he has *by force*; and it is not in nature that he should *thank* any body for it, and least of all the party *from whom it is forced*. Then, if this sort of force be insufficient to obtain him *enough* to eat and to keep him warm, is it surprising, if he think it *no great offence against God* (who created no man to starve) to use *another sort of force* more within his own controul? Is it, in short, surprising, if he resort to *theft* and *robbery*?

This is not only the *natural* progress, but it *has been* the progress in England. The blame is not justly imputed to 'SQUIRE CHARINGTON and his like; the blame belongs to the infernal stock-jobbing system. There was no reason to expect that farmers would not endeavour to keep pace, in point of show and luxury, with fund-holders, and with all the tribes that *war* and *taxes* created. Farmers were not the authors of

D

the mischief; and *now* they are compelled to shut the labourers out of their houses, and to pinch them in their wages, in order to be able to pay their own taxes; and, besides this, the manners and the principles of the working class are so changed, that a sort of self-preservation bids the farmer (especially in some counties) to keep them from beneath his roof.

I could not quit this farm-house without reflecting on the thousands of scores of bacon and thousands of bushels of bread that had been eaten from the long oak-table which, I said to myself, is now perhaps, going, at last, to the bottom of a bridge that some stock-jobber will stick up over an artificial river in his cockney garden. 'By——it shant,' said I, almost in a real passion: and so I requested a friend to buy it for me; and if he do so, I will take it to Kensington, or to Fleet-street, and keep it for the good it has done in the world.

When the old farm-houses are down (and down they must come in time) what a miserable thing the country will be! Those that are now erected are mere painted shells, with a Mistress within, who is stuck up in a place she calls a *parlour*, with, if she have children, the 'young ladies and gentlemen' about her: some showy chairs and a sofa (a *sofa* by all means): half a dozen prints in gilt frames hanging up: some swinging book-shelves with novels and tracts upon them: a dinner brought in by a girl that is perhaps better 'educated' than she: two or three nick-nacks to eat instead of a piece of bacon and a pudding: the house too neat for a dirty-shoed carter to be allowed to come into; and every thing proclaiming to every sensible beholder, that there is here a constant anxiety to make a *show* not warranted by the reality. The children (which is the worst part of it) are all too clever to *work*: they are all to be *gentlefolks*. Go to plough! Good God! What, 'young gentlemen' go to plough! They become *clerks*, or some skimmy-dish thing or other. They flee from the dirty *work* as cunning horses do from the bridle. What misery is all this! What a mass of materials for producing that general and *dreadful convulsion* that must, first or last, come and blow this funding and jobbing and enslaving and starving system to atoms!

From William Cobbett, 'Rural Rides', Penguin ed., pp. 226-9.

Further Reading

Raymond Williams, 'Culture and Society', chap. 1.
E. P. Thompson, 'The Making of the English Working Class', 1965, chap.
    XVI.ii

See also C 6, J 8, J 9.

'The Oldham Weaver'

The folk-songs in which the industrial workers commented upon their lives remained until recently a sort of evidence which existed only in performance. Only in the 1950s was a serious attempt made to record and transcribe them, as the folk-song revival of the 1900s had concentrated, naturally enough, on the rural tradition which migration, literacy, a standardised vocabulary and a written culture were destroying. Mrs Gaskell's is therefore a pioneer effort, although this particular song was popular under various titles in Lancashire as a broadsheet ballad from about 1820 on.

The song itself would be more relevant to Oldham at the time Mrs Gaskell wrote 'Mary Barton' in 1848 than when it was originally composed. Until the 1830s Oldham hand-loom weavers enjoyed a considerable degree of prosperity — wages in 1820 were two guineas a week — exercised a fair amount of control over their work, and even imposed within the town itself a sort of 'dictatorship of the proletariat'. In the thirties weaving was mechanised, and control of the town passed into the hands of the middle-class ratepayers. A 'Morning Chronicle' reporter who visited it in 1849 called it 'the most repulsive working-place I have seen in Lancashire'; the weavers he met were earning four shillings a week.

F 2

I

Oi'm a poor cotton-weyver, as mony a one knoowas,
Oi've nowt for t' yeat, and oi've woorn eawt my clooas,
Yo'ad hardly gi' tuppence for aw as oi've on,
My clogs are boath brosten, and stuckins oi've none,
      Yo'd think it wur hard
      To be browt into th' warld,
To be — clemmed,* an do th' best as yo con.

II

Owd Dicky o' Billy's kept telling me lung,
Wee s'd ha' better toimes if I'd but howd my tung,
Oi've howden my tung, till oi've near stopped my breath,
Oi think i' my heeart oi'se soon clem to deeath,
      Owd Dicky's weel crammed,
      He never wur clemmed,
An' he ne'er picked ower† i' his loife.

III

We tow'rt on six week — thinking aitch day wur th' last,
We shifted, an' shifted, till neaw we're quoite fast;
We lived upo' nettles, whoile nettles wur good,
An' Waterloo porridge the best o' eawr food,
      Oi'm tellin' yo' true,
      Oi can find folk enow,
As wur livin' na better nor me.

* 'Clem,' to starve with hunger. 'Hard is the choice, when the valiant must eat their arms or *clem*.' — Ben Jonson.
† To 'pick ower' means to throw the shuttle in hand-loom weaving.

IV

Owd Billy o' Dans sent th' baileys one day,
Fur a shop deebt oi eawd him, as oi coud na pay,
But he wer too lat, fur owd Billy o' th' Bent,
Had sowd th' tit an' cart, an' ta'en goods fur th' rent,
    We'd neawt left bo' th' owd stoo',
      That wur seeats fur two,
An' on it ceawred Marget an' me.

V

Then t' baileys leuked reawnd as sloy as a meawse,
When they seed as aw t' goods were ta'en eawt o' t' heawse,
Says one chap to th' tother, 'Aws gone, theaw may see;'
Say oi, 'Ne'er freet, mon, yeaur welcome ta' me.'
    They made no moor ado
      But whopped up th' eawd stoo',
An' we booath leet, whack — upo' t' flags!

VI

Then oi said to eawr Marget, as we lay upo' t' floor,
'We's never be lower i' this warld, oi'm sure,
If ever things awtern, oi'm sure they mun mend,
For oi think i' my heart we're booath at t' far eend;
    For meeat we ha' none;
      Nor looms t' weyve on, —
Edad! they're as good lost as fund.'

VII

Eawr Marget declares had hoo cloo'as to put on,
Hoo'd goo up to Lunnon an' talk to th' greet mon;
An' if things were na awtered when there hoo had been,
Hoo's fully resolved t' sew up meawth an' eend;
    Hoo's neawt to say again t' king,
      But hoo loikes a fair thing,
An' hoo says hoo can tell when hoo's hurt.

From Mrs Gaskell, 'Mary Barton', 1848, pp. 32-3.

Further Reading

A. L. Lloyd, 'Folk Song in England', 1967, chap. 5.
E. P. Thompson, 'The Making of the English Working Class', 1965, chap. IX.

See also C 6, F 7.

The Masons on Strike and at Play

Hugh Miller (1802–56)

Hugh Miller, starting as a stonemason in Cromarty, became an important Scots religious leader, geologist and journalist. His paper, 'The Witness', became the organ of the 'Free Church' in Scotland which broke away from the Established Church in 1843, believing in the right of congregations to select their own minister instead of having him imposed on them by the local landowner. Such disputes, and causes like temperance and foreign missions, which were socially neutral, occupied the energies of the middle class in the areas most affected by industrial expansion. Rather like George Eliot, their admonitions to the working class have something of the tone of a bystander telling a drowning man that he ought to have learned to swim, that his poverty is his own responsibility and can be remedied only by his own hard work on the terms laid down by society. The suppression of traditional holidays and recreations and the imposition of the horrors of the Victorian Sabbath were also part of this ethic, and can be seen as attempts to impose a 'labour discipline' attuned to the demands of industry. Miller's dismissal of the strike meeting, and his disgust at the blood-sports of the workers, are typical of this approach, and the manufacturers who supported the Free Church would have concurred. But we should not forget that the concern about violence and cruelty was genuine, and the suppression of the worst barbarities of the criminal code, cruelty to children and animals, and exposure of atrocities against subject races abroad owed much to the 'Nonconformist conscience'.

F 3

... when, on coming to the work-shed on the Monday morning, I found my comrades gathered in front of it in a group, and learned that there was a grand strike all over the district, I received the intelligence with as little of the enthusiasm of the 'independent associated mechanic' as possibly may be. 'You are right in your claims,' I said to Charles; 'but you have taken a bad time for urging them, and will be beaten to a certainty. The masters are much better prepared for a strike than you are. How, may I ask, are you yourself provided with the sinews of war?' 'Very ill indeed,' said Charles, scratching his head: 'if the masters don't give in before Saturday, it's all up with me; but never mind; let us have one day's fun: there's to be a grand meeting at Bruntsfield Links; let us go in as a deputation from the country masons, and make a speech about our rights and duties; and then, if we see matters going very far wrong, we can just step back again, and begin work tomorrow.' 'Bravely resolved,' I said: 'I shall go with you by all means, and take notes of your speech.' We marched into town, about sixteen in number; and, on joining the crowd already assembled on the Links, were recognised, by the deep hue of our clothes and aprons, which differed considerably from that borne by workers in the paler Edinburgh stone, as a reinforcement from a distance, and were received with loud cheers. Charles, however, did not make his speech: the meeting, which was about eight hundred strong, seemed fully in the possession of a few crack orators, who spoke with a fluency to which he could make no pretension; and so he replied to the various calls from among his comrades, of 'Cha, Cha,' by assuring them that he could not catch the eye of the gentleman in the chair. The meeting had, of course, neither chair nor chairman; and after a good deal of idle speech-making, which seemed to satisfy the speakers themselves remarkably well, but which at least some of their auditory regarded as nonsense, we found that the only motion on which we could harmoniously agree was a motion for an adjournment. And so we adjourned until the evening, fixing as our place of meeting one of the humbler halls of the city.

My comrades proposed that we should pass the time until the hour of meeting in a public-house; and, desirous of securing a glimpse of the sort of enjoyment for which they sacrificed so much, I accompanied them. Passing not a few more inviting-looking places, we entered a low tavern in the upper part of the Canongate, kept in an old, half-ruinous building, which has since disappeared. We passed on through a narrow passage to a low-roofed room in the centre of the erection, into which the light of day never penetrated, and in which the gas was burning dimly in a close sluggish atmosphere, rendered still more stifling by tobacco-smoke, and a strong smell of ardent spirits. In the middle of the crazy floor there was a trap-door which lay open at the time; and a wild combination of sounds, in which the yelping of a dog, and a few gruff voices that seemed cheering him on, were most noticeable, rose from the apartment below. It was customary for dram-shops to keep badgers housed in long narrow boxes, and for working men to keep dogs, and it was part of the ordinary sport of such places to set the dogs to unhouse the badgers. . . . Our party, like most others, had its dog – a repulsive-looking brute, with an earth-directed eye, as if he carried about with him an evil conscience; and my companions were desirous of getting his earthing ability tested upon the badger of the establishment; but on summoning the tavern-keeper, we were told that the party below had got the start of us: their dog was, as we might hear, 'just drawing the badger; and before our dog could be permitted to draw him, the poor brute would require to get an hour's rest.' I need scarce say that the hour was spent in hard drinking in that stagnant atmosphere; and then we all descended through the trap-door, by means of a ladder, into a bare-walled dungeon, dark and damp, and where the pestiferous air smelt like that of a burial-vault. The scene which followed was exceedingly repulsive and brutal – nearly as much so as some of the scenes furnished by those otter hunts in which the aristocracy of the country delight occasionally to indulge. Amid shouts and yells the badger, with the blood of his recent conflict still fresh upon him, was again drawn to the box mouth; and the party returning satisfied to the apartment above, again betook themselves to hard drinking. . . . The conversation became very loud, very involved, and, though highly seasoned with oaths, very insipid. . . . I stole out to the King's Park, and passed an hour to better purpose among the trap-rocks than I could possibly have spent it beside the trap-door.

From Hugh Miller, 'My Schools and Schoolmasters', 1852.

Further Reading

G. Kitson Clark, 'The Making of Victorian England', pp. 20-1, 58-62, chap. VI.

E. P. Thompson, 'The Making of the English Working Class', chap. XII.i.

See also B 1, G 6.

Women in the Mines, 1842

F 4

Betty Harris, aged thirty-seven, drawer, in a coal-pit at Little Bolton: I have a belt round my waist, and a chain passing between my legs, and I go on my hands and feet. The road is very steep, and we have to hold by a rope; and when there is no rope, by anything we can catch hold of. . . . I am not as strong as I was, and cannot stand the work so well as I used to. I have drawn till I have had the skin off me; the belt and chain is worse when we are in the family way. . . .

From Children's Employment Commission: First Report
of the Commissioners (Mines), Parliamentary
Papers, 1842, vol. xv, p. 84.

Working Conditions in Scottish Mines

Alexander MacDonald (1821–81)

A Royal Commission is the most authoritative of official bodies in the investigation of economic and social problems. Today it tends to be composed in such a way as to give a 'balanced' consideration to its subject. This was not always the case. The famous Commissions on the Poor Law (1832-4), Municipal Corporations (1834-5) and Oxford and Cambridge Universities (1850-2) had their conclusions more or less determined for them by the reforming Whig Governments which appointed them, and were simply intended to expose the expected abuses in the situations they inquired into. There is a greater similarity between them and Chadwick's one-man sanitary report of 1842 than between them and later bodies which bore the same title.

The Commission on the Trades Unions (1867-9) comes at the transitional stage. Pressures from two opposed viewpoints led to its being set up: the unions were campaigning for legal recognition and for the repeal of the 'Master and Servant' laws, which placed the employee at a grave disadvantage in suing or being sued by his employer over breach of contract; and conservatively minded M.P.s, seizing reports of coercion by union officials during a strike at Sheffield as evidence that trade unions were terroristic organisations, wanted to prove that they were. The Commission, however, was not weighted greatly on either side, and eventually recommended the granting of a rather qualified legal recognition to the unions; while a minority report, the work of its most radical members Tom Hughes, author of 'Tom Brown's Schooldays', and Frederic Harrison, urged straightforward legalisation.

Government action followed the report of the Commission in being ambiguous: an Act was passed in 1871 legalising the unions but prohibiting picketing. However, following further agitation and another Commission, the 'Master and Servant' laws and the prohibition of picketing were ended in 1875.

F 5

15,252. (*Lord Elcho.*) What year was it in which you entered the mines? — About the year 1835 I think; I could not fix the year. When I entered the mines at eight years of age or so, at that time workings were not so large for we had not sunk in Scotland to the thicker seams which are now being worked.

15,253. What mine did you enter? — A mine called the Dyke Head Ironstone Mine.

15,254. Not a coal mine? — Not a coal mine at first.

15,255. Where is that mine? — In Lanarkshire.

15,256. Does that mine still exist? — It does not exist now, it has long since been closed. The condition of the miner's boy then was to be raised about 1 o'clock or 2 o'clock in the morning if the distance was very far to travel, and I at that time had to travel a considerable distance, more than three miles; I was raised at that time at 2 o'clock, and never later than 3 o'clock.

15,257. Do you mean that someone went round the place to call the boys? — No. The men lived more then in their own cottages in that part of the country. We got up in the morning, I being called by my father at 1, or very often at 2 o'clock. We remained then in the mine until 5 and 6 at night. It was an ironstone mine, very low, working about 18 inches, and in some instances not quite so high.

15,258. That is, you remained 16 or 17 hours in the pit? — Yes, as a rule.

15,259. Was the work constant for a boy of that age for that time? — The work was perfectly constant.

15,260. No break? — No break. Then I removed to coal mines after that. There we had low seams also, very low seams. There we had no rails to draw upon, that is, tramways laid like rails now for our tubs, or corves, or whirlies as we call them, to run upon. We had leather belts for our shoulders. One was before and another behind, and the wheels were cutting the pavements or floor (we called it pavement) and we had to keep dragging the coal with these ropes over our shoulders, and sometimes round the middle with a chain between our legs. Then there was always another behind pushing with his head.

15,261. That work was done with children? — That work was done by boys, such as I was, from 10 or 11 down to eight, and I have known them as low as seven years old. In the mines at that time the state of ventilation was frightful.

15,262. (*Mr Mathews.*) Are you now speaking of ironstone mines or coal mines? — Of coal and ironstone mines together. The gases pervading the mines in Scotland at that time were, for the most part, carbonic acid gas, not carburetted hydrogen; and I remember well often having three or four lamps put together for the purpose of keeping so much light as to enable us to see by. A very great deal of our drawing, as we call it, was performed in the dark in consequence of the want of ventilation in the mines.

15,263. (*Lord Elcho.*) Did that want of ventilation at that time lead to frequent accidents? — It did not lead to frequent accidents; but it lead to premature death.

15,264. Not to explosion? — No; carbonic acid gas in no case leads to explosion. There was no explosive gas in those mines I was in, or scarcely any. I may state incidentally here that in the first ironstone mine I was in there were some 20 or more boys besides myself, and I am not aware at this moment that there is one alive excepting myself.

Alexander MacDonald, Evidence given before the Royal Commission on Trades Unions, Wednesday 28 April 1868. (Parliamentary Papers, 1867-8, vol. 39, pp. 38-9.)

Further Reading

Henry Pelling. 'A History of British Trade Unionism', 1966, chap. IV.
Asa Briggs, 'Thomas Hughes' and 'Robert Applegarth', in 'Victorian People', 1965.
'The History of the T.U.C. 1868-1968', pp. 11-28.

See also D 1, G 1.

Alexander MacDonald

F 6

MacDonald, Alexander. b. New Monkland, Lanarkshire, June 1821; commenced working in a coal pit 1831; at the age of 21 he had saved £250; ed. Glasgow univ. 1851 still working as a collier during the summer and autumn; a teacher 1853; agitated for release of women and children from working in coal mines 1852-72, and on laws of contract and hiring, and on the truck system; contested Kilmarnock Burghs, 1868; M.P. Stafford 1874 to death, the first working man member, known as the Working Men's member of parliament; sec. of Miners' Association of Scotland; president of Miners' national union 1863; visited the U.S. America 3 times; presented by the miners with £1500, Jany., 1873; member of royal commission on trade unions 1874. d. Well hall near Hamilton 31 Oct. 1881. bur. New Monkland ch. yd. 7 Nov. 'The Biograph', Aug. 1880 pp. 148-57; I.L.N. ('Illustrated London News') lxiv 551, 552 (1874) portrait.

Extract from Frederic Boase, 'Modern English Biography: containing many thousand concise memoirs of persons who have died between the years 1851-1900 with an index of the most interesting matter' (ii, 580). Published between 1892 and 1921 in six volumes, this is the best source of biographical information for Victorian Britain. The 'Dictionary of National Biography' has only a third of Boase's 30,000 entries for this period. Besides, it tends to have a certain Oxbridge and metropolitan exclusiveness.

The Manchester Cotton Workers

James Phillips Kay (1804–77)

'. . . if history judged men less by the noise than by the difference they make, it is hard to think of any name in the Victorian age which deserves to stand above or even beside Kay-Shuttleworth's'. What Edwin Chadwick was to public health reform, James Phillips Kay, later Kay-Shuttleworth, was to public education. A Lancashire man of farming background, he studied medicine at Edinburgh, practised in Manchester, and went on to become the nineteenth-century equivalent of Permanent Secretary at the Ministry of Education. But he was a civil servant with a tendency to act on his own, and his pioneer work in setting up the machinery which trained teachers for elementary schools, commended so enthusiastically by G. M. Young, was paid for out of his own pocket.

His investigation of the Manchester cotton-mill labour force, undertaken in the wake of a terrible cholera epidemic, was in the tradition of the methodical approach to social investigation of the Scottish 'March of Mind' school which many of the livelier minds in the English provinces shared. The rosy, rather complacent optimism of this school was not absent; at the conclusion of his report he observed of the workers he described:

. . .that they are in great measure the architects of their own fortune; that what others can do for them is trifling indeed, compared with what they can do for themselves; that they are infinitely more interested in the preservation of public tranquillity than any other class of society; that mechanical inventions and discoveries are always supremely advantageous to them; and that their real interests can only be effectually promoted, by displaying greater prudence and forethought.

The remedy lay in better educational provision to inculcate those last two qualities, and the implication of this was a degree of public intervention which had no sanction in the individualist ideology. Thus

Kay-Shuttleworth, like Chadwick, represents a vital transitional stage between 'laissez-faire' and state intervention.

F 7

The population employed in the cotton factories rises at five o'clock in the morning, works in the mills from six till eight o'clock, and returns home for half an hour or forty minutes to breakfast. This meal generally consists of tea or coffee with a little bread. Oatmeal porridge is sometimes, but of late rarely used, and chiefly by the men; but the stimulus of tea is preferred, and especially by the women. The tea is almost always of a bad, and sometimes of a deleterious quality, the infusion is weak, and little or no milk is added. The operatives return to the mills and workshops until twelve o'clock, when an hour is allowed for dinner. Amongst those who obtain the lower rates of wages this meal generally consists of boiled potatoes. The mess of potatoes is put into one large dish; melted lard and butter are poured upon them, and a few pieces of fried fat bacon are sometimes mingled with them, and but seldom a little meat. Those who obtain better wages, or families whose aggregate income is larger, add a greater proportion of animal food to this meal, at least three times in the week; but the quantity consumed by the labouring population is not great. The family sits round the table, and each rapidly appropriates his portion on a plate, or, they all plunge their spoons into the dish, and with an animal eagerness satisfy the cravings of their appetite. At the expiration of the hour, they are all again employed in the workshops or mills, where they continue until seven o'clock or a later hour, when they generally again indulge in the use of tea, often mingled with spirits accompanied by a little bread. Oatmeal or potatoes are however taken by some a second time in the evening.

The comparatively innutritious qualities of these articles of diet are most evident. We are, however, by no means prepared to say that an individual living in a healthy atmosphere, and engaged in active employment in the open air, would not be able to continue protracted and severe labour, without any suffering, whilst nourished by this food. We should rather be disposed on the contrary to affirm, that any ill effects must necessarily be so much diminished, that, from the influence of habit, and the benefits derived from the constant inhalation of an uncontaminated atmosphere, during healthy exercise in agricultural pursuits, few if any evil results would ensue. But the population nourished on this aliment is crowded into one dense mass, in cottages separated by narrow, unpaved, and almost pestilential streets; in an atmosphere loaded with the smoke and exhalations of a large manufacturing city. The operatives are congregated in rooms and workshops during twelve hours in the day, in an enervating, heated atmosphere, which is frequently loaded with dust or filaments of cotton, or impure from constant respiration, or from other causes. They are engaged in an employment which absorbs their attention, and unremittingly employs their physical energies.* They are drudges who watch the movements, and assist the operations, of a mighty material force, which toils with an energy ever unconscious of fatigue. The persevering labour of the operative must rival the mathematical precision, the incessant motion, and the exhaustless power of the machine.

Hence, besides the negative results — the total abstraction of every moral and intellectual stimulus — the absence of variety — banishment from the grateful air and the cheering influences of light, the physical energies are exhausted by incessant toil, and imperfect nutrition. Having been subjected to the prolonged labour of an animal—his physical energy wasted — his mind in supine inaction — the artizan has neither moral dignity nor intellectual nor organic strength to resist the seductions of appetite. His wife and children, too frequently subjected to the same process, are unable to cheer his remaining moments of leisure. Domestic economy is neglected, domestic comforts are unknown. A meal of the coarsest food is prepared with heedless haste, and devoured with equal precipitation. Home has no other relation to him than that of shelter — few pleasures are there — it chiefly presents to

---

* A gentleman, whose opinions on these subjects command universal respect, suggests to me, that the intensity of this application is exceedingly increased by the system of paying, not for time, but according to the result of labour.

him a scene of physical exhaustion, from which he is glad to escape. Himself impotent of all the distinguishing aims of his species, he sinks into sensual sloth, or revels in more degrading licentiousness. His house is ill furnished, uncleanly, often ill ventilated, perhaps damp; his food, from want of forethought and domestic economy, is meagre and innutritious; he is debilitated and hypochondriacal, and falls the victim of dissipation.

These artizans are frequently subject to a disease, in which the sensibility of the stomach and bowels is morbidly excited; the alvine secretions are deranged, and the appetite impaired. Whilst this state continues, the patient loses flesh, his features are sharpened, the skin becomes pale, leaden coloured, or of the yellow hue which is observed in those who have suffered from the influence of tropical climates. The strength fails, all the capacities of physical enjoyment are destroyed, and the paroxysms of corporeal suffering are aggravated by the horrors of a disordered imagination, till they lead to gloomy apprehension, to the deepest depression, and almost to despair. We cannot wonder that the wretched victim of this disease, invited by those haunts of misery and crime the gin shop and the tavern, as he passes to his daily labour, should endeavour to cheat his suffering of a few moments, by the false excitement procured by ardent spirits; or that the exhausted artizan, driven by ennui and discomfort from his squalid home, should strive, in the delirious dreams of a continued debauch, to forget the remembrance of his reckless improvidence, of the destitution, hunger, and uninterrupted toil, which threaten to destroy the remaining energies of his enfeebled constitution.

The contagious example which the Irish have exhibited of barbarous habits and savage want of economy, united with the necessarily debasing consequences of uninterrupted toil, have demoralized the people.

From J. P. Kay, 'The Moral and Physical Conduct of the Working Classes employed in the Cotton Manufacture in Manchester', 1832, pp. 9-12.

Further Reading

Asa Briggs, 'Manchester', in 'Victorian Cities', 1963.
G. Kitson Clark, 'The Making of Victorian England', 1962, pp. 95-107.
G. M. Young, 'Victorian England', 1936, pp. 55-62.

See also B 3, C 1, E 2, F 8, G 4.

The Factory Girls' Dinner Hour, Wigan

Eyre Crowe (1824–1910)

F 8

Painting of 1874 in City Art Gallery, Manchester.

So long as the hours do not include overtime, the work is as healthful to body and mind as it well could be. Sitting by the hands at work, watching the invigorating quickness of the machinery, the pleasant fellowship of men, women and children, the absence of care and the presence of common interest — the general well-being of well-earned and well-paid work — one was tempted to think that here, indeed, was happiness — unknown to the strained brain-worker, the idle and overfed rich, or the hardly pressed very poor.

From Beatrice Webb: 'My Apprenticeship'.

The London Scavenger

Henry Mayhew (1812–87)

Henry Mayhew, in E. P. Thompson's estimation 'Incomparably the greatest social investigator in the mid-century', absorbed himself, in his monumental 'London Labour and the London Poor' (1851-62), less in investigation of the casualties of industrialisation than of the casualties of non-industrialisation. His subjects were that urban mass whose expansion did not directly result from the expansion of industry, and whose apparent social degeneracy alarmed other commentators. 'The Ghetto folk', the American socialist Jack London called them half a century later, 'unable to render efficient service to England in the world struggle for industrial supremacy', they were the product not of the organisation of industry but of the disorganisation of urban growth.

Unlike London, however, Mayhew was a sympathetic interviewer who got his subjects to talk to him with a rare frankness and lack of inhibition. The individual components of the urban mass, whom some commentators treated at best as inanimate statistics or at worst as anonymous brutes, gain an identity as they talk to him. Mayhew came from the same milieu as Dickens: he was a playwright and journalist. Occasionally the theatrical and the sensational show through, but this detracts little from his value in providing a direct contact with the forgotten masses of the Victorian city.

F 9

'I don't know how old I am and I can't see what that consarns any one, as I's old enough to have a jolly rough beard, and so can take care of myself. . . .

'I likes to hear the paper read well enough, if I's resting; but old Bill, as often wolunteers to read, has to spell the hard words so, that one can't tell what the devil he's reading about. I never heers anything about books. . . . I don't know much good that ever anybody as I knows ever got out of books; they're fittest for idle people. . . .

'I never goes to any church or chapel. . . . I was once in a church but felt queer, as one does in them strange places, and never went again. They're fittest for rich people. Yes, I've heered about religion and about God Almighty. *What* religion have I heered on? Why, the regular religion. I'm satisfied with what I knows and feels about it, and that's enough about it. . . . I cares nothing about politics neither; but I'm a chartist.

'I'm not a married man. I was a-going to be married to a young woman as lived with me a goodish bit as my housekeeper' (this he said very demurely); 'but she went to the hopping to yarn a few shillings for herself, and never came back. I heered that she'd taken up with an Irish Hawker, but I can't say as to the rights on it. Did I fret about her? Perhaps not; but I was wexed.'

'I'm sure I can't say what I spends my wages in. I sometimes makes 12s. 6d a week, and sometimes better than 21s. with night-work. I suppose grub costs 1s. a day, and beer 6d.; but I keeps no accounts. I buy ready-cooked meat; often cold b'iled beef, and eats it at any tap room. I have meat every day; mostly more than once a day. Wegetables I don't care about, only ingans and cabbage, if you can get it smoking hot, with plenty of pepper. The rest of my tin goes for rent and baccy and togs, and a little drop of gin now and then.'

From Henry Mayhew, 'London Labour and the London Poor' (1851-62), vol. ii, pp. 224-6.

A Walk in a Workhouse

Charles Dickens (1812–70)

Because of the famous scenes in 'Oliver Twist', there is a popular tendency to see Dickens as a critic of the 'bastilles' of the New Poor Law of 1834. In fact as 'Oliver Twist' appeared in 1837, and few if any of the new workhouses had then been erected, Bumble the Beadle can be taken as a caricature of the old-style corrupt local official rather than as a new utilitarian taskmaster. There are several descriptions of the new mixed workhouses in Dickens's writings, and in these the element of satire gives way to a deeper social criticism. Here there is no attack on the personnel who run the institution, nor are the inmates pictured as martyred saints, but as representatives of all conditions of distress, from honest poverty through to downright criminality. It is on this lumping together, on this failure to use the workhouse as anything other than a social dustbin, that the attack is made. And, by fixing on this particular point, Dickens attacks also the rationale which commended the workhouse as an institution to most Boards of Guardians: the use of the workhouse not as a means of relieving distress but as a deterrent. Edwin Chadwick and his colleagues on the Poor Law Commission had hoped to make the workhouses cater suitably for the non-able-bodied poor, but uppermost in their minds was the task, which they believed to be a necessary and humane one, of transferring labour from the land, where it was redundant, to the industrial market, where it was needed. If, to attain this, the workhouse had to become the 'bastille', then they reckoned that the misery of the few who would be forced to enter them would be outweighed by the general social good. To criticise this was to criticise the mechanistic utilitarianism, the conception of men as economic units rather than human personalities, which underlay Britiain's industrial success.

F 10

On a certain Sunday, I formed one of the congregation assembled in the chapel of a large metropolitan Workhouse. With the exception of the clergyman and clerk, and a very few officials, there were none but paupers present. The children sat in the galleries; the women in the body of the chapel, and in one of the side aisles; the men in the remaining aisle. The service was decorously performed, though the sermon might have been much better adapted to the comprehension and to the circumstances of the hearers. The usual supplications were offered, with more than the usual significancy in such a place, for the fatherless children and widows, for all sick persons and young children, for all that were desolate and oppressed, for the comforting and helping of the weak-hearted, for the raising-up of them that had fallen; for all that were in danger, necessity, and tribulation. The prayers of the congregation were desired 'for several persons in the various wards dangerously ill;' and others who were recovering returned their thanks to Heaven.

Among this congregation, were some evil-looking young women, and beetle-browed young men; but not many — perhaps that kind of characters kept away. Generally, the faces (those of the children excepted) were depressed and subdued, and wanted colour. Aged people were there, in every variety. Mumbling, blear-eyed, spectacled, stupid, deaf, lame; vacantly winking in the gleams of sun that now and then crept in through the open doors, from the paved yard; shading their listening ears, or blinking eyes, with their withered hands; poring over their books, leering at nothing, going to sleep, crouching and drooping in corners. There were weird old women, all skeleton within, all bonnet and cloak without, continually wiping their eyes with dirty dusters of pocket-handkerchiefs; and there were ugly old crones, both male and female, with a ghastly kind of contentment upon them which was not at all comforting to see. Upon the whole, it was the dragon, Pauperism, in a very weak and impotent condition; toothless, fangless, drawing his breath heavily enough, and hardly worth chaining up.

When the service was over, I walked with the humane and conscientious gentleman whose duty it was to take that walk, that Sunday morning, through the little world of poverty enclosed within the workhouse walls. It was inhabited by a population of some fifteen hundred or two thousand paupers, ranging from the infant newly born or not yet come into the pauper world, to the old man dying on his bed. . . .

Groves of babies in arms; groves of mothers and other sick women in bed; groves of lunatics; jungles of men in stone-paved down-stairs day-rooms, waiting for their dinners; longer and longer groves of old people in up-stairs Infirmary wards, wearing out life, God knows how — this was the scenery through which the walk lay, for two hours. In some of these latter chambers, there were pictures stuck against the wall, and a neat display of crockery and pewter on a kind of sideboard; now and then it was a treat to see a plant or two; in almost every ward there was a cat.

In all of these Long Walks of aged and infirm, some old people were bedridden, and had been for a long time; some were sitting on their beds half-naked; some dying in their beds; some out of bed, and sitting at a table near the fire. A sullen or lethargic indifference to what was asked, a blunted sensibility to everything but warmth and food, a moody absence of complaint as being of no use, a dogged silence and resentful desire to be left alone again, I thought were generally apparent. On our walking into the midst of one of these dreary perspectives of old men, nearly the following little dialogue took place, the nurse not being immediately at hand:

'All well here?'

No answer. An old man in a Scotch cap sitting among others on a form at the table, eating out of a tin porringer, pushes back his cap a little to look at us, claps it down on his forehead again with the palm of his hand, and goes on eating.

'All well here?' (repeated.)

No answer. Another old man sitting on his bed, paralytically peeling a boiled potato lifts his head and stares.

'Enough to eat?'

No answer. Another old man, in bed, turns himself and coughs.

'How are you to-day?' To the last old man.

That old man says nothing; but another old man, a tall old man of very good address, speaking with perfect correctness, comes forward from somewhere, and volunteers an answer. The reply almost always proceeds from a volunteer, and not from the person looked at or spoken to.

'We are very old, sir,' in a mild, distinct voice. 'We can't expect to be well, most of us.'

'Are you comfortable?'

'I have no complaint to make, sir.' With a half shake of his head, a half shrug of his shoulders, and a kind of apologetic smile.

'Enough to eat?'

'Why, sir, I have but a poor appetite,' with the same air as before; 'and yet I get through my allowance very easily.'

'But,' showing a porringer with a Sunday dinner in it; 'here is a portion of mutton, and three potatoes. You can't starve on that?'

'Oh dear no, sir,' with the same apologetic air. 'Not starve.'

'What do you want?'

'We have very little bread, sir. It's an exceedingly small quantity of bread.'

The nurse, who is now rubbing her hands at the questioner's elbow, interferes with, 'It ain't much raly, sir. You see they've only six ounces a day, and when they've took their breakfast, there *can* only be a little left for night, sir.'

Another old man, hitherto invisible, rises out of his bed-clothes, as out of a grave, and looks on.

'You have tea at night?' The questioner is still addressing the well-spoken old man.

'Yes, sir, we have tea at night.'

'And you can save what bread you can from the morning, to eat with it?'

'Yes, sir — if we can save any.'

'And you want more to eat with it?'

'Yes, sir.' With a very anxious face.

The questioner, in the kindness of his heart, appears a little discomposed, and changes the subject.

'What has become of the old man who used to lie in that bed in the corner?'

The nurse don't remember what old man is referred to. There has been such a many old men. The well-spoken old man is doubtful. The spectral old man who has come to life in bed, says, 'Billy Stevens.' Another old man who has previously had his head in the fire-place, pipes out,

'Charley Walters.'

Something like a feeble interest is awakened. I suppose Charley Walters had conversation in him.

'He's dead,' says the piping old man.

Another old man, with one eye screwed up, hastily displaces the piping old man, and says:

'Yes! Charley Walters died in that bed, and — and —— '

'Billy Stevens,' persists the spectral old man.

'No, no! and Johnny Rogers died in that bed, and — and — they're both on 'em dead — and Sam'l Bowyer;' this seems very extraordinary to him; 'he went out!'

With this he subsides, and all the old men (having had quite enough of it) subside, and the spectral old man goes into his grave again, and takes the shade of Billy Stevens with him.

As we turn to go out at the door, another previously invisible old man, a hoarse old man in a flannel gown, is standing there, as if he had just come up through the floor.

'I beg your pardon, sir, could I take the liberty of saying a word?'

'Yes; what is it?'

'I am greatly better in my health, sir; but what I want, to get me quite round,' with his hand on his throat, 'is a little fresh air, sir. It has always done my complaint so much good, sir. The regular leave for going out, comes round so seldom, that if the gentlemen, next Friday, would give me leave to go out walking, now and then — for only an hour or so, sir! —— '

Who could wonder, looking through those weary vistas of bed and infirmity, that it should do him good to meet with some other scenes, and assure himself that there was something else on earth? Who could help wondering why the old men lived on as they did; what grasp they had on life; what crumbs of interest or occupation they could pick up from its bare board; whether Charley Walters had ever described to them the days when he kept company with some old pauper woman in the bud, or Billy Stevens ever told them of the time when he was a dweller in the far-off foreign land called Home!

The morsel of burnt child, lying in another room, so patiently, in bed, wrapped in lint, and looking stedfastly at us with his bright quiet eyes when we spoke to him kindly, looked as if the knowledge of these things, and of all the tender things there are to think about, might have been in his mind — as if he thought, with us, that there was a fellow-feeling in the pauper nurses which appeared to make them more kind to their charges than the race of common nurses in the hospitals — as if he mused upon the Future of some older children lying around him in the same place, and thought it best, perhaps, all things considered, that he should die — as if he knew, without fear, of those many coffins, made and unmade, piled up in the store below — and of his unknown friend, 'the dropped child,' calm upon the box lid covered with a cloth. But there was something wistful and appealing, too, in his tiny face, as if, in the midst of all the hard necessities and incongruities he pondered on, he pleaded, in behalf of the helpless and the aged poor, for a little more liberty — and a little more bread.

> Charles Dickens, 'A Walk in a Workhouse',
> from 'Household Words', reprinted in
> 'The Uncommercial Traveller', 1860.

Further Reading

G. Kitson Clark, 'The Making of Victorian England', p. 140.

See also G 3, H 2.

Section G

Responses

Trade Unionism

Friedrich Engels (1820–95)

Engels, the son of a Rhineland cotton manufacturer, was already a socialist radical when his father posted him to his Manchester business in 1842. His collaboration with Karl Marx was still in the future, but he observed in the structure of industrial society elements of the theory of the class struggle which he and Marx were to announce in the 'Communist Manifesto' of 1848, and which Marx was to elaborate in 'Capital' (1867-94). He used as evidence 'Blue Books' — the collective term for official publications like reports of Royal Commissions, Select Committees, government inspectors' reports on working conditions — and social studies of individuals like Kay, newspaper reports, and the social criticism of Chartist commentators and writers like Carlyle.

Engels was intent on discovering a radical party within the industrial working class, and saw trade unionism as a means to this end, rather than as a practical instrument for raising the material standards of the workers by successful action against the employers. Leaving this political aim out, orthodox economists reached the same conclusion (politics aside, the economics of Marx and Engels were always impeccably orthodox). In fact, the subsequent success of the trade unions was regarded by them with a great deal of suspicion. Not only had the disastrous slump Engels expected in 1845 failed to appear, but living standards showed, from the 1850s on, a perceptible improvement. By the sixties the power of the unions, considerable within the skilled trades, was having a real effect on wage levels and conditions of work, but their political tendencies were towards collaboration with middle-class radicalism. In 1879 Engels wrote:

At the present time and for many years past the English working-class movement has confined itself within a narrow circle of strikes for higher wages and shorter hours. These strikes are an end in themselves and are not an expedient or a means of propaganda. The trade unions in their charters actually bar all political action on principle and in this way they stop the proletariat as a class from taking part in any working-class movement.

It was not until mechanisation struck at the skilled trades in the 1880s and the unskilled workers were unionised that a militant and class-conscious movement of the sort envisaged by Engels started to emerge.

G 1

When, on the other hand, the working-men received in 1824 the right of free association, these combinations were very soon spread over all England and attained great power. In all branches of industry Trades Unions were formed with the outspoken intention of protecting the single working-man against the tyranny and neglect of the bourgeoisie. The objects were: to fix wages and to deal, en masse, as a power, with the employers; to regulate the rate of wages according to the profit of the latter, to raise it when opportunity offered, and to keep it uniform in each trade throughout the country. Hence they tried to settle with the capitalists a scale of wages to be universally adhered to, and ordered out on strike the employees of such individuals as refused to accept the scale. They aimed further to keep up the demand for labour by limiting the number of apprentices, and so to keep wages high; to counteract, as far as possible, the indirect wages reductions which the manufacturers brought about by means of new tools and machinery; and finally, to assist unemployed working-men financially. This they do either directly or by means of a card to legitimate the bearer as a 'society man', and with which the working-man wanders from place to place, supported by his fellow-workers, and instructed as to the best opportunity for finding employment. This is tramping, and the wanderer a tramp. To attain these ends, a President and Secretary are engaged at a salary (since it is to be expected that no manufacturer will employ such persons), and a committee collects the weekly contributions and watches over their expenditure for the purposes of the association. When it proved possible and advantageous, the various trades of single districts united in a federation and held delegate conventions at set times. The attempt has been made in single cases to unite the workers of one branch over all England in one great Union; and several times (in 1830 for the first time) to form one universal trades association for the whole United Kingdom, with a separate organization for each trade. These associations, however, never held together long, and were seldom realized even for the moment, since an exceptionally universal excitement is necessary to make such a federation possible and effective.

The means usually employed by these Unions for attaining their ends are the following: If one or more employers refuse to pay the wage specified by the Union, a deputation is sent or a petition forwarded (the working-men, you see, know how to recognize the absolute power of the lord of the factor in his little State); if this proves unavailing, the Union commands the employees to stop work, and all hands go home. This strike is either partial when one or several, or general when all employers in the trade refuse to regulate wages according to the proposals of the Union. So far go the lawful means of the Union, assuming the strike to take effect after the expiration of the legal notice, which is not always the case. But these lawful means are very weak, when there are workers outside the Union, or when members separate from it for the sake of the momentary advantage offered by bourgeoisie. Especially in the case of partial strikes can the manufacture readily secure recruits from these black sheep (who are known as knobsticks), and render fruitless the efforts of the united workers. Knobsticks are usually threatened, insulted, beaten, or otherwise maltreated by the members of the Union; intimidated, in short, in every way. Prosecution follows, and as the law-abiding bourgeoisie has the power in its own hands, the force of the Union is broken almost every time by the first unlawful act, the first judicial procedure against its members.

The history of these unions is a long series of defeats of the working-men, interrupted by a few isolated victories. All these efforts naturally cannot alter the economic law according to which wages are determined by the relation between supply and demand in the labour market. Hence the Unions remain powerless against all *great* forces which influence this relation. In a commercial crisis the Union itself must reduce wages or dissolve wholly; and in a time of considerable increase in the demand for labour, it cannot fix the rate of wages higher than would be reached spontaneously by the competition of the capitalists among themselves. But in dealing with minor, single influences they are powerful. If the employer had no concentrated, collective opposition to expect, he would in his own interest gradually reduce wages to a lower and lower point: indeed, the battle of competition which he has to wage against his fellow-manufacturers would force him to do so, and wages would soon reach the minimum. But this competition of the manufacturers among themselves is, *under average conditions*, somewhat restricted by the opposition of the working-men.

Every manufacturer knows that the consequence of a reduction not justified by conditions to which his competitors also are subjected, would be a strike, which would most certainly injure him, because his capital would be idle as long as the strike lasted, and his machinery would be rusting, whereas it is very doubtful whether he could, in such a case, enforce his reduction. Then he has the certainty that if he should succeed, his competitors would follow him, reducing the price of the goods so produced, and thus depriving him of the benefit of his policy. Then, too, the Unions often bring about a more rapid increase of wages after a crisis than would otherwise follow. For the manufacturer's interest is to delay rising wages until forced by competition, but now the working-men demand an increased wage as soon as the market improves, and they can carry their point, by reason of the smaller supply of workers at his command under such circumstances. But, for resistance to more considerable forces which influence the labour market, the Unions are powerless. In such cases hunger gradually drives the strikers to resume work on any terms, and when once a few have begun, the force of the Union is broken, because these few knobsticks, with the reserve supplies of goods in the market, enable the bourgeoisie to overcome the worst effects of the interruption of business. The funds of the Union are soon exhausted by the great numbers requiring relief, the credit which the shopkeepers give at high interest is withdrawn after a time, and want compels the working-man to place himself once more under the yoke of the bourgeoisie. But strikes end disastrously for the workers mostly, because the manufacturers, in their own interest (which has, be it said, become their interest only through the resistance of the workers), are obliged to avoid all useless reductions, while the workers feel in every reduction imposed by the state of trade a deterioration of their condition, against which they must defend themselves as far as in them lies.

It will be asked, 'Why, then, do the workers strike in such cases, when the uselessness of such measures is so evident?' Simply because they *must* protest against every reduction, even if dictated by necessity; because they feel bound to proclaim that they, as human beings, shall not be made to bow to social circumstances, but social conditions ought to yield to them as human beings. . . . But what gives these Unions and the strikes arising from them their real importance is this, that they are the first attempt of the workers to abolish competition. They imply the recognition of the fact that the supremacy of the bourgeoisie is based wholly upon the competition of the workers among themselves: i.e. upon their want of cohesion. . . .

Wages depend upon the relation of demand to supply, upon the accidental state of the labour market, simply because the workers have hitherto been content to be treated as chattels, to be bought and sold. The moment the workers resolve to be bought and sold no longer, when, in the determination of the value of labour, they take the part of men possessed of a will as well as of working-power, at that moment the whole Political Economy of today is at an end.

> From Friedrich Engels, 'The Conditions of the
> Working Class in England', 1844,
> Panther Books ed., 1969, pp. 241-5.

Further Reading

Henry Pelling, 'A History of British Trade Unionism', 1966, chap. 3.

See also F 5, F 7, H 2.

The Amalgamated Society of Engineers (1851): a membership certificate of one of the 'new model' unions which organised the skilled trades at the mid-century.

Conclusions from the Sanitary Report, 1842

Edwin Chadwick (1800–90)

'Modern communities', noted Aneurin Bevan in 1946, 'have been made tolerable by the behaviour patterns imposed upon them by the activities of the sanitary inspector and the medical officer of health. It is true, those rarely work out what they do in terms of socialist philosophy; but that does not alter the fact that the whole significance of their contribution is that the claims of the individual shall subordinate themselves to social codes that have the collective well-being for their aim. . . .' The early stages of such sanitary legislation in Britain are virtually the biography of Edwin Chadwick. Born appropriately enough in Manchester, Chadwick became the disciple of Bentham, and proceeded to reform in a logical Benthamite manner the statutory social services of the country. Starting with the Poor Law, he then pursued pauperism to its roots in diseases which urban conditions allowed to spread rapidly. It is a measure of how bad the situation was, that, on a scientifically false diagnosis — the 'atmospheric impurities' he indicated were innocent, disease was borne by polluted water supplies — he and other resolute sanitary reformers were able to abate the worst of the evils by the late 1860s simply through terrorising lackadaisical local government bodies. Chadwick also represents a movement within the utilitarian mainstream from the spirit of laissez-faire to one of collectivist intervention to secure by direct legislation 'the greatest good to the greatest number', a movement given qualified support by John Stuart Mill.

G3

After as careful an examination of the evidence collected as I have been able to make, I beg leave to recapitulate the chief conclusions which that evidence appears to me to establish.

First, as to the extent and operation of the evils which are the subject of the inquiry: —

That the various forms of epidemic, endemic, and other disease caused, or aggravated, or propagated chiefly amongst the labouring classes by atmospheric impurities produced by decomposing animal and vegetable substances, by damp and filth, and close and overcrowded dwellings prevail amongst the population in every part of the kingdom, whether dwelling in separate houses, in rural villages, in small towns, in the larger towns — as they have been found to prevail in the lowest districts of the metropolis.

That such disease, wherever its attacks are frequent, is always found in connexion with the physical circumstances above specified, and that where those circumstances are removed by drainage, proper cleansing, better ventilation, and other means of diminishing atmospheric impurity, the frequency and intensity of such disease is abated; and where the removal of the noxious agencies appears to be complete, such disease almost entirely disappears.

That high prosperity in respect to employment and wages, and various and abundant food, have afforded to the labouring classes no exemptions from attacks of epidemic disease, which have been as frequent and as fatal in periods of commercial and manufacturing prosperity than in any others.

That the formation of all habits of cleanliness is obstructed by defective supplies of water.

That the annual loss of life from filth and bad ventilation is greater than the loss from death and wounds in any wars in which the country has been engaged in modern times.

That of the 43,000 cases of widowhood, and 112,000 cases of destitute orphanage relieved from the poor's rates in England and Wales alone, it appears that the greatest proportion of deaths of the heads of families occurred from the above specified and other removable causes; that their ages were under 45 years; that is to say, 13 years below the natural probabilities of life as shown by the experience of the whole population of Sweden.

That the public loss from the premature deaths of the heads of families is greater than can be represented by any enumeration of the pecuniary burdens consequent upon their sickness and death.

That, measuring the loss of working ability amongst large classes by the instances of gain, even from incomplete arrangements for the removal of noxious influences from places of work or from abodes, that this loss cannot be less than eight or ten years.

That the ravages of epidemics and other diseases do not diminish but tend to increase the pressure of population.

That in the districts where the mortality is the greatest the births are not only sufficient to replace the numbers removed by death, but to add to the population.

That the younger population, bred up under noxious physical agencies, is inferior in physical organisation and general health to a population preserved from the presence of such agencies.

That the population so exposed is less susceptible of moral influences, and the effects of education are more transient than with a healthy population.

That these adverse circumstances tend to produce an adult population short-lived, improvident, reckless, and intemperate, and with habitual avidity for sensual gratification.

That these habits lead to the abandonment of all the conveniences and decencies of life, and especially lead to the overcrowding of their homes, which is destructive to the morality as well as the health of large classes of both sexes.

That defective town cleansing fosters habits of the most abject degradation and tends to the demoralisation of large numbers of human beings, who subsist by means of what they find amidst the noxious filth accumulated in neglected streets and bye-places.

That the expenses of local public works are in general unequally and unfairly assessed, oppressively and uneconomically collected, by separate collections, wastefully expended in separate and inefficient operations by unskilled and practically irresponsible officers.

That the existing law for the protection of the public health and the constitutional machinery for reclaiming its execution, such as the Courts Leet, have fallen into desuetude, and are in the state indicated by the prevalence of the evils they were intended to prevent.

Secondly, as to the means by which the present sanitary condition of the labouring classes may be improved: —

The primary and most important measures, and at the same time the most practicable, and within the recognized province of public administration, are drainage, the removal of all refuse of habitations, streets, and roads, and the improvement of the supplies of water.

That the chief obstacles to the immediate removal of decomposing refuse of towns and habitations have been the expense and annoyance of the hand labour and cartage requisite for the purpose.

That this expense may be reduced to one-twentieth or to one-thirtieth, or rendered inconsiderable, by the use of water and self-acting means of removal by improved and cheaper sewers and drains.

That refuse when thus held in suspension in water may be most cheaply and innoxiously conveyed to any distance out of towns, and also in the best form for productive use, and that the loss and injury by the pollution of natural streams may be avoided.

That for all these purposes, as well as for domestic use, better supplies of water are absolutely necessary.

That for succesful and economical drainage the adoption of geological areas as the basis of operations is requisite.

That appropriate scientific arrangements for public drainage would afford important facilities for private land-drainage, which is important for the health as well as sustenance of the labouring classes.

That for the protection of the labouring classes and of the ratepayers against inneficiency and waste in all new structural arrangements for the protection of the public health, and to ensure public confidence that the expenditure will be beneficial, securities should be taken that all local public works are devised and conducted by responsible officers qualified by the possession of the science and the skill of civil engineers.

That the oppressiveness and injustice of levies for the whole immediate outlay on such works upon persons who have only short interests in the benefits may be avoided by care in spreading the expense over periods coincident with the benefits.

That by appropriate arrengements, 10 or 15 per cent. on the ordinary outlay for drainage might be saved, which on an estimate of the expense of the necessary structural alterations of one-third only of the existing tenements would be a saving of one million and a half sterling, besides the reduction of the future expenses of management.

That for the prevention of the disease occasioned by defective ventilation, and other causes of impurity in places of work and other places in which large numbers are assembled, and for the general promotion of the means necessary to prevent disease, it would be good economy to appoint a district medical officer independent of private practice, and with the securities of special qualifications and responsibilities to initiate sanitary measures and reclaim the execution of the law.

That by the combinations of all these arrangements, it is probable that the full ensurable period of life indicated by the Swedish tables; that is, an increase of 13 years at least, may be extended to the whole of the labouring classes.

That the attainment of these and the other collateral advantages of reducing existing charges and expenditure are within the power of the legislature, and are dependent mainly on the securities taken for the application of practical science, skill and economy in the direction of public works.

And that the removal of noxious physical circumstances, and the promotion of civic, household, and personal cleanliness, are necessary to the improvement of the moral condition of the population; for that sound morality and refinement in manners and health are not long found co-existent with filthy habits amongst any class of the community.

> From Edwin Chadwick, 'Report on the Sanatory Condition of the Labouring Population', Parliamentary Papers, 1842, vol. xxvi, pp. 369—72.

Further Reading

G. Kitson Clark, 'The Making of Victorian England', pp. 95-107.
G. M. Young, 'Victorian England', pp. 11, 40-2.

See also B 3, F 10, G 6.

Introduction of the Education Bill, 1870

William Edward Forster, M.P. (1818–86)

When the second Reform Bill passed into law in 1867, Robert Lowe, who had led the opposition to any further extension of the franchise, remarked, 'I believe it will be absolutely necessary to compel our future masters to learn their letters.' Lowe had been the Minister responsible for education at the beginning of the decade when his policy — summed up by his maxim 'If it [education] is not cheap it shall be efficient, if it is not efficient it shall be cheap' — led to the curriculum being restricted and expenditure, which took the form of state grants to religious bodies, being cut.

But if the enfranchisement of the urban workers was one motive for the introduction of a Bill which, according to Brian Simon, 'would have been rejected out of hand in 1860', another was supplied by external events which seemed to have ominous implications for Britain's military and commercial supremacy. In 1866 Prussia rapidly defeated Austria in the Seven Weeks War. She had had compulsory elementary education since the 1840s and her troops were intelligent and adaptable. Contemporary commentators despaired of the performance in such a conflict of a British army 'picked up from the dregs of the population'. The lesson, alluded to obliquely by Forster in his peroration, was obvious. The Paris Exhibition of 1867, in which European manufactures were seen to be catching Britain up, and the Prussian victory over France in 1870, were to ram it home.

G 4

... I have said that this is a very serious question; I would further say that whatever we do in the matter should be done quickly. We must not delay. Upon the speedy provision of elementary education depends our industrial prosperity. It is of no use trying to give technical teaching to our artizans without elementary education; uneducated labourers — and many of our labourers are utterly uneducated — are, for the most part, unskilled labourers, and, if we leave our work-folk any longer unskilled, notwithstanding their strong sinews and determined energy, they will become overmatched in the competition of the world. Upon this speedy provision depends also, I fully believe, the good, the safe working of our constitutional system. To its honour, Parliament has lately decided that England shall in future be governed by popular government. I am one of those who would not wait until the people were educated before I would trust them with political power. If we had thus waited we might have waited long for education; but now that we have given them political power we must not wait any longer to give them education. There are questions demanding answers, problems which must be solved, which ignorant constituencies are ill fitted to solve. Upon this speedy provision of education depends also our national power. Civilized communities throughout the world are massing themselves together, each mass being measured by its force; and if we are to hold our position among men of our own race or among the nations of the world we must make up the smallness of our numbers by increasing the intellectual force of the individual. . . .

> Conclusion of W. E. Forster's speech in Parliament
> introducing his Education Bill, 17 February 1870,
> 'Hansard', series iii, vol. 199, cols. 465-6.

Further Reading

Brian Simon, 'Studies in the History of Education, 1780-1870', chap. 7.
G. Kitson Clark, 'The Making of Victorian England', pp. 173-6.

See also F 7, H 5.

Co-operation and Nonconformity in Bacup

Beatrice Webb (1858–1943)

Beatrice Potter's father was a Lancashire man who had made good as a railway director and international financier, and in the process moved from his Manchester School radicalism to formal Toryism. The family also became integrated into the traditional administrative and professional class, and Beatrice found herself related to a good proportion of the academics, senior civil servants and leading legal men of the capital. On the other hand she still possessed her Lancashire forebears who had not managed to make the transition. Stimulated by the family's acquaintanceship with the sociologist Herbert Spencer, the rather paternalistic social work expected of young middle-class ladies by bodies like the Charity Organisation Society, and especially by the great survey of London poverty undertaken in the 1880s by her cousin Charles Booth, nephew of the moving spirit of the Liverpool and Manchester Railway, she embarked upon her own programme of social research. The description of co-operation here was to be succeeded by a major work on the co-operative movement and, in collaboration with her husband Sidney Webb, by complex studies of trade unions and local government. Both in the practical nature of their social investigations and in the pragmatism of the programme of Fabian socialism with which they became closely identified, they represent a continuation of the interventionist utilitarianism of Edwin Chadwick.

G 5

We dined this morning in a most comfortable cottage, owned by a mill-hand with three sons, mill-hands. (The) afternoon I spent in going over two or three mills, introduced by my friends to their managers, and finished up by going through the Co-op. stores with the manager. I told him I had been sent by my father to enquire into the management of Co-ops. as you wanted to start one; and he took me into his counting-house, showed me his books and explained the whole thing. It is entirely owned and managed by working men. Membership entails spending a certain amount there; and the dividend is paid according to the amount spent per quarter, though it is not paid out until the share is paid up through accumulation. In this way there is a double check on the management; the shareholder requiring his dividend, and the consumer requiring cheap and good articles, and as the manager remarked, 'Females look pretty sharp arter that.' It has been established twenty years or more and has never paid less than 12½ per cent.; the working expenses only come to 5 per cent. on capital turned over. No member can have more than £100 in stock, and any one can become a member on the payment of three shillings and sixpence entrance fee, and on the original terms. The manager gave me a graphic account of his trouble with the committee of working men; and interested me by explaining the reasons of the failure of most of the Co-op. mills, all of which I will tell you over our cigarettes. . . .

I have spent the day in the chapels and schools. After dinner, a dissenting minister dropped in and I had a long talk with him; he is coming for a cigarette this evening after chapel. He told me that in all the chapels there was a growing desire among the congregation to have political and social subjects treated in the pulpit, and that it was very difficult for a minister, now, to please. He also remarked that, in districts where co-operation amongst the workmen (in industrial enterprise) existed, they were a much more independent and free-thinking set.

There is an immense amount of co-operation in the whole of this district; the stores seem to succeed well, both as regards supplying the people with cheap articles and as savings banks paying good interest. Of course I am just in the centre of the dissenting organisation; and as our host is the chapel keeper and entertains all the ministers who come here, I hear all about the internal management. Each chapel, even of the same denomination, manages its own affairs; and there are monthly meetings of all the members (male and female) to discuss questions of expenditure, etc. In fact each chapel is a self-governing community, regulating not only chapel matters but overlooking the private life of its members.

One cannot help feeling what an excellent thing these dissenting organisations have been for educating this class for self-government. I can't help thinking, too, that one of the best preventives against the socialistic tendency of the coming democracy would lie in local government; which would force the respectable working man to consider political questions as they come up in local administration. Parliament is such a far-off thing, that the more practical and industrious lot say that it is 'gormless meddling with it' (useless), and they leave it to the 'gabblers.' But they are keen enough on any local question which comes within their own experiences, and would bring plenty of shrewd sound sense to bear on the actual management of things.

Certainly the earnest successful working man is essentially conservative as regards the rights of property and the non-interference of the central government; and though religious feeling still has an immense hold on this class, and forms a real basis for many lives, the most religious of them agree that the younger generation are looking elsewhere for subjects of thought and feeling.

It seems to me of great importance that the political thought should take a practical instead of a theoretical line; that each section of the community should try experiments on a small scale, and that the promoters should see and reap the difficulties, and disadvantages of each experiment as it is executed. There is an immense amount of spare energy in this class, now that it is educated, which is by no means used up in their mechanical occupation. When the religious channel is closed up it must go somewhere. It can be employed either in the *practical* solution of social and economic questions, or in the purely intellectual exercise of political theorising and political discussion about problems considered in the abstract. . . .

Forgive all these crudely expressed ideas. I have jotted them down just as they have crossed my mind. I am immensely interested in what I hear and see. But it is a daring thing in a young woman to drop 'caste'; and that is why I am anxious it should not be talked about. I have sufficient knowledge of men to make them be to me as I choose; but not every one would understand that one had that power, and without it it would not be a profitful or wise adventure.

In living amongst mill-hands of East Lancashire [I reflect a few months later] I was impressed with the depth and realism of their religious faith. It seemed to absorb the entire nature, to claim as its own all the energy unused in the actual struggle for existence. Once the simple animal instincts were satisfied the surplus power, whether physical, intellectual or moral, was devoted to religion. Even the social intercourse was based on religious sympathy and common religious effort. It was just this one-idea'd-ness and transparentness of life which attracted my interest and admiration. For a time it contrasted favourably with the extraordinarily complex mental activity arising in the cosmopolitan life of London — an activity which in some natures tends to paralyse action and dissipate thought.

The same quality of one-idea'd-ness is present in the Birmingham Radical set, earnestness and simplicity of motive being strikingly present. Political conviction takes the place here of religious faith; and intolerance of scepticism of the main articles of the creed is as bitter in the one case as in the other. Possibly the Bible, from its inherent self-contradiction, is a more promising ground for the individualism than the Radical programme and the less likely to favour the supremacy of one interpreter. Heine said some fifty years ago, 'Talk to an Englishman on religion and he is a fanatic; talk to him on politics and he is a man of the world.' It would seem to me from my slight experience of Bacup and Birmingham, that that part of the Englishmans's nature which has found gratification in religion is now drifting into political life. When I suggested this to Mr Chamberlain he answered, 'I quite agree with you, and I rejoice in it. I have always had a grudge against religion for absorbing the passion in man's nature.' It is only natural then that, this being his view, he should find in the uncompromising belief of his own set more sympathetic atmosphere wherein to recruit his forces to battle with powers of evil, than in the somewhat cynical, or at any rate indefinately varied and qualified, political opinions of London society. [MS. diary, March 16, 1884.]

From Beatrice Webb, 'My Apprenticeship', Penguin ed., i, pp. 182-9.

Further Reading

Henry Pelling, 'Origins of the Labour Party', 1954.   See also E 1, G 4.

Part Two

Section H

Prophets and Sceptics

Prophets and Sceptics

The March of Mind

The most remarkable feature of the nineteenth-century writers who praised and defended the mores of industrial society is their insignificance today. We know the age through its critics — Carlyle, Ruskin, Morris — not through its enthusiasts: who now reads Andrew Ure, Harriet Martineau or Herbert Spencer? The critics probably survive to a great extent because they combined their social criticism with intellectual and artistic criticism, and mounted their attack in the language of a traditional and continuing culture. The enthusiasts adopted the language of economics and the infant 'social sciences', disciplines which have changed so radically since their time that to rediscover the thread of their argument is to have to embark on a taxing exploration of archaic economic and social philosophy.

As Karl Marx indicated in his description of the liberal ideologues of the 1850s, economic and social philosophy was to them merely a practical extension of their business interests. They were content to pronounce economic judgements on the basis of an acquaintance with the more self-evident propositions of the 'classical' economics of Adam Smith, Jeremy Bentham (1748-1832) and David Ricardo (1772-1823), restated by John Stuart Mill in his 'Principles of Political Economy' of 1848. They could rest their case on the theory of 'enlightened self-interest', arguing that if each man pursued his own ends the self-acting mechanism of the market ensured that a general good resulted. This is the burden of Goldwin Smith's panegyric. The notion was an attractive one both to businessmen who had done well out of the free-for-all and to intellectuals captivated by the prospect of extending the laws which appeared to govern 'economic man' 'to the estimation of a hair' to other aspects of social behaviour. Individualist economics were taken for granted by businessmen and civil servants who made a pastime out of lecturing the rest of society, notably the working class, on the importance of abiding by their 'iron laws'. In 1885 Henry Sidgwick (1838-1900) wrote of the senior body of British economists, the Political Economy Club: 'It is astonishing how little political economy these people know. The bankers come to the front . . . I think they read Mill some time ago and look at him from time to time on Sundays.' Sidgwick, however, demonstrated in his own career that this compact and coherent approach to the study of man in society could be stimulating. Although he was Professor of Moral Philosophy at Cambridge, his mind ranged over the fields of politics, economics and theology as well as ethics.

But the free market, to operate satisfactorily, required social stability, which in turn required civil and legal equality. The great industrial labour force had either to be incorporated into the political system, or left to itself it would create institutions of its own — a state within the state. The problem became acute in the 1860s with the growing prosperity and internal organisation of the working class, and social and economic theorists like Mill, James Bryce and Goldwin Smith urged, in the words of one of the essays in the book from which the passage from Bryce is taken, 'the admission of the working classes as part of our social system; and their recognition for all purposes as part of the nation'.

At the same time such theorists were concerned that popular government might imply the coercion of minorities by the majority. Partly this was the fear of the propertied at government passing to a mass electorate, partly the concern of genuine believers in the rights of individuals who feared the tyranny of a narrow-minded public opinion. 'The greatest enemy of freedom,' said a character in one of Ibsen's plays, 'is the damned compact liberal majority', a sentiment which later rebels against Victorian orthodoxy, like Bernard Shaw, took as a sacred text.

Critics

John Stuart Mill's defence of individual liberty represents, even if only tentatively, a movement away from the notion of 'economic man', and towards the position of observers of the industrial experience whose disagreement with its ruling ideology was more fundamental. For individuality as Mill understood it had an intrinsic value which the mechanism of 'individualist' economics denied. If a common factor can be detected in the criticism of industrial society which follows, it is precisely this: the individual and his work had been made subordinate to the system, and the corollary of this was that the value in human terms of both had been reduced.

The value of a commodity in an economic calculation is not fixed. It varies according to the relations of supply and demand, and this applies to labour as much as to, say, soap. Thomas Carlyle's concern in his observations on the Irish is to point out the destructive effect such a conception of value has on the human beings involved. The master of horses' speech to his 'quadrupeds' — correct in terms of political economy — is nevertheless inhuman in practice. The same point — in the context of the opposition of what he calls 'political' and 'mercantile' economy — is made by Ruskin. Where true 'political' economy conserves and enhances individual values and skills, 'mercantile' economy exploits these, and exploits them in such a way that the individual is further threatened by the narrowness of the tasks expected of him.

Division of labour, praised so eloquently by Adam Smith, had for them human implications which were destructive of the individual personality. As Ruskin wrote: '*It is not, truly speaking, the labour that is divided; but the men: — divided into mere segments of men — broken into small fragments and crumbs of life. . . . You must either make a tool of the creature, or a man of him.*' This led to the linked observation, that '*It is verily this degradation of the operative into a machine, which, more than any other evil of the times, is leading the mass of the nations everywhere into vain, incoherent, destructive struggling for a freedom of which they cannot explain the nature to themselves.*'

Carlyle and Ruskin were critical of the social thought which saw democracy and 'free institutions' as an end in itself. Matthew Arnold, like Mill assenting in general to liberal politics, deprecated the elevation of the 'machinery' of politics over a rational consideration of the purposes to which such machinery should be applied:

Freedom is a very good horse to ride, but to ride somewhere. You think that you have only to get on the back of your horse Freedom . . . and to ride away as hard as you can, to be sure of coming to the right destination.

'May not every man in England say what he likes?' — Mr Roebuck perpetually asks; and that, he thinks, is quite sufficient, and when every man says what he likes, our aspirations ought to be satisfied. But the aspirations of culture, which is the study of perfection, are not satisfied, unless what men say, when they may say what they like, is worth saying, — has good in it, and more good than bad.

'Culture, which is the study of perfection' was Arnold's measure of value, Ruskin's was art:

The art of any country is the exponent of its social and political virtues. The art, or general productive and formative energy of any country, is an exact exponent of its ethical life. You can have art only from noble persons, associated under laws fitted to their time and circumstances.

Although Ruskin's criterion seems a narrower one than Arnold's it fastened on the critical point — the harm inflicted on the individual by craft specialisation and commercial exploitation — which intellectual critics of the industrial experience shared with those who had been forced to participate in it.

The actual remedies which Carlyle and Ruskin advanced were less significant than their perceptions. Carlyle's grasp of the implications, good as well as bad, of industrialism, was probably firmer than that of the other critics, but his remedy, an hierarchical state ruled by the aristocracy and the 'Captains of Industry', seems as constricting as the actuality of the order it was supposed to replace. Ruskin's, if milder, was little less archaic. William Morris, on the other hand, who had been Ruskin's disciple, grafted on to his master's perception the 'scientific socialist' analysis of the development of capitalist society propounded by Karl Marx and his English followers. He associated the commercial-isation of art with the same divorce of art and life which Ruskin had seen, but he extended this analysis to comprehend the position of those whose lives were warped and whose talents were exploited by capitalist industry:

Surely any one who professes to think that the question of art and cultivation must go before that of the knife and fork (and there are some who do propose that) does not understand what art means, or how that its roots must have a soil of thriving and unanxious life.

Morris's socialism rested fundamentally on the identification of art with life and work. The good life was that in which man's work expressed the highest aspects of his personality; it could only be achieved when society was reorganised in such a way that specialisation of function was replaced by the co-operation of men whose adapta-bility was the result of all their talents being fully developed. In such a context machinery would continue to play a part — there is no justification for seeing Morris as an indiscriminate machine-wrecker — but that part would be determined by the specific needs of the individuals who constitute a given society, and where the use of machinery threatened to unbalance these, it would be discarded.

Further Reading

S. G. Checkland, 'The Rise of Industrial Society in England', chap. 10.
Asa Briggs, 'The Age of Improvement', chap. 9.4.
Raymond Williams, 'Culture and Society', chaps. 4, 6, 7.

The Division of Labour

Adam Smith (1723–90)

Adam Smith passed the greater part of a tranquil life in Scotland, as a professor at Glasgow University between 1751 and 1764, and in semi-retirement in Kirkcaldy and Edinburgh from 1766 to his death. In 1776 he published his 'Inquiry into the Nature and Causes of the Wealth of Nations', the Bible of individualist economics.

H 1

The greatest improvement in the productive powers of labour, and the greater part of the skill, dexterity, and judgment with which it is anywhere directed, or applied, seem to have been the effects of the division of labour. . . .

To take an example from a very trifling manufacture; but one in which the division of labour has been very often taken notice of, the trade of the pin-maker; a workman not educated to this business (which the division of labour has rendered a distinct trade), nor acquainted with the use of the machinery employed in it (to the invention of which the same division of labour has probably given occasion), could scarce, perhaps, with his utmost industry, make one pin in a day, and certainly could not make twenty. But in the way in which this business is now carried on, not only the whole work is a peculiar trade, but it is divided into a number of branches, of which the greater part are likewise peculiar trades. One man draws out the wire, another straights it, a third cuts it, a fourth points it, a fifth grinds it at the top for receiving the head; to make the head requires two or three distinct operations; to put it on is a peculiar business, to whiten the pins is another; it is even a trade by itself to put them into the paper; and the important business of making a pin is, in this manner, divided into about eighteen distinct operations, which, in some manufactories, are all performed by distinct hands, though in others the same man will sometimes perform two or three of them. I have seen a small manufactory of this kind where ten men only were employed, and where some of them consequently performed two or three distinct operations. But though they were very poor, and therefore but indifferently accommodated with the necessary machinery, they could, when they exerted themselves, make among them about twelve pounds of pins in a day. There are in a pound upwards of four thousand pins of a middling size. Those ten persons, therefore, could make among them upwards of forty-eight thousand pins in a day. Each person therefore, making a tenth part of forty-eight thousand pins, might be considered as making four thousand eight hundred pins in a day. But if they had all wrought separately and independently, and without any of them having been educated to this peculiar business, they certainly could not each of them have made twenty, perhaps not one pin in a day; that is, certainly, not the two hundred and fortieth, perhaps not the four thousand eight hundredth part of what they are at present capable of performing, in consequence of a proper division and combination of their different operations.

In every other art and manufacture, the effects of the division of labour are similar to what they are in this very trifling one; though, in many of them, the labour can neither be so much subdivided, nor reduced to so great a simplicity of operation. The division of labour, however, so far as it can be introduced, occasions, in every art, a proportionable increase of the productive powers of labour. The separation of different trades and employments from one another seems to have taken place in consequence of this advantage. This separation, too, is generally carried furthest in those countries which enjoy the highest degree of industry and improvement; what is the work of one man in a rude state of society being generally that of several in an improved one. In every improved society, the farmer is generally nothing but a farmer; the manufacturer, nothing but a manufacturer. The labour, too, which is necessary to produce any one complete manufacture is almost always divided among a great number of hands. How many different trades are employed in each branch of the linen and woollen manufactures from the growers of the flax and the wool, to the bleachers and smoothers of the linen, or to the dyers and dressers of the cloth! . . .

It is the great multiplication of the productions of all the different arts, in consequence of the division of labour, which occasions, in a well-governed society, that universal opulence which extends itself to the lowest ranks of the people. Every workman has a great quantity of his own work to dispose of beyond what he himself has occasion for; and every other workman being exactly in the same situation, he is enabled to exchange a great quantity of his own goods for a great quantity, or, what comes to the same thing, for the price of a great quantity of theirs. He supplies them abundantly with what they have occasion for, and they accommodate him as amply with what he has occasion for, and a general plenty diffuses itself through all the different ranks of the society.

> Adam Smith, 'Of the Division of Labour',
> from 'The Wealth of Nations', 1776, Everyman ed., i 4-9.

See also M3, P 10.

The Manchester Party

Karl Marx (1818–83)

Karl Marx spent about half his life in exile in London following his part in the German revolutions of 1848. Besides much 'bread and butter' journalism like this article for an American paper, and his political activities which included the founding of the First International in 1864, he produced the vast analysis of 'Capital', of which the first volume appeared in 1867, and the other two after his death, edited by his patron and collaborator, Engels.

H 2

While the Tories, the Whigs, the Peelites — in fact, all the parties we have hitherto commented upon — belong more or less to the past, the Free Traders (the men of the Manchester School, the Parliamentary and Financial Reformers) are the *official representatives of modern English society*, the representatives of that England which rules the market of the world. They represent the party of the self-conscious Bourgeoisie, of industrial capital striving to make available its social power as a political power as well, and to eradicate the last arrogant remnants of feudal society. This party is led on by the most active and most energetic portion of the English Bourgeoisie — the *manufacturers*. What they demand is the complete and undisguised ascendancy of the Bourgeoisie, the open, official subjection of society at large under the laws of modern, bourgeois production, and under the rule of those men who are the directors of that production. By Free Trade they mean the unfettered movement of capital, freed from all political, national, and religious shackles. The soil is to be a marketable commodity, and the exploitation of the soil is to be carried on according to the common commercial laws. There are to be manufacturers of food as well as

F

manufacturers of twist and cottons, but no longer any lords of the land. There are, in short, not to be tolerated any political or social restrictions, regulations or monopolies, unless they proceed from 'the eternal laws of political economy', that is, from the conditions under which Capital produces and distributes. The struggle of this party against the old English institutions, products of a superannuated, an evanescent stage of social development, is resumed in the watchword: *Produce as cheap as you can, and do away with all the* faux frais *of production* (with all superfluous, unnecessary expenses in production). And this watchword is addressed not only to the private individual, but to the *nation at large* principally.

Royalty, with its 'barbarous splendours', its court, its civil list and its flunkeys — what else does it belong to but to the *faux frais* of production? The nation can produce and exchange without royalty; away with the crown. The sinecures of the nobility, the House of Lords? — *faux frais* of production. The large standing army? — *faux frais* of production. The State Church, with its riches, the spoils of plunder or of mendicity? — *faux frais* of production. Let parsons compete freely with each other, and everyone pay them according to his own wants. The whole circumstantial routine of English law, with its Court of Chancery? — *faux frais* of production. National wars? — *faux frais* of production. England can exploit foreign nations more cheaply while at peace with them.

You see, to these champions of the British Bourgeoisie, to the men of the Manchester School, every institution of Old England appears in the light of a piece of machinery as costly as it is useless, and which fulfils no other purpose but to prevent the nation from producing the greatest possible quantity at the least possible expense, and to exchange its products in freedom. Necessarily, their last word is the *Bourgeois Republic*, in which free competition rules supreme in all spheres of life; in which there remains altogether that *minimum* only of government which is indispensable for administration, internally and externally, of the common class interest and business of the Bourgeoisie; and where this *minimum* of government is as soberly, as economically organized as possible. Such a party, in other countries, would be called *democratic*. But it is necessarily revolutionary, and the complete annihilation of Old

England as an aristocratic country is the end which it follows up with more or less consciousness. Its nearest object, however, is the attainment of a Parliamentary reform which should transfer to its hands the legislative power necessary for such a revolution.

But the British Bourgeois are not excitable Frenchmen. When they intend to carry a Parliamentary reform they will not make a Revolution of February. On the contrary. Having obtained, in 1846, a grand victory over the landed aristocracy by the repeal of the Corn Laws, they were satisfied with following up the material advantages of this victory, while they neglected to draw the necessary political and economic conclusions from it, and thus enabled the Whigs to reinstate themselves into their hereditary monopoly of government. During all the time, from 1846 to 1852, they exposed themselves to ridicule by their battle-cry: Broad principles and practical (read *small*) measures. And why all this? Because in every violent movement they are obliged to appeal to the *working class*. And if the aristocracy is their vanishing opponent, the working class is their arising enemy. They prefer to compromise with the vanishing opponent rather than to strengthen the arising enemy, to whom the future belongs, by concessions of a more than apparent importance. Therefore, they strive to avoid every forcible collision with the aristocracy; but historical necessity and the Tories press them onwards. They cannot avoid fulfilling their mission, battering to pieces Old England, the England of the Past; and the very moment when they will have conquered exclusive political dominion, when political dominion and economical supremacy will be united in the same hands, when, therefore, the struggle against capital will no longer be distinct from the struggle against the existing Government — from that very moment will date the *social revolution of England*.

Karl Marx, 'The Chartists', in
'New York Daily Tribune',
25 August 1852.

See also B 3, F 1, P 7.

Art in the Service of Political Economy

Marriott's Free-Trade Hat, 1844

H 3

THE FREE-TRADE HAT.

The Laws of Political Economy

Goldwin Smith (1823–1911)

Goldwin Smith was appointed Regius Professor of Modern History at Oxford in 1859, and led the liberal dons at the university until he put his enthusiasm for democracy into practice by emigrating to America in 1868, moving subsequently to Toronto.

H 4

The laws of the production and distribution of wealth are not the laws of duty or affection. But they are the most beautiful and wonderful of the natural laws of God, and through their beauty and their wonderful wisdom they, like the other laws of nature which science explores, are not without a poetry of their own. Silently, surely, without any man's taking thought, if human folly will only refrain from hindering them, they gather, store, dispense, husband, if need be, against scarcity, the wealth of the great community of nations. They take from the consumer in England the wages of the producer in China, his just wages; and they distribute those wages among the thousand or hundred thousand Chinese workmen, who have contributed to the production, justly, to 'the estimation of a hair', to the estimation of a fineness far passing human thought. They call on each nation with silent bidding to supply of its abundance that which the other wants; and make all nations labourers for the common store; and in them lies perhaps the strongest natural proof that the earth was made for the sociable being, man. To buy in the cheapest and sell in the dearest market, the supposed concentration of economic selfishness, is simply to fulfil the command of the Creator, who provides for all the wants of His creatures through each other's help; to take from those who have abundance, and to carry to those who have need. It would be an exaggeration to erect trade into a moral agency; but it does unwittingly serve agencies higher than itself, and make one heart as well as one harvest for the world.

From Goldwin Smith's inaugural lecture
as Regius Professor of Modern History, Oxford, 1859,
in 'Lectures on Modern History',
Oxford and London, 1861, pp. 32-3.

The Approaching Democracy

James Bryce (1838–1922)

The tendency of the last seven centuries of European history has been to an equalisation of the conditions of men — an equalisation not so much (in England at least) of wealth as of physical force, of manners, and of intelligence. The feeling of subordination — that reverence of the lower classes for the upper, which was at once the cause and justification of feudal polity — has disappeared; political equality has become a passion in some countries, legal or civil equality is admitted to be necessary in all. (Speaking, of course, of civilised communities only.) Exclusive systems of government are therefore out of date. In enforcing this principle De Tocqueville is not, what he has sometimes been represented as being, a fatalist who predicts the universal sway of democratic institutions. Applying his argument to England, it would rather seem to be in this wise. Those things which are the basis of political power — knowledge and self-respect, and the capacity for combined action — have formerly been possessed by the few only, are now possessed by the many and among them by persons who do not enjoy civic privileges, though they feel themselves in every other respect the equals of those who do. Or, in other words, the social progress of democracy has outrun its political progress. This is dangerous, because it makes the organs of our political life no longer an adequate expression of our national will; and because there is nothing more dangerous than a democratic society without democratic institutions. The possessors of power ought therefore to admit others to share it, lest a worse thing befal them — lest class hatreds and jealousies arise, lest the people be alienated from their old institutions, and lest power be at last suddenly and violently seized by hands untrained to use it. The force of this view, which, like all those of its author, is an eminently practical one, founded on a careful observation of the phenomena of his own and other countries, seems to lie in this, that it suggests no vague or random extension of the franchise, but the inclusion of those persons only who are already powerful — powerful not by mere numbers, but also by their intelligence and organisation. Once received within the pale of the Constitution, such persons will learn to give their wishes a legitimate expression through its ancient organs: and they will themselves become its defenders if it should ever be threatened by the ignorance and turbulence of that lowest class to whom it is not now possible to entrust electoral rights.

From James Bryce, 'The Historical Aspect of Democracy' in 'Essays on Reform', 1867, pp. 272-3.

See also B 3, E 7, F 5.

The Peril of Uniformity

John Stuart Mill (1806–73)

John Stuart Mill, after a rigorous education by his father James, succeeded him as a senior administrator of the East India Company. He published his 'Logic' in 1843 and his 'Principles of Political Economy' in 1848. After his retirement he was radical M.P. for Westminster between 1865 and 1868, advocating, during his parliamentary career, female suffrage and representation for minorities.

H 6

We have a warning example in China — a nation of much talent, and, in some respect, even wisdom, owing to the rare good fortune of having been provided at an early period with a particularly good set of customs, the work, in some measure, of men to whom even the enlightened European must accord, under certain limitations, the title of sages and philosophers. They are remarkable, too, in the excellence of their apparatus for impressing, as far as possible, the best wisdom they possess upon every mind in the community, and securing that those who have appropriated most of it shall occupy the posts of honour and power. Surely the people who did this have discovered the secret of human progressiveness, and must have kept themselves steadily at the head of the movement of the world. On the contrary, they have become stationary — have remained so for thousands of years; and if they are ever to be further improved, it must be by foreigners. They have succeeded beyond all hope in what English philanthropists are so industriously working at — in making a people all alike, all governing their thoughts and conduct by the same maxims and rules; and these are the fruits. The modern régime of public opinion is, in an unorganised form, what the Chinese educational and political systems are in an organised; and unless individuality shall be able successfully to assert itself against this yoke, Europe, notwithstanding its noble antecedents and its professed Christianity, will tend to become another China.

What is it that has hitherto preserved Europe from this lot? What has made the European family of nations an improving, instead of a stationary portion of mankind? Not any superior excellence in them, which, when it exists, exists as the effect not as the cause; but their remarkable diversity of character and culture. Individuals, classes, nations, have been extremely unlike one another: they have struck out a great variety of paths, each leading to something valuable; and although at every period those who travelled in different paths have been intolerant of one another, and each would have thought it an excellent thing if all the rest could have been compelled to travel his road, their attempts to thwart each other's development have rarely had any permanent success, and each has in time endured to receive the good which the others have offered. Europe is, in my judgment, wholly indebted to this plurality of paths for its progressive and many-sided development. But it already begins to possess this benefit in a considerably less degree. It is decidedly advancing towards the Chinese ideal of making all people alike. M. de Tocqueville, in his last important work, remarks how much more the Frenchmen of the present day resemble one another than did those even of the last generation. The same remark might be made of Englishmen in a far greater degree. [In a passage already quoted from] Wilhelm von Humboldt [he] points out two things as necessary conditions of human development, because necessary to render people unlike one another; namely, freedom, and variety of situations. The second of these two conditions is in this country every day diminishing. The circumstances which surround different classes and individuals, and shape their characters, are daily becoming more assimilated. Formerly, different ranks, different neighbourhoods, different trades and professions, lived in what might be called different worlds; at present to a great degree in the same. Comparatively speaking, they now read the same things, listen to the same things, see the same things, go to the same places, have their hopes and fears directed to the same objects, have the same rights and liberties, and the same means of asserting them. Great as are the differences of position which remain, they are nothing to those which have ceased. And the assimilation is still proceeding. All the political changes of the age promote it, since they all tend to raise the low and to lower the high. Every extension of education promotes it, because education brings people under common influences, and gives them access to the general stock of facts and sentiments. Improvement in the means of communication promotes it, by bringing the inhabitants of distant places into personal contact, and keeping up a rapid flow of changes of residence between one place and another. The increase of commerce and manufactures promotes it, by diffusing more widely the advantages of easy circumstances, and opening all objects of ambition, even the highest, to general competition, whereby the desire of rising becomes no longer the character of a particular class, but of all classes. A more powerful agency than all these, in bringing about a general similarity among mankind, is the complete establishment, in this and other free countries, of the ascendancy of public opinion in the State. As the various social eminences which enabled persons entrenched on them to disregard the opinion of the multitude gradually become levelled; as the very idea of resisting the will of the public, when it is positively known that they have a will, disappears more and more from the minds of practical politicians; there ceases to be any social support for nonconformity — any substantive power in society which, itself opposed to the ascendancy of numbers, is interested in taking under its protection opinions and tendencies at variance with those of the public.

The combination of all these causes forms so great a mass of influences hostile to Individuality, that it is not easy to see how it can stand its ground. It will do so with increasing difficulty, unless the intelligent part of the public can be made to feel its value — to see that it is good there should be differences, even though not for the better, even though, as it may appear to them, some should be for the worse. If the claims of Individuality are ever to be asserted, the time is now, while much is still wanting to complete the enforced assimilation. It is only in the earlier stages that any stand can be successfully made against the encroachment. The demand that all other people shall resemble ourselves grows by what it feeds on. If resistance waits till life is reduced *nearly* to one uniform type, all deviations from that type will come to be considered impious, immoral, even monstrous and contrary to nature. Mankind speedily become unable to conceive diversity, when they have been for some time unaccustomed to see it.

From John Stuart Mill, 'On Liberty', 1859, Fontana ed., pp. 202-4.

Notes

Karl Wilhelm von Humboldt (1767-1835) was a Prussian statesman, educationalist and linguistic expert.

Culture and Machinery
Matthew Arnold (1822–88)

Matthew Arnold, poet and critic, was the son of the public-school reformer Thomas Arnold of Rugby and spent most of his life as a government inspector of schools. W. E. Forster was his brother-in-law.

H 7

If culture, then, is a study of perfection, and of harmonious perfection, general perfection, and perfection which consists in becoming something rather than in having something, in an inward condition of the mind and spirit, not in an outward set of circumstances, — it is clear that culture, instead of being the frivolous and useless thing which Mr Bright, and Mr Frederic Harrison, and many other Liberals are apt to call it, has a very important function to fulfil for mankind. And this function is particularly important in our modern world, of which the whole civilisation is, to a much greater degree than the civilisation of Greece and Rome, mechanical and external, and tends constantly to become more so. But above all in our own country has culture a weighty part to perform, because here that mechanical character, which civilisation tends to take everywhere, is shown in the most eminent degree. Indeed nearly all the characters of perfection, as culture teaches us to fix them, meet in this country with some powerful tendency which thwarts them and sets them at defiance. The idea of perfection as an *inward* condition of the mind and spirit is at variance with the mechanical and material civilisation in esteem with us, and nowhere, as I have said, so much in esteem as with us. The idea of perfection as a *general* expansion of the human family is at variance with our strong individualism, our hatred of all limits to the unrestrained swing of the individual's personality, our maxim of 'every man for himself.' **Above** all the idea of perfection as a *harmonious* expansion of human nature is at variance with our want of flexibility, with our inaptitude for seeing more than one side of a thing, with our intense energetic absorption in the particular pursuit we happen to be following. So culture has a rought task to achieve in this country. Its preachers have, and are likely long to have, a hard time of it, and they will much oftener be regarded, for a great while to come, as elegant or spurious Jeremiahs, than as friends and benefactors. That, however, will not prevent their doing in the end good service if they persevere. And meanwhile, the mode of action they have to pursue, and the sort of habits they must fight against, ought to be made quite clear for every one to see who may be willing to look at the matter attentively and dispassionately.

Faith in machinery is, I said, our besetting danger; often in machinery most absurdly disproportioned to the end which this machinery, if it is to do any good at all, is to serve; but always in machinery, as if it had a value in and for itself. What is freedom but machinery? what is population but machinery? what is coal but machinery? what are railroads but machinery? what is wealth but machinery? what are, even, religious organisations but machinery? Now almost every voice in England is accustomed to speak of these things as if they were precious ends in themselves, and therefore had some of the characters of perfection indisputably joined to them. I have before now noticed Mr Roebuck's stock argument for proving the greatness and happiness of England as she is, and for quite stopping the mouths of all gainsayers. Mr Roebuck is never weary of reiterating this argument of his, so I do not know why I should be weary of noticing it. 'May not every man in England say what he likes?' — Mr Roebuck perpetually asks; and that, he thinks, is quite sufficient, and when every man may say what he likes, our aspirations ought to be satisfied. But the aspirations of culture, which is the study of perfection, are not satisfied, unless what men say, when the may say what they like, is worth saying, — has good in it, and more good than bad. . . .

And in the same way with respect to railroads and coal. Every one must have observed the strange language current during the late discussions as to the possible failure of our supplies of coal. Our coal, thousands of people were saying, is the real basis of our national greatness; if our coal runs short, there is an end of the greatness of England. But what *is* greatness? — culture makes us ask. Greatness is a spiritual condition worthy to excite love, interest, and admiration; and the outward proof of possessing greatness is that we excite love, interest, and admiration. If England were swallowed up by the sea to-morrow, which of the two, a hundred years hence, would most excite the love, interest, and admiration of mankind, — would most, therefore, show the evidences of having possessed greatness — the England of the last twenty years, or the England of Elizabeth, of a time of splendid spiritual effort, but when our coal, and our industrial operations depending on coal, were very little developed? Well, then, what an unsound habit of mind it must be which makes us talk of things like coal or iron as constituting the greatness of England, and how salutary a friend is culture, bent on seeing things as they are, and thus dissipating delusions of this kind and fixing standards of perfection that are real!

Wealth, again, that end to which our prodigious works for material advantage are directed, — the commonest of commonplaces tells us how men are always apt to regard wealth as a precious end in itself; and certainly they have never been so apt thus to regard it as they are in England at the present time. Never did people believe anything more firmly, than nine Englishmen out of ten at the present day believe that our greatness and welfare are proved by our being so very rich. Now, the use of culture is that it helps us, by means of its spiritual standard of perfection, to regard wealth as but machinery, and not only to say as a matter of words that we regard wealth as but machinery, but really to perceive and feel that it is so. If it were not for this purging effect wrought upon our minds by culture, the whole world, the future as well as the present, would inevitably belong to the Philistines. The people who believe most that our greatness and welfare are proved by our being very rich, and who most give their lives and thoughts to becoming rich, are just the very people whom we call Philistines. Culture says: 'Consider these people, then, their way of life, their habits, their manners, the very tones of their voice; look at them attentively; observe the literature they read, the things which give them pleasure, the words which come forth out of their mouths, the thoughts which make the furniture of their minds; would any amount of wealth be worth having with the condition that one was to become just like these people by having it?' And thus culture begets a dissatisfaction which is of the highest possible value in stemming the common tide of men's thoughts in a wealthy and industrial community, and which saves the future, as one may hope, from being vulgarised, even if it cannot save the present.

From Matthew Arnold, 'Culture and Anarchy', 1869, pp. 9-13.

Notes

John Bright (1811-89) was the leader of the radical wing of the Liberal Party.

Frederic Harrison (1831-1923) was an extreme radical lawyer and journalist whose attack on an earlier lecture of Arnold's provoked the publication of 'Culture and Anarchy'.

John Arthur Roebuck (1801-79) had been a radical M.P. but was now to the right of the Liberal Party.

See also G 5, P 7, P 9.

The Irish

Thomas Carlyle

Thomas Carlyle, a stonemason's son from Dumfriesshire, educated at Edinburgh University, broke on the public with 'Signs of the Times' (1829). The radicalism of his social criticism in 'Chartism' (1849) caused Engels to declare that he 'had found the right path', but his subsequent writing, with its preoccupation with the heroic, tended to an increasing authoritarianism.

H 8

But the thing we had to state here was our inference from that mournful fact of the third Sanspotato, — coupled with this other well-known fact that the Irish speak a partially intelligible dialect of English, and their fare across by steam is fourpence sterling! Crowds of miserable Irish darken all our towns. The wild Milesian features, looking false ingenuity, restlessness, unreason, misery and mockery, salute you on all highways and byways. The English coachman, as he whirls past, lashes the Milesian with his whip, curses him with his tongue; the Milesian is holding out his hat to beg. He is the sorest evil this country has to strive with. In his rags and laughing savagery, he is there to undertake all work that can be done by mere strength of hand and back; for wages that will purchase him potatoes. He needs only salt for condiment; he lodges to his mind in any pighutch or doghutch, roosts in outhouses; and wears a suit of tatters, the getting off and on of which is said to be a difficult operation, transacted only in festivals and the hightides of the calendar. The Saxon man if he cannot work on these terms, finds no work. He too may be ignorant; but he has not sunk from decent manhood to squalid apehood: he cannot continue there. American forests lie untilled across the ocean; the uncivilised

Irishman, not by his strength, but by the opposite of strength, drives out the Saxon native, takes possession in his room. There abides he, in his squalor and unreason, in his falsity and drunken violence, as the ready-made nucleus of degradation and disorder. Whosoever struggles, swimming with difficulty, may now find an example how the human being can exist not swimming but sunk. Let him sink; he is not the worst of men; not worse than this man. We have quarantines against pestilence; but there is no pestilence like that; and against it what quarantine is possible? It is lamentable to look upon. This soil of Britain, these Saxon men have cleared it, made it arable, fertile and a home for them; they and their fathers have done that. Under the sky there exists no force of men who with arms in their hands could drive them out of it; all force of men with arms these Saxons would seize, in their grim way, and fling (Heaven's justice and their own Saxon humour aiding them) swiftly into the sea. But behold, a force of men armed only with rags, ignorance and nakedness; and the Saxon owners, paralysed by invisible magic of paper formula, have to fly far, and hide themselves in Transatlantic forests. 'Irish repeal'? 'Would to God,' as Dutch William said, '*you* were King of Ireland, and could take yourself and it three thousand miles off,' — there to repeal it!

And yet these poor Celtiberian Irish brothers, what can *they* help it? They cannot stay at home, and starve. It is just and natural that they come hither as a curse to us. Alas, for them too it is not a luxury. It is not a straight or joyful way of avenging their sore wrongs this; but a most sad circuitous one. Yet a way it is, and an effectual way. The time has come when the Irish population must either be improved a little, or else exterminated. Plausible management, adapted to this hollow outcry or to that, will no longer do; it must be management grounded on sincerity and fact, to which the truth of things will respond — by an actual beginning of improvement to these wretched brother-men. In a state of perennial ultra-savage famine, in the midst of civilisation, they cannot continue. For that the Saxon British will ever submit to sink along with them to such a state, we assume as impossible. There is in these latter, thank God, an ingenuity which is not false; a methodic spirit, of insight, of perseverant well-doing; a rationality and veracity which Nature with her truth does *not* disown; — withal there is a

'Berserkir rage' in the heart of them, which will prefer all things, including destruction and self-destruction, to that. Let no man awaken it, this same Berserkir rage! Deep-hidden it lies, far down in the centre, like genial central-fire, with stratum after stratum of arrangement, traditionary method, composed productiveness, all built above it, vivified and rendered fertile by it: justice, clearness, silence, perseverance, unhasting unresting diligence, hatred of disorder, hatred of injustice, which is the worst disorder, characterise this people; their inward fire we say, as all such fire should be, is hidden at the centre. Deep-hidden; but awakenable, but immeasurable; — let no man awaken it! With this strong silent people have the noisy vehement Irish now at length got common cause made. Ireland, now for the first time, in such strange circuitous way, does find itself embarked in the same boat with England, to sail together, or to sink together; the wretchedness of Ireland, slowly but inevitably, has crept over to us, and become our own wretchedness. The Irish population must get itself redressed and saved, for the sake of the English if for nothing else. Alas, that it should, on both sides, be poor toiling men that pay the smart for unruly Striguls, Henrys, Macdermots, and O'Donoghues! The strong have eaten sour grapes, and the teeth of the weak are set on edge. 'Curses,' says the Proverb, 'are like chickens, they return always *home*.'

But now, on the whole, it seems to us, English Statistic Science, with floods of the finest peasantry in the world steaming in on us daily, may fold up her Danaides reticulations on this matter of the Working Classes; and conclude, what every man who will take the statistic spectacles off his nose, and look, may discern in town or country: That the condition of the lower multitude of English labourers approximates more and more to that of the Irish competing with them in all markets; that whatsoever labour, to which mere strength with little skill will suffice, is to be done, will be done not at the English price, but at an approximation to the Irish price: at a price superior as yet to the Irish, that is, superior to scarcity of third-rate potatoes for thirty weeks yearly; superior, yet hourly, with the arrival of every new steamboat, sinking nearer to an equality with that. Half-a-million handloom weavers, working fifteen hours a-day, in perpetual inability to procure thereby enough of the coarsest food; English farm-labourers at nine shillings and at seven shillings a-week; Scotch farm-labourers who, 'in districts the half of whose husbandry is that of cows, taste no milk, can procure no milk:' all these things are credible to us; several of them are known to us by the best evidence, by eyesight. With all this it is consistent that the wages of 'skilled labour,' as it is called, should in many cases be higher than they ever were: the giant Steamengine in a giant English Nation will here create violent demand for labour, and will there annihilate demand. But, alas, the great portion of labour is not skilled: the millions are and must be skilless, where strength alone is wanted; ploughers, delvers, borers; hewers of wood and drawers of water; menials of the Steamengine, only the *chief* menials and immediate *body*-servants of which require skill. English Commerce stretches its fibres over the whole earth; sensitive literally, nay quivering in convulsion, to the farthest influences of the earth. The huge demon of Mechanism smokes and thunders, panting at his great task, in all sections of English land; changing his *shape* like a very Proteus; and infallibly, at every change of shape, *oversetting* whole multitudes of workmen, and as if with the waving of his shadow from afar, hurling them asunder, this way and that, in their crowded march and course of work or traffic; so that the wisest no longer knows his whereabout. With an Ireland pouring daily in on us, in these circumstances; deluging us down to its own waste confusion, outward and inward, it seems a cruel mockery to tell poor drudges that *their* condition is improving.

New Poor-Law! *Laissez faire, laissez passer!* The master of horses, when the summer labour is done, has to feed his horses through the winter. If he said to his horses: 'Quadrupeds, I have no longer work for you; but work exists abundantly over the world: are you ignorant (or must I read you Political-Economy Lectures) that the Steamengine always in the long-run creates additional work? Railways are forming in one quarter of this earth, canals in another, much cartage is wanted; somewhere in Europe, Asia, Africa or America, doubt it not, ye will find cartage: go and seek cartage, and good go with you!' They, with protrusive upper lip, snort dubious; signifying that Europe, Asia, Africa and America lie somewhat out of their beat; that what cartage may be wanted there is not too well known to them. *They* can find no cartage. They gallop distracted along highways, all fenced in to the right and to the left: finally, under pains of hunger they take to leaping fences; eating foreign property, and — we know the rest. Ah, it is not a joyful mirth, it is sadder than tears, the laugh Humanity is forced to, at *Laissez-faire* applied to poor peasants, in a world like our Europe of the year 1839!

From Thomas Carlyle, 'Chartism', 1839, pp. 28-33.

Notes

'Sanspotato' was from the French 'sansculottes' — the ragged street-mobs of the Revolution. Milesius was a legendary Spanish conqueror of Ireland, so 'Milesian' meant 'Irish'. 'Berserkir rage' referred to the battle-trance of the Norse warriors. In Greek mythology the daughters of Danaus — the Danaides — who murdered their husbands on their wedding night, were doomed eternally to fill sieves — 'reticulations' — with water. Also from the Greek, Proteus was the sea god who ventured on land, changing shape and form.

See also A 1, B 3, F 7.

Hudson's Statue

Thomas Carlyle

Hudson the railway king, if Popular Election be the rule, seems to me by far the most authentic king extant in this world. Hudson has been 'elected by the people' so as almost none other is or was. Hudson solicited no vote; his votes were silent voluntary ones, not liable to be false: he *did* a thing which men found, in their inarticulate hearts to be worthy of paying money for; and they paid it. What the desire of every heart was, Hudson had or seemed to have produced: Scrip out of which profit could be made. They 'voted' for him by purchasing his scrip with a profit to him. Every vote was the spontaneous product of those men's deepest insights and most practical convictions, about Hudson and themselves and this Universe: I say, it was not a spoken vote, but a silently acted one; a vote for one incapable of being insincere. What their appetites, intelligences, stupidities, and pruriences had taught these men, they authentically told you there. I beg you to mark that well. Not by all the ballot-boxes in Nature could you have hoped to get, with such exactness, from these men, what the deepest inarticulate voice of the gods and of the demons in them was, as by this their spontaneous purchase of scrip. It is the ultimate rectified quintessence of these 'men's votes;' the distillation of their very souls; the sincerest sincerity that was in them. Without gratitude to Hudson, or even without thought of him, they raised Hudson to his bad eminence, not by their voice given once at some hustings under the influence of balderdash and beer, but by the thought of their heart, by the inarticulate, indisputable dictate of their whole being. Hudson inquired of England: 'What precious thing can I do for you, O enlightened Countrymen; what may be the value to you, by popular election, of this stroke of work that lies in me?' Popular election, with universal, with household and other suffrage, free as air, deep as life and death, free and deep as *spoken* suffrage never was or could be, has answered: 'Pounds sterling to such and such amount; that is the apparent value of thy stroke of work to *us*, — blockheads as we are.' Real value differs from apparent to a frightful extent in this world, try it by what suffrage you will!

Hudson's value as a demigod being what is was, his value as a maker of railways shall hardly concern us here. What Hudson's real worth to mankind in the matter of railways might be, I cannot pretend to say. Fact knows it to the uttermost fraction, and will pay it him yet; but men differ widely in opinion, and in general do not in the least know. From my own private observation and conjecture, I should say, Trifling if any worth.

Much as we love railways, there is one thing undeniable: Railways are shifting all Towns of Britain into new places; no Town will stand where it did, and nobody can tell for a long while yet where it will stand. This is an unexpected, and indeed most disastrous result. I perceive, railways have set all the Towns of Britain a-dancing. Reading is coming up to London, Basingstoke is going down to Gosport or Southampton, Dumfries to Liverpool and Glasgow; while at Crewe, and other points, I see new ganglions of human population establishing themselves, and the prophecy of metallurgic cities which were not heard of before. Reading, Basingstoke and the rest, the unfortunate Towns, subscribed money to get railways; and it proves to be for cutting their own throats. Their business has gone elsewhither; and they — cannot stay behind their business! They are set a-dancing, as I said; confusedly waltzing, in a state of progressive dissolution, towards the four winds; and know not where the end of the death-dance will be for them, in what point of space they will be allowed to rebuild themselves. That is their sad case.

And what an affair it is in each of the shops and houses of those Towns, thus silently bleeding to death, or what we call dancing away to other points of the British territory: how Joplin of Reading, who had anchored himself in that pleasant place, and fondly hoping to live by upholstery and paperhanging, had wedded, and made friends there, — awakens some morning, and finds that his trade has flitted away! Here it is not any longer; it is gone to London, to Bristol: whither has it gone? Joplin knows not whither; knows and sees only that gone it is; and that he by preternatural sagacity must scent it out again, follow it over the world, and catch it again, or else die. Sad news for Joplin: — indeed I fear, should his sagacity be too inconsiderable, he is not unlikely to break his heart, or take to drinking in these inextricable circumstances! And it is the history, more or less, in every town, house, shop and industrial dwelling-place of the British Empire at this moment; — and the cipher of afflicted Joplins; and the amount of private distress, uncertainty, discontent; and withal of 'revolutionary movement' created hereby, is tragical to think of. This is 'revolutionary movement' with a witness; revolution brought home to everybody's hearth and moneysafe and heart and stomach — Which miserable result, with so many others from the same source, what method was there of avoiding or indefinitely mitigating? This surely, as the beginning of all: That you had made your railways *not* in haste; that, at least, you had spread the huge process, sure to alter all men's mutual position and relations, over a reasonable breadth of time!

For all manner of reasons, how much could one have wished that the making of our British railways had gone on with deliberation; that these great works had made themselves not in five years but in fifty-and-five! Hudson's 'worth' to railways, I think, will mainly resolve itself into this. That he carried them to completion within the former short limit of time; that he got them made, — in extremely improper directions I am told, and surely with endless confusion to the innumerable passive Joplins, and likewise to the numerous active scrip-holders, a widespread class, once rich, now coinless, — hastily in five years, not deliberately in fifty-five. His worth to railways? His worth, I take it, to English railways, much more to English men, will turn out to be extremely inconsiderable; to be incalculable damage rather! Foolish railway people gave him two millions, and thought it not enough without a Statue to boot. But Fact thought, and is now audibly saying, far otherwise! . . .

Fact and Suffrage: what a discrepancy! Fact decided for some coalshaft such as we describe. Suffrage decides for such a column. Suffrage having money in its pocket, carries it hollow, for the moment.

And so there is Rayless Majesty exalted far above the chimney-pots, with a potential Copper Likeness, twenty-five thousand pounds worth of copper over and above; and a King properly belonging only to *this* epoch. — That there are greedy blockheads in huge majority, in all epochs, is certain; but that any sane mortal should think of counting *their* heads to ascertain who or what is to be King, this is a little peculiar. All Democratic men, and members of the Suffrage Movement, it appears to me, are called upon to think seriously, with a seriousness approaching to despair, of these things.

From Thomas Carlyle, 'Latter-Day Pamphlets', 1850, pp. 228-30.

Notes

George Hudson (1800-71) was the York draper who rose to dominate over a third of the British railway system. The people of York intended to commemorate him with a statue, but following his disgrace after allegations of fraud were proved against him, the money was used to erect a statue to his opponent in local politics.

See also E 2.

Contrasted Towns

A. W. N. Pugin (1812–52)

Augustus Welby Northmore Pugin was a gifted architect who combined his acquired Catholicism with enthusiasm for medieval architecture to attack both the architecture and the organisation of contemporary society. The technique of juxtaposing scenes of medieval harmony and modern barbarism Pugin shared with Carlyle in 'Past and Present' (1842), and Benjamin Disraeli in 'Sybil' (1845).

H 10

A Catholic town in 1440.

The same town in 1840

from *'Contrasts: or a Parallel between the Noble Edifices of the Middle Ages and the Present Day, showing the present Decay of Taste'*, 1836.

True and False Economy

John Ruskin (1819–1900)

John Ruskin, the son of a wealthy wine merchant, was educated at Oxford. He gained a reputation first as an art critic in the 1840s, then moved towards social criticism. In 1869 he was appointed Slade Professor of the Fine Arts at Oxford, and became a major influence on the students and among working man. But his last years, spent by Coniston Water, were clouded by mental illness.

H 11

27. Primarily, which is very notable and curious, I observe that men of business rarely know the meaning of the word 'rich.' At least, if they know, they do not in their reasonings allow for the fact, that it is a relative word, implying its opposite 'poor' as positively as the word 'north' implies its opposite 'south.' Men nearly always speak and write as if riches were absolute, and it were possible, by following certain scientific percepts, for everybody to be rich. Whereas riches are a power like that of electricity, acting only through inequalities or negations of itself. The force of the guinea you have in your pocket depends wholly on the default of a guinea in your neighbour's pocket. If he did not want it, it would be of no use to you; the degree of power it possesses depends accurately upon the need or desire he has for it, — and the art of making yourself rich, in the ordinary mercantile economist's sense, is therefore equally and necessarily the art of keeping your neighbour poor.

I would not contend in this matter (and rarely in any matter) for the acceptance of terms. But I wish the reader clearly and deeply to understand the difference between the two economies, to which the terms 'Political' and 'Mercantile' might not unadvisedly be attached.

28. Political economy (the economy of a State, or of citizens) consists simply in the production, preservation, and distribution, at fittest time and place, of useful or pleasurable things. The farmer who cuts his hay at the right time; the shipwright who drives his bolts well home in sound wood; the builder who lays good bricks in well-tempered mortar; the housewife who takes care of her furniture in the parlour, and guards against all waste in her kitchen; and the singer who rightly disciplines, and never overstrains her voice, are all political economists in the true and final sense: adding continually to the riches and well-being of the nation to which they belong.

But mercantile economy, the economy of 'merces' or of 'pay,' signifies the accumulation, in the hands of individuals, of legal or moral claim upon, or power over, the labour of others; every such claim implying precisely as much poverty or debt on one side, as it implies riches or right on the other.

It does not, therefore, necessarily involve an addition to the actual property, or well-being of the State in which it exists. But since this commercial wealth, or power over labour, is nearly always convertible at once into real property, while real property is not always convertible at once into power over labour, the idea of riches among active men in civilized nations, generally refers to commercial wealth; and in estimating their possessions, they rather calculate the value of their horses and fields by the number of guineas they could get for them, than the value of their guineas by the number of horses and fields they could buy with them.

29. There is, however, another reason for this habit of mind: namely, that an accumulation of real property is of little use to its owner, unless, together with it, he has commercial power over labour. Thus, suppose any person to be put in possession of a large estate of fruitful land, with rich beds of gold in its gravel; countless herds of cattle in its pastures; houses, and gardens, and storehouses full of useful stores: but suppose, after all, that he could get no servants? In order that he may be able to have servants, some one in his neighbourhood must be poor, and in want of his gold — or his corn. Assume that no one is in want of either, and that no servants are to be had. He must, therefore, bake his own bread, make his own clothes, plough his own

ground, and shepherd his own flocks. His gold will be as useful to him as any other yellow pebbles on his estate. His stores must rot, for he cannot consume them. He can eat no more than another man could eat, and wear no more than another man could wear. He must lead a life of severe and common labour to procure even ordinary comforts; he will be ultimately unable to keep either houses in repair, or fields in cultivation; and forced to content himself with a poor man's portion of cottage and garden, in the midst of a desert of waste land, trampled by wild cattle, and encumbered by ruins of palaces, which he will hardly mock at himself by calling 'his own.'

30. The most covetous of mankind would, with small exultation, I presume, accept riches of this kind on these terms. What is really desired, under the name of riches, is, essentially, power over men; in its simplest sense, the power of obtaining for our own advantage the labour of servant, tradesman, and artist; in wider sense, authority of directing large masses of the nation to various ends (good, trivial, or hurtful, according to the mind of the rich person). And this power of wealth of course is greater or less in direct proportion to the poverty of the men over whom it is exercised, and in inverse proportion to the number of persons who are as rich as ourselves, and who are ready to give the same price for an article of which the supply is limited. If the musician is poor, he will sing for small pay, as long as there is only one person who can pay him; but if there be two or three, he will sing for the one who offers him most. And thus the power of the riches of the patron (always imperfect and doubtful, as we shall see presently, even when most authoritative) depends first on the poverty of the artist, and then on the limitation of the number of equally wealthy persons, who also want seats at the concert. So that, as above stated, the art of becoming 'rich,' in the common sense, is not absolutely nor finally the art of accumulating much money for ourselves, but also of contriving that our neighbours shall have less. In accurate terms, it is 'the art of establishing the maximum inequality in our own favour.'

From John Ruskin, 'The Veins of Wealth',
in 'Unto this Last', 1862, pp. 40-6.

See also M 1-5, p 17.

How I Became a Socialist

William Morris (1834–96)

William Morris was initially involved in the medievalism of the Pre-Raphaelites but concentrated on the design of furniture and fabrics and the revival of hand-craftsmanship. He was involved in the Eastern Question agitation of the 1870s, joined the Marxist Social Democratic Federation in 1883, and to his death remained a committed revolutionary socialist.

H 12

I am asked by the Editor to give some sort of a history of the above conversation, and I feel that it may be of some use to do so, if my readers will look upon me as a type of a certain group of people, but not so easy to do clearly, briefly, and truly. Let me, however, try. But first, I will say what I mean by being a Socialist, since I am told that the word no longer expresses definitely and with certainty what it did ten years ago. Well, what I mean by Socialism is a condition of society in which there should be neither rich nor poor, neither master nor master's man, neither idle nor overworked, neither brain-sick brain workers, nor heart-sick hand workers, in a word, in which all men would be living in equality of condition, and would manage their affairs unwastefully, and with the full consciousness that harm to one would mean harm to all – the realization at last of the meaning of the word 'commonwealth'.

Now this view of Socialism which I hold today, and hope to die holding, is what I began with; I had no transitional period, unless you may call such a brief period of political radicalism during which I saw my ideal clear enough, but had no hope of any realization of it. That came to an end some months before I joined the (then) Democratic

Federation, and the meaning of my joining that body was that I had conceived a hope of the realization of my ideal. If you ask me how much of a hope, or what I thought we Socialists then living and working would accomplish towards it, or when there would be effected any change in the face of society, I must say, I do not know. I can only say that I did not measure my hope, nor the joy that it brought me at the time. For the rest, when I took that step I was blankly ignorant of economics; I had never so much as opened Adam Smith, or heard of Ricardo, or of Karl Marx. Oddly enough, I *had* read some of Mill, to wit, those posthumous papers of his (published, was it, in the 'West-minster Review' or the 'Fortnightly'?' in which he attacks Socialism in its Fourierist guise. In those papers he put the arguments, as far as they go, clearly and honestly, and the result, so far as I was concerned, was to convince me that Socialism was a necessary change, and that it was possible to bring it about in our own days. Those papers put the finishing touch to my conversion to Socialism. Well, having joined a Socialist body (for the Federation soon became definitely Socialist), I put some conscience into trying to learn the economical side of Socialism, and even tackled Marx, though I must confess that, whereas I thoroughly enjoyed the historical part of 'Capital', I suffered agonies of confusion of the brain over reading the pure economics of that great work. Anyhow, I read what I could, and will hope that some information stuck to me from my reading; but more, I must think, from continuous conversation with such friends as Bax and Hyndman and Scheu, and the brisk course of propaganda meetings which were going on at the time, and in which I took my share. Such finish to what of education in practical Socialism as I am capable of I received afterwards from some of my Anarchist friends, from whom I learned, quite against their intention, that Anarchism was impossible, much as I learned from Mill against *his* intention that Socialism was necessary.

But in this telling how I fell into *practical* Socialism I have begun, as I perceive, in the middle, for in my position of a well-to-do man, not suffering from the disabilities which oppress a working man at every step, I feel that I might never have been drawn into the practical side of the question if an ideal had not forced me to seek towards it. For politics as politics, i.e., not regarded as a necessary if cumbersome and disgustful means to an end, would never have attracted me, nor when I had become conscious of the wrongs of society as it now is, and the oppression of poor people, could I have ever believed in the possibility of a *partial* setting right of those wrongs. In other words, I could never have been such a fool as to believe in the happy and 'respectable' poor.

If, therefore, my ideal forced me to look for practical Socialism, what was it that forced me to conceive of an ideal? Now, here comes in what I said of my being (in this paper) a type of a certain group of mind.

Before the uprising of *modern* Socialism almost all intelligent people either were, or professed themselves to be, quite contented with the civilization of this century. Again, almost all of these really were thus contented, and saw nothing to do but to perfect the said civilization by getting rid of a few ridiculous survivals of the barbarous ages. To be short, this was the *Whig* frame of mind, natural to the modern prosperous middle-class men, who, in fact, as far as mechanical progress is concerned, have nothing to ask for, if only Socialism would leave them alone to enjoy their plentiful style.

But besides these contented ones there were others who were not really contented, but had a vague sentiment of repulsion to the triumph of civilization, but were coerced into silence by the measureless power of Whiggery. Lastly, there were a few who were in open rebellion against the said Whiggery — a few, say two, Carlyle and Ruskin. The latter, before my days of practical Socialism, was my master towards the ideal aforesaid, and, looking backward, I cannot help saying, by the way, how deadly dull the world would have been twenty years ago but for Ruskin! It was through him that I learned to give form to my discontent, which I must say was not by any means vague. Apart from the desire to produce beautiful things, the leading passion of my life has been and is hatred of modern civilization. What shall I say of it now, when the words are put into my mouth, my hope of its destruction — what shall I say of its supplanting by Socialism?

What shall I say concerning its mastery of and its waste of mechanical power, its commonwealth so poor, its enemies of the commonwealth so rich, its stupendous organization — for the misery of life! Its contempt of simple pleasures which everyone could enjoy but for its folly? Its eyeless vulgarity which has destroyed art, the one certain solace of labour? All this I felt then as now, but I did not know why it was so. The hope of the past times was gone, the struggles of mankind for many ages had produced nothing but this sordid, aimless, ugly confusion; the immediate future seemed to me likely to intensify all the present evils by sweeping away the last survivals of the days before the dull squalor of civilization had settled down on the world. This was a bad look-out indeed, and, if I may mention myself as a personality and not as a mere type, especially so to a man of my disposition, careless of metaphysics and religion, as well as of scientific analysis, but with a deep love of the earth and the life on it, and a passion for the history of the past of mankind. Think of it! Was it all to end in a counting-house on the top of a cinder-heap, with Podsnap's drawing-room in the offing, and a Whig committee dealing out champagne to the rich and margarine to the poor in such convenient proportions as would make all men contented together, though the pleasure of the eyes was gone from the world, and the place of Homer was to be taken by Huxley? Yet, believe me in my heart, when I really forced myself to look towards the future, that is what I saw in it, and, as far as I could tell, scarce anyone seemed to think it worth while to struggle against such a consummation of civilization. So there I was in for a fine pessimistic end of life, if it had not somehow dawned on me that amidst all this filth of civilization the seeds of a great change, what we others call Social-Revolution, were beginning to germinate. The whole face of things was changed to me by that discovery, and all I had to do then in order to become a Socialist was to hook myself on to the practical movement which, as before said, I have tried to do as well as I could.

To sum up, then, the study of history and the love and practice of art forced me into a hatred of the civilization which, if things were to stop as they are, would turn history into inconsequent nonsense, and make art a collection of the curiosities of the past, which would have no serious relation to the life of the present.

But the consciousness of revolution stirring amidst our hateful modern society prevented me, luckier than many others of artistic perceptions, from crystallizing into a mere railer against 'progress' on the one hand, and on the other from wasting time and energy in any of the numerous schemes by which the quasi-artistic of the middle classes hope to make art grow when it has no longer any root, and thus I became a practical Socialist.

A last word or two. Perhaps some of our friends will say, what have we to do with these matters of history and art? We want by means of Social-Democracy to win a decent livelihood, we want in some sort to live, and that at once. Surely anyone who professes to think that the question of art and cultivation must go before that of the knife and fork (and there are some who do propose that) does not understand what art means, or how that its root must have a soil of a thriving and unanxious life. Yet it must be remembered that civilization has reduced the workman to such a skinny and pitiful existence, that he scarcely knows how to frame a desire for any life much better than that which he now endures perforce. It is the province of art to set the true ideal of a full and reasonable life before him, a life to which the perception and creation of beauty, the enjoyment of real pleasure that is, shall be felt to be as necessary to man as his daily bread, and that no man, and no set of men, can be deprived of this except by mere opposition, which should be resisted to the utmost.

William Morris, 'How I Became a Socialist', in 'Justice', 16 June 1894.

Notes

François Marie Charles Fourier (1772-1837) was a French theorist who conceived social reorganisation taking the form of co-operative communities, rather like those of Robert Owen in Britain. Henry Mayers Hyndman (1842-1921), Andreas Scheu (1844-1927) and Ernest Belfort Bax (1854-1926) were leading lights of the socialist movement in Britain during the 1880s. 'Justice', for which Morris wrote this article, was the organ of the Social Democratic Federation, founded as the Democratic Federation in 1881. 'Podsnap' was Charles Dickens's caricature of the middle-class philistine in 'Our Mutual Friend' (1865).

See also G 1, N 1-11.

Art in the Service of Socialism

H 13

Membership card of William Morris's Hammersmith Branch of the Socialist League, designed by Walter Crane, c. 1885.

Section J

Religion and Materialist Philosophy

Religion and Materialist Philosophy

Two tendencies, one intellectual and one social, made for the collision in the 1860s between scientific thought and religion.

Religion of a fundamentalist sort was losing the utility as a social discipline it had possessed in the first critical years of the industrial experience. The performance of the industrial economy seemed to indicate the claims of individualism to provide a viable framework for social behaviour. Leslie Stephen wrote that his generation, reared on John Stuart Mill,

claimed with complete confidence to be in possession of a definite and scientific system of economical, political and ethical truth. They were calmly convinced that all objectors, from Carlyle downwards, were opposed to him [Mill] as dreamers to logicians; and the recent triumph of free trade [1846] had given special plausibility to their claims.

('Some Early Impressions', 1903, pp. 74-5)

The implication of this 'definite and scientific system' was that codes of social behaviour were not affected by whether or not God existed. W. K. Clifford put this politely:

Duty to one's countrymen and fellow-citizens, which is the social instinct guided by reason [my emphasis], is in all healthy communities the one thing sacred and supreme. If the course of things is guided by some unseen intelligent person [God], then this instinct is his highest and clearest voice, and because of it we may call him good. But if the course of things is not so guided, that voice loses nothing of its sacredness, nothing of its clearness, nothing of its obligation.

Clifford's politeness masked a deep hostility to any notion of man's ethical sense being derived from some innate, and presumably God-implanted, 'conscience'. John Stuart Mill shared his position:

The notion that truths external to the mind may be known by intuition or consciousness, independently of observation and experience, is, I am persuaded, in these times the great intellectual support of false doctrines and bad institutions. By the aid of this theory, every inveterate belief and every intense feeling, of which the origin is not remembered, is enabled to dispense with the object of justifying itself by reason, and is erected into its own all-sufficient voucher and justification.

('Autobiography', 1873, p. 191)

Moreover, by appealing to 'observation and experience' the 'materialist' philosophers were able to marshal on their side the body of research in the sciences which by the 1850s was undermining belief in the literal truth of the Scriptures and in any supernatural intervention in the physical world.

In particular the Darwinian idea that plants and animals do not belong to fixed and unchanging species — but develop by a process whereby the mutant best adapted to its environment survives, and transmits those characteristics that make it the fittest to survive — conflicted with the idea that God created each species as it now is, and set apart one species, the human, by the gift of an immortal soul.

If man evolved from the lower animals through such a process of 'natural selection', then the same physical laws which govern their behaviour govern his. In Huxley's words:

The consciousness of brutes would appear to be related to the mechanism of their body simply as a collateral product of its working, and to be as completely without any power of modifying that working. ... Their volition, if they have any, is an emotion indicative of physical changes, not a cause of such changes ... the argumentation which applies to brutes holds equally good of men ... our mental conditions are simply the symbols in consciousness of the changes which take place automatically in the organism.

The theological, or rather anti-theological implication of this was obvious. If consciousness were an effect produced by changes in the substance of the brain, and were only known in this context, then notions of intelligence or volition — the modes of consciousness — occurring apart from a physically existent brain were untenable.

Arguments for the existence of God, therefore, were not susceptible to scientific proof.

Against this assault defenders of religious authority could adopt an argument which amounted to a defence of religious belief on grounds of social psychology. Henry Longueville Mansel did not advance in his Bampton lectures any logical argument for God's existence, but argued that:

the instinctive confession of all mankind, that the moral nature of man, as subject to a law of obligation, reflects and represents, in some degree, the moral nature of a Deity by whom that obligation is imposed.

or, in the religious context of 1859:

accept the traditional doctrines of the Church, because they have in practice endured and revealed a human need for them and do not attempt to question them by using methods of science.

At this point the argument lapses from the intellectual to the social. Mansel was a last-ditch defender of the prerogatives of the Church in the universities and an active Tory organiser; Clifford, Stephen and Huxley were all political radicals as well as secularists and campaigners for the removal of education from clerical domination. For them the dismantling of the intellectual fabric of religion was part of a general process of destroying or remodelling anomalous social institutions which had depended on irrational factors — prejudice or tradition — for their survival, and of substituting in the mind of the mass public the values of rational investigation and discussion.

Further Reading

Noel Annan, 'Leslie Stephen', 1951.
Asa Briggs, 'The Age of Improvement', chap. 9.5.
J. W. Burrow, 'Evolution and Society', 1966.
G. N. A. Vesey (ed.), 'Body and Mind', 1964, chaps. 11, 14, 15, 16, 17, 20.

See also A 1, G 5, P 9.

The Automatism of Animals

T. H. Huxley (1825–95)

Thomas Henry Huxley began his career as a naval surgeon, a post which enabled him to pursue his inclination towards biological studies. He became Professor of Natural History at the Royal School of Mines in 1854, but his eminence really dates from the 1860s, when he supported energetically Charles Darwin's evolutionary theory, and became a leading consultant to the Government on scientific research and education. He did not fail to draw conclusions from scientific advance which were hostile to accepted religious thought, and we owe to him the term 'agnostic'.

J 1

The first half of the seventeenth century is one of the great epochs of biological science. For though suggestions and indications of the conceptions which took definite shape, at that time, are to be met with in works of earlier date, they are little more than the shadows which coming truth casts forward; men's knowledge was neither extensive enough, nor exact enough, to show them the solid body of fact which threw these shadows.

But, in the seventeenth century, the idea that the physical processes of life are capable of being explained in the same way as other physical phenomena, and, therefore, that the living body is a mechanism, was proved to be true for certain classes of vital actions; and, having thus taken firm root in irrefragable fact, this conception has not only successfully repelled every assault which has been made upon it, but has steadily grown in force and extent of application, until it is now the expressed or implied fundamental proposition of the whole doctrine of scientific Physiology.

If we ask to whom mankind are indebted for this great service, the general voice will name William Harvey. For, by his discovery of the circulation of the blood in the higher animals, by his explanation of the nature of the mechanism by which that circulation is effected, and by his no less remarkable, though less known, investigation of the process of development, Harvey solidly laid the foundations of all those physical explanations of the functions of sustentation and reproduction which modern physiologists have achieved.

But the living body is not only sustained and reproduced: it adjusts itself to external and internal changes; it moves and feels. The attempt to reduce the endless complexities of animal motion and feeling to law and order is, at least, as important a part of the task of the physiologist as the elucidation of what are sometimes called the vegetative processes. Harvey did not make this attempt himself: but the influence of his work upon the man who did make it is patent and unquestionable. This man was René Descartes, who, though by many years Harvey's junior, died before him and yet in his short span of fifty-four years, took an undisputed place, not only among the chiefs of philosophy, but amongst the greatest and most original of mathematicians; while, in my belief, he is no less certainly entitled to the rank of a great and original physiologist; inasmuch as he did for the physiology of motion and sensation that which Harvey had done for the circulation of the blood, and opened up that road to the mechanical theory of these processes, which has been followed by all his successors.

Thus far, the propositions respecting the physiology of the nervous system which are stated by Descartes have simply been more clearly defined, more fully illustrated, and, for the most part, demonstrated, by modern physiological research. But there remains a doctrine to which Descartes attached great weight, so that full acceptance of it became a sort of note of a thoroughgoing Cartesian, but which, nevertheless, is so opposed to ordinary prepossessions that it attained more general notoriety, and gave rise to more discussion, than almost any other Cartesian hypothesis. It is the doctrine that brute animals are mere machines or automata, devoid not only of reason, but of any kind of consciousness, which is stated briefly in the 'Discours de la

Méthode', and more fully in the 'Réponses aux Quartièmes Objections', and in the correspondence with Henry More.

The process of reasoning by which Descartes arrived at this startling conclusion is well shown in the following passage of the 'Réponses': —

But as regards the souls of beasts, although this is not the place for considering them, and though, without a general exposition of physics, I can say no more on this subject than I have already said in the fifth part of my Treatise on Method; yet, I will further state, here, that it appears to me to be a very remarkable circumstance that no movement can take place, either in the bodies of beasts, or even in our own, if these bodies have not in themselves all the organs and instruments by means of which the very same movements would be accomplished in a machine. So that, even in us, the spirit, or the soul, does not directly move the limbs, but only determines the course of that very subtle liquid which is called the animal spirits, which, running continually from the heart by the brain into the muscles, is the cause of all the movements of our limbs, and often may cause many different motions, one as easily as the other.

And it does not even always exert this determination; for among the movements which take place in us, there are many which do not depend on the mind at all, such as the beating of the heart, the digestion of food, the nutrition, the respiration of those who sleep; and even in those who are awake, walking, singing, and other similar actions, when they are performed without the mind thinking about them. And, when one who falls from a height throws his hands forward to save his head, it is in virtue of no ratiocination that he performs this action; it does not depend upon his mind, but takes place merely because his senses being affected by the present danger, some change arises in his brain which determines the animal spirits to pass thence into the nerves, in such a manner as is required to produce this motion, in the same way as in a machine, and without the mind being able to hinder it. Now since we observe this in ourselves, why should we be so much astonished if the light reflected from the body of a wolf into the eye of a sheep has the same force to excite in it the motion of flight?

After having observed this, if we wish to learn by reasoning, whether certain movements of beasts are comparable to those which are effected in us by the operation of the mind, or, on the contrary, to those which depend only on the animal spirits and the disposition of the organs, it is necessary to consider the difference between the two, which I have explained in the fifth part of the 'Discourse on Method' (for I do not think that any others are discoverable), and then it will easily be seen, that all the actions of beasts are similar only to those which we perform without the help of our minds. For which reason we shall be forced to conclude, that we know of the existence in them of no other principle of motion than the disposition of their organs and the continual affluence of animal spirits produced by the heat of the heart, which attenuates and subtilizes the blood; and, at the same time, we shall acknowledge that we have had no reason for assuming any other principle, except that, not having distinguished these two principles of motion, and seeing that the one, which depends only on the animal spirits and the organs, exists in beasts as well as in us, we have hastily concluded that the other, which depends on mind and on thought, was also possessed by them.

Descartes' line of argument is perfectly clear. He starts from reflex action in man, from the unquestionable fact that, in ourselves, co-ordinate, purposive, actions may take place, without the intervention of consciousness or volition, or even contrary to the latter. As actions of a certain degree of complexity are brought about by mere mechanism, why may not actions of still greater complexity be the result of a more refined mechanism? What proof is there that brutes are other than a superior race of marionettes, which eat without pleasure, cry without pain, desire nothing, know nothing, and only simulate intelligence as a bee simulates a mathematician?

Suppose that the anterior division of the brain of a frog — so much of it as lies in front of the 'optic lobes' — is removed. If that operation is performed quickly and skilfully, the frog may be kept in a state of full bodily vigour for months, or it may be for years; but it will sit unmoved. It sees nothing: it hears nothing. It will starve sooner than feed itself, although food put into its mouth is swallowed. On irritation, it jumps or walks; if thrown into the water it swims. If it be put on the hand, it sits there, crouched, perfectly quiet, and would sit there for ever. If the hand be inclined very gently and slowly, so that the frog would naturally tend to slip off, the creature's fore paws are shifted on to the edge of the hand, until he can just prevent himself from falling. If the turning of the hand be slowly continued, he mounts up with great care and deliberation, putting first one leg forward and then another, until be balances himself with perfect precision upon the edge; and if the turning of the hand is continued, he goes through the needful set of muscular operations, until he comes to be seated in security, upon the back of the hand. The doing of all this requires a delicacy of co-ordination, and a precision of adjustment of the muscular apparatus of the body, which are only comparable to those of a rope-dancer. To the ordinary influences of light, the frog, deprived of its cerebral hemispheres, appears to be blind. Nevertheless, if the animal be put upon a table, with a book at some little distance between it and the light, and the skin of the hinder part of its body is then irritated, it will jump forward, avoiding the book by passing to the right or left of it. Therefore, although the frog appears to have no sensation of light, visible objects act through its brain upon the motor mechanisms of its body.*

It is obvious, that had Descartes been acquainted with these remarkable results of modern research, they would have furnished him with far more powerful arguments than he possessed in favour of his view of the automatism of brutes. The habits of a frog, leading its natural life, involve such simple adaptations to surrounding conditions, that the machinery which is competent to do so much without the intervention of consciousness, might well do all. And this argument is vastly strengthened by what has been learned in recent times of the marvellously complex operations which are performed mechanically, and to all appearance without consciousness, by men, when, in consequence of injury or disease, they are reduced to a condition more or less comparable to that of a frog, in which the anterior part of the brain has been removed.

* See the remarkable essay of Göltz, 'Beiträge zur Lehre von den Functionen der Nervencentren des Frosches', published in 1869. I have repeated Göltz's experiments, and obtained the same results.

If such facts as these had come under the knowledge of Descartes, would they not have formed an apt commentary upon that remarkable passage in the 'Traité de l' Homme', which I have quoted elsewhere, but which is worth repetition?: —

All the functions which I have attributed to this machine (the body), as the digestion of food, the pulsation of the heart and of the arteries; the nutrition and the growth of the limbs; respiration, wakefulness, and sleep; the reception of light, sounds, odours, flavours, heat, and such like qualities, in the organs of the external senses; the impression of the ideas of these in the organ of common sensation and in the imagination; the retention or the impression of these ideas on the memory; the internal movements of the appetites and the passions, and lastly the external movements of all the limbs, which follow so aptly, as well the action of the objects which are presented to the senses, as the impressions which meet in the memory, that they imitate as nearly as possible those of a real man; I desire, I say, that you should consider that these functions in the machine naturally proceed from the mere arrangement of its organs, neither more nor less than do the movements of a clock or other automaton, from that of its weights and its wheels; so that, so far as these are concerned, it is not necessary to conceive any other vegetative or sensitive soul, nor any other principle of motion or of life, than the blood and the spirits agitated by the fire which burns continually in the heart, and which is no wise essentially different from all the fires which exist in inanimate bodies.

And would Descartes not have been justified in asking why we need deny that animals are machines, when men, in a state of unconsciousness, perform, mechanically, actions as complicated and as seemingly rational as those of any animals?

But though I do not think that Descartes' hypothesis can be positively refuted, I am not disposed to accept it. The doctrine of continuity is too well established for it to be permissible to me to suppose that any complex natural phenomenon comes into existence suddenly, and without being preceded by simpler modifications; and very strong arguments would be needed to prove that such complex phenomena as those of consciousness, first make their appearance in man. We know, that, in the individual man, consciousness grows from a dim glimmer to its full light, whether we consider the infant advancing in years, or the adult emerging from slumber and swoon. We know, further, that the lower animals possess, though less developed, that part of the brain which we have every reason to believe to be the organ of consciousness in man; and, as in other cases, function and organ are proportional, so we have a right to conclude it is with the brain; and that the brutes, though they may not possess our intensity of consciousness, and though, from the absence of language, they can have no trains of thoughts, but only trains of feelings, yet have a consciousness which, more or less distinctly, foreshadows our own.

I confess that, in view of the struggle for existence which goes on in the animal world, and of the frightful quantity of pain with which it must be accompanied, I should be glad if the probabilities were in favour of Descartes' hypothesis; but, on the other hand, considering the terrible practical consequences to domestic animals which might ensue from any error on our part, it is as well to err on the right side, if we err at all, and deal with them as weaker brethren, who are bound, like the rest of us, to pay their toll for living, and suffer what is needful for the general good. As Hartley finely says, 'We seem to be in the place of God to them'; and we may justly follow the precedents He sets in nature in our dealings with them.

But though we may see reason to disagree with Descartes' hypothesis that brutes are unconscious machines, it does not follow that he was wrong in regarding them as automata. They may be more or less conscious, sensitive, automata; and the view that they are such conscious machines is that which is implicitly, or explicitly, adopted by most persons. When we speak of the actions of the lower animals being guided by instinct and not by reason, what we really mean is that, though they feel as we do, yet their actions are the results of their physical organization. We believe, in short, that they are machines, one part of which (the nervous system) not only sets the rest in motion, and co-ordinates its movements in relation with changes in surrounding bodies, but is provided with special apparatus, the function of which is the calling into existence of those states of consciousness which are termed sensations, emotions and ideas. I believe that this generally accepted view is the best expression of the facts at present known.

It is experimentally demonstrable — any one who cares to run a pin into himself may perform a sufficient demonstration of the fact — that a mode of motion of the nervous system is the immediate antecedent of a state of consciousness. All but the adherents of 'Occasionalism', or of the doctrine of 'Pre-established Harmony' (if any such now exist), must admit that we have as much reason for regarding the mode of motion of the nervous system as the cause of the state of consciousness, as we have for regarding any event as the cause of another. How the one phenomenon causes the other we know, as much or as little, as in any other case of causation; but we have as much right to believe that the sensation is an effect of the molecular change, as we have to believe that motion is an effect of impact; and there is as much propriety in saying that the brain evolves sensation, as there is in saying that an iron rod, when hammered, evolves heat.

As I have endeavoured to show, we are justified in supposing that something analogous to what happens in ourselves takes place in the brutes, and that the affections of their sensory nerves give rise to molecular changes in the brain, which again give rise to, or evolve, the corresponding states of consciousness. Nor can there be any reasonable doubt that the emotions of brutes, and such ideas as they possess, are similarly dependent upon molecular brain changes. Each sensory impression leaves behind a record in the structure of the brain — an 'ideagenous' molecule, so to speak, which is competent, under certain conditions, to reproduce, in a fainter condition, the state of consciousness which corresponds with that sensory impression; and it is these 'ideagenous molecules' which are the physical basis of memory.

It may be assumed, then, that molecular changes in the brain are the causes of all the states of consciousness of brutes. Is there any evidence that these states of consciousness may, conversely, cause those molecular changes which give rise to muscular motion? I see no such evidence. The frog walks, hops, swims, and goes through his gymnastic performances quite as well without consciousness, and consequently without volition, as with it; and, if a frog, in his natural state, possesses anything corresponding with what we call volition, there is no reason to think that it is anything but a concomitant of the molecular changes in the brain which form part of the series involved in the production of motion.

The consciousness of brutes would appear to be related to the mechanism of their body simply as a collateral product of its working, and to be as completely without any power of modifying that working as the steam-whistle which accompanies the working of a locomotive engine is without influence upon its machinery. Their volition, if they have any, is an emotion indicative of physical changes, not a cause of such changes.

This conception of the relations of states of consciousness with molecular changes in the brain — of *psychoses* with *neuroses* — does not prevent us from ascribing free will to brutes. For an agent is free when there is nothing to prevent him from doing that which he desires to do. If a greyhound chases a hare, he is a free agent, because his action is in entire accordance with his strong desire to catch the hare; while so long as he is held back by the leash he is not free, being prevented by external force from following his inclination. And the ascription of freedom to the greyhound under the former circumstances is by no means inconsistent with the other aspect of the facts of the case — that he is a machine impelled to the chase, and caused, at the same time, to have the desire to catch the game by the impression which the rays of light proceeding from the hare make upon his eyes, and through them upon his brain.

Much ingenious argument has at various times been bestowed upon the question: How is it possible to imagine that volition, which is a state of consciousness, and, as such, has not the slightest community of nature with matter in motion, can act upon the moving matter of which the body is composed, as it is assumed to do in voluntary acts? But if, as is here suggested, the voluntary acts of brutes — or, in other words, the acts which they desire to perform — are as purely mechanical as the rest of their actions, and are simply accompanied by the state of consciousness called volition, the inquiry, so far as they are concerned, becomes superfluous. Their volitions do not enter into the chain of causation of their actions at all.

The hypothesis that brutes are conscious automata is perfectly consistent with any view that may be held respecting the often discussed and curious question whether they have souls or not; and, if they have souls, whether those souls are immortal or not. It is obviously harmonious with the most literal adherence to the text of Scripture concerning 'the beast that perisheth'; but it is not inconsistent with the amiable conviction ascribed by Pope to his 'untutored savage', that when he passes to the happy hunting-grounds in the sky, 'his faithful dog shall bear him company'. If the brutes have consciousness and no souls, then it is clear that, in them, consciousness is a direct function of material changes; while, if they possess immaterial subjects of consciousness, or souls, then, as consciousness is brought into existence only as the consequence of molecular motion of the brain, it follows that it is an indirect product of material changes. The soul stands related to the body as the bell of a clock to the works, and consciousness answers to the sound which the bell gives out when it is struck.

Thus far I have strictly confined myself to the problem with which I proposed to deal at starting — the automatism of brutes. The question is, I believe, a perfectly open one, and I feel happy in running no risk of either Papal or Presbyterian condemnation for the views which I have ventured to put forward. And there are so very few interesting questions which one is, at present, allowed to think out scientifically — to go as far as reason leads, and stop where evidence comes to an end — without speedily being deafened by the tattoo of 'the drum ecclesiastic' — that I have luxuriated in my rare freedom, and would now willingly bring this disquisition to an end if I could hope that other people would go no farther. Unfortunately, past experience debars me from entertaining any such hope, even if

> . . . *that drum's discordant sound*
> *Parading round and round and round,*

were not, at present, as audible to me as it was to the mild poet who ventured to express his hatred of drums in general, in that well-known couplet.

It will be said, that I mean that the conclusions deduced from the study of the brutes are applicable to man, and that the logical consequences of such application are fatalism, materialism, and atheism — whereupon the drums will beat the *pas de charge*.

One does not do battle with drummers; but I venture to offer a few remarks for the calm consideration of thoughtful persons, untrammelled by foregone conclusions, unpledged to shore-up tottering dogmas, and anxious only to know the true bearings of the case.

It is quite true that, to the best of my judgment, the argumentation which applies to brutes holds equally good of men; and, therefore, that all states of consciousness in us, as in them, are immediately caused by molecular changes of the brain substance. It seems to me that in men, as in brutes, there is no proof that any state of consciousness is the cause of change in the motion of the matter of the organism. If these positions are well based, it follows that our mental conditions are simply the symbols in consciousness of the changes which take place automatically in the organism; and that, to take an extreme illustration, the feeling we call volition is not the cause of a voluntary act, but the symbol of that state of the brain which is the immediate cause of that act. We are conscious automata, endowed with free will in the only intelligible sense of that much-abused term — inasmuch as in many respects we are able to do as we like — but none the less parts of the great series of causes and effects which, in unbroken continuity, composes that which is, and has been, and shall be — the sum of existence.

As to the logical consequences of this conviction of mine, I may be permitted to remark that logical consequences are the scarecrows of fools and the beacons of wise men. The only question which any wise man can ask himself, and which any honest man will ask himself, is whether a doctrine is true or false. Consequences will take care of themselves; at most their importance can only justify us in testing with extra care the reasoning process from which they result.

So that if the view I have taken did really and logically lead to fatalism, materialism, and atheism, I should profess myself a fatalist, materialist, and atheist; and I should look upon those who, while they believed in my honesty of purpose and intellectual competency, should raise a hue and cry against me, as people who by their own admission preferred lying to truth, and whose opinions therefore were unworthy of the smallest attention.

But, as I have endeavoured to explain on other occasions, I really have no claim to rank myself among fatalistic, materialistic, or atheistic philosophers. Not among fatalists, for I take the conception of necessity to have a logical, and not a physical foundation; not among materialists, for I am utterly incapable of conceiving the existence of matter if there is no mind in which to picture that existence; not among atheists, for the problem of the ultimate cause of existence is one which seems to me to be hopelessly out of reach of my poor powers. Of all the senseless babble I have ever had occasion to read, the demonstrations of these philosophers who undertake to tell us all about the nature of God would be the worst, if they were not surpassed by the still greater absurdities of the philosophers who try to prove that there is no God.

From T. H. Huxley, 'On the Hypothesis that Animals
are Automata, and its History', lecture delivered
to British Association, Belfast, 1874.

Body and Mind

W. K. Clifford (1845–79)

William Kingdon Clifford became Professor of Applied Mathematics at University College London, at the age of twenty-six, after a brilliant Cambridge career.

J 2

The subject of this Lecture is one in regard to which a great change has recently taken place in the public mind. Some time ago it was the custom to look with suspicion upon all questions of a metaphysical nature as being questions that could not be discussed with any good result, and which, leading inquirers round and round in the same circle, never came to an end. But quite of late years there is an indication that a large number of people are waking up to the fact that Science has something to say upon these subjects; and the English people have always been very ready to hear what Science can say — understanding by Science what we shall now understand by it, that is, organised common sense.

...there is evidence which is sufficient to satisfy any competent scientific man of this day — that every fact of consciousness is parallel to some disturbance of nerve matter, although there are some nervous disturbances which have no parallel in consciousness, properly so called ; that is to say, disturbances of my nerves may exist which have no parallel in my consciousness.

We have now observed two classes of facts and the parallelism between them. Let us next observe what an enormous gulf there is between these two classes of facts.

The state of a man's brain and the actions which go along with it are things which every other man can perceive, observe, measure, and tabulate; but the state of a man's own consciousness is known to him only, and not to any other person. Things which appear to us and which we can observe are called *objects* or *phenomena*. Facts in a man's consciousness are not objects or phenomena to any other man; they are capable of being observed only by him. We have no possible ground, therefore, for speaking of another man's consciousness as in any sense a part of the physical world of objects or phenomena. It is a thing entirely separate from it; and all the evidence that we have goes to show that the physical world gets along entirely by itself, according to practically universal rules. That is to say, the laws which hold good in the physical world hold good everywhere in it — they hold good with practical universality, and there is no reason to suppose anything else but those laws in order to account for any physical fact; there is no reason to suppose anything but the universal laws of mechanics in order to account for the motion of organic bodies. The train of physical facts between the stimulus sent into the eye, or to any one of our senses, and the exertion which follows it, and the train of physical facts which goes on in the brain, even when there is no stimulus and no exertion, — these are perfectly complete physical trains, and every step is fully accounted for by mechanical conditions. In order to show what is meant by that, I will endeavour to explain another supposition which might be made. When a stimulus comes into the eye there is a certain amount of energy transferred from the ether, which fills space, to this nerve; and this energy travels along into the ganglion, and sets the ganglion into a state of disturbance which may use up some energy previously stored in it. The amount of energy is the same as before by the law of the conservation of energy. That energy is spread over a number of threads which go out to the brain, and it comes back again and is reflected from there. It may be supposed that a very small portion of energy is created in that process, and that while the stimulus is going round this loop-line it gets a little push somewhere, and then, when it comes back to the ganglia, it goes away to the muscle and sets loose a store of energy in the muscle so that it moves the limb. Now the question is, Is there any creation of energy anywhere? Is there any part of the physical progress which cannot be included within ordinary physical laws? It has been supposed, I say, by some people, as it seems to me merely by a confusion of ideas, that there is, at some part or other of this process, a creation of energy; but there is no reason whatever why we should suppose this. The difficulty in proving a negative in these cases is similar to that in proving a negative about anything which exists on the other side of the moon. It is quite true that I am not absolutely certain that the law of the conservation of energy is exactly true; but there is no more reason why I should suppose a particular exception to occur in the brain than anywhere else. . . .

Therefore it is not a right thing to say, for example, that the mind is a force, because if the mind were a force we should be able to perceive it. I should be able to perceive your mind and to measure it, but I cannot; I have absolutely no means of perceiving your mind. I judge by analogy that it exists, and the instinct which leads me to come to that conclusion is the social instinct, as it has been formed in me by generations during which men have lived together; and they could not have lived together unless they had gone upon that supposition. But I may very well say that among the physical facts which go along at the same time with mental facts there are forces at work. That is perfectly true, but the two things are on two utterly different platforms — the physical facts go along by themselves, and the mental facts go along by themselves. There is a parallelism between them, but there is no inter-ference of one with the other. Again, if anybody says that the will influences matter, the statement is not untrue, but it is nonsense. The will is not a material thing, it is not a mode of material motion. Such an assertion belongs to the crude materialism of the savage. The only thing which influences matter is the position of surrounding matter or the motion of surrounding matter. It may be conceived that at the same time with every exercise of volition there is a disturbance of the physical laws; but this disturbance, being perceptible to me, would be a physical fact accompanying the volition, and could not be the volition itself, which is not perceptible to me. Whether there is such a disturbance of the physical laws or no is a question of fact to which we have the best of reasons for giving a negative answer; but the assertion that another man's volition, a feeling in his consciousness which I cannot perceive, is part of the train of physical facts which I may perceive, — this is neither true nor untrue, but nonsense; it is a combination of words whose corresponding ideas will not go together.

Thus we are to regard the body as a physical machine, which goes by itself according to a physical law, that is to say, is automatic. An automaton is a thing which goes by itself when it is wound up, and we go by ourselves when we have had food. Excepting the fact that other men are conscious, there is no reason why we should not regard the human body as merely an exceedingly complicated machine which is wound up by putting food into the mouth. But it is not *merely* a machine, because consciousness goes with it. The mind, then, is to be regarded as a stream of feelings which runs parallel to, and simultaneous with, a certain part of the action of the body, that is to say, that particular part of the action of the brain in which the cerebrum and the sensory tract are excited.

Then, you say, if we are automata what becomes of the freedom of the will? The freedom of the will, according to Kant, is that property which enables us to originate events independently of foreign determining causes; which, it seems to me, amounts to saying precisely that we are automata, that is, that we go by ourselves, and do not want anybody to push or pull us. . . .

If, on the contrary, we suppose that in the action of the brain there is some point where physical causes do not apply, and where there is a discontinuity, then it will follow that some of our actions are not dependent upon our character. Provided the action which goes on in my brain is a continuous one, subject to physical rules, then it will depend upon what the character of my brain is; or if I look at it from the mental side, it will depend upon what my mental character is; but if there is a certain point where the law of causation does not apply, where my action does not follow by regular physical causes from what I am, then I am not responsible for it, because it is not I that do it. So you see the notion that we are not automata destroys responsibility; because, if my actions are not determined by my character in accordance with the particular circumstances which occur, then I am not responsible for them, and it is not I that do them. . . .

I want now, very briefly indeed, to consider to what extent these doctrines furnish a bridge between the two classes of facts. I have said that the series of mental facts corresponds to only a portion of the action of the organism. But we have to consider not only ourselves, but also those animals which are next below us in the scale of organisation, and we cannot help ascribing to them a consciousness which is analogous to our own. We find, when we attempt to enter into that, and to judge by their actions what sort of consciousness they possess, that it differs from our own in precisely the same way that their brains differ from our brains. There is less of the co-ordination which is implied by a message going round the loop-line. A much larger number of the messages which go in at a cat's eyes and out at her paws go straight through without any loop-line at all than do so in the case of a man; but still there is a little loop-line left. And the lower we go down in the scale of organisation the less of this loop-line there is; yet we cannot suppose that so enormous a jump from one creature to another should have occurred at any point in the process of evolution as the introduction of a fact entirely different and absolutely separate from the physical fact. It is impossible for anybody to point out the particular place in the line of descent where that event can be supposed to have taken place. The only thing that we can come to, if we accept the doctrine of evolution at all, is that even in the very lowest organisms, even in the Amoeba which swims about in our own blood, there is something or other, inconceivably simple to us, which is of the same nature with our own consciousness, although not of the same complexity — that is to say (for we cannot stop at organic matter, knowing as we do that it must have arisen by continuous physical processes out of inorganic matter), we are obliged to assume, in order to save continuity in our belief, that along with every motion of matter, whether organic or inorganic, there is some fact which corresponds to the mental fact in ourselves. The mental fact in ourselves is an exceedingly complex thing; so also our brain is an exceedingly complex thing. We may assume that the quasi-mental fact which corresponds and which goes along with the motion of every particle of matter is of such inconceivable simplicity, as compared with our own mental fact, with our consciousness, as the motion of a molecule of matter is of inconceivable simplicity when compared with the motion in our brain. . . .

With the exception of just this last bridge connecting the two great regions of inquiry that we have been discussing, the whole of what I have said is a body of doctrine which is accepted now, as far as I know, by all competent people who have considered the subject. There are, of course, individual exceptions with regard to particular points, such as that I have mentioned about the possible creation of energy in the brain; but these are few, and they occur mainly, I think, among those who are so exceedingly well acquainted with one side of the subject that they regard the whole of it from the point of view of that side, and do not sufficiently weigh what may come from the other side. With such exceptions as those, and with the exception of the last speculation of all, the doctrine which I have expounded to you is the doctrine of Science at the present day.

These results may now be applied to the consideration of certain questions which have always been of great interest. The application which I shall make is a purely tentative one, and must be regarded as merely indicating that such an application becomes more possible every day. The first of these questions is that of the possible existence of consciousness apart from a nervous system, of mind without body. Let us first of all consider the effect upon this question of the doctrines which are admitted by all competent scientific men. All the consciousness that we know of is associated with a brain in a certain definite manner, namely, it is built up out of elements in the same way as part of the action of the brain is built up out of elements; an element of one corresponds to an element in the other; and the mode of connection, the shape of the building, is the same in the two cases. The mere fact that all the consciousness we know of is associated with certain complex forms of matter need only make us exceedingly cautious not to imagine any consciousness apart from matter without very good reason indeed; just as the fact of all swans having turned out white up to a certain time made us quite rightly careful about accepting stories that involved black swans. But the fact that mind and brain are associated in a definite way, and in that particular way that I have mentioned, affords a very strong presumption that we have here something which can be *explained*; that it is possible to find a reason for this exact correspondence. If such a reason can be found, the case is entirely altered; instead of a provisional probability which may rightly make us cautious we should have the highest assurance that Science can give, a practical certainty on which we are bound to act, that there is no mind without a brain. Whatever, therefore, is the probability that an explanation exists of the connection of mind with brain in action, such is also the probability that each of them involves the other.

If, however, that particular explanation which I have ventured to offer should turn out to be the true one, the case becomes even stronger. If mind is the reality or substance of that which appears to us as brain-action, the supposition of mind without brain is the supposition of an organised material substance not affecting other substances (for if it did it might be perceived), and therefore not affected by them; in other words, it is the supposition of immaterial matter, a contradiction in terms to the fundamental assumption of the uniformity of nature, without practically believing in which we should none of us have been here to-day. . . .

The other question which may be asked is this: Can we regard the universe, or that part of it which immediately surrounds us, as a vast brain, and therefore the reality which underlies it as a conscious mind? This question has been considered by the great naturalist Du Bois Reymond, and has received from him that negative answer which I think we also must give. For we found that the particular organisation of the brain which enables its action to run parallel with consciousness amounts to this — that disturbances run along definite channels, and that two disturbances which occur together establish links between the channels along which they run, so that they naturally occur together again. It will, I think, be clear to every one that these are not characteristics of the great interplanetary spaces. Is it not possible, however, that the stars we can see are just atoms in some vast organism, bearing some such relation to it as the atoms which make up our brains bear to us? I am sure I do not know. But it seems clear that the knowledge of such an organism could not extend to events taking place on the earth, and that its volition could not be concerned in them. And if some vast brain existed far away in space, being invisible because not self-luminous, then, according to the laws of matter at present known to us, it could affect the Solar system only by its weight.

On the whole, therefore, we seem entitled to conclude that during such time as we can have evidence of, no intelligence or volition has been concerned in events happening within the range of the Solar system, except that of animals living on the planets. The weight of such probabilities is, of course, estimated differently by different people, and the questions are only just beginning to receive the right sort of attention. But it does seem to me that we may expect in time to have negative evidence on this point of the same kind and of the same cogency as that which forbids us to assume the existence between the Earth and Venus of a planet as large as either of them.

Now, about these conclusions which I have described as probable ones, there are two things that may be said. In the first place, it may be said that they make the world a blank, because they take away the objects of very important and widespread emotions of hope and reverence and love, which are human faculties and require to be exercised, and that they destroy the motives for good conduct. To this it may be answered that we have no right to call the world a blank while it is full of men and women, even though our one friend may be lost to us. And in the regular everyday facts of this common life of men, and in the promise which it holds out for the future, there is room enough and to spare for all the high and noble emotions of which our nature is capable. Moreover, healthy emotions are felt about facts and not about phantoms; and the question is not 'What conclusion will be most pleasing or elevating to my feelings?' but 'What is the truth?' For it is not all human faculties that have to be exercised, but only the good ones. It is not right to exercise the faculty of feeling terror or of resisting evidence. And if there are any faculties which prevent us from accepting the truth and guiding our conduct by it, these faculties ought not to be exercised. As for the assertion that these conclusions destroy the motive for good conduct, it seems to me that it is not only utterly untrue, but, because of its great influence upon human action, one of the most dangerous doctrines that can be set forth. The two questions which we have last discussed are exceedingly difficult and complex questions; the ideas and the knowledge which we used in their discussion are the product of long centuries of laborious investigation and thought; and perhaps, although we all make our little guesses, there is not one man in a million who has any right to a definite opinion about them. But it is not necessary to answer these questions in order to tell an honest man from a rogue. The distinction of right and wrong grows up in the broad light of day out of natural causes wherever men live together; and the only right motive to right action is to be found in the social instincts which have been bred into mankind by hundreds of generations of social life. In the target of every true Englishman's allegiance the bull's-eye belongs to his countrymen, who are visible and palpable and who stand around him; not to any far-off shadowy centre beyond the hills, *ultra montes*, either at Rome or in heaven. Duty to one's countrymen and fellow-citizens, which is the social instinct guided by reason, is in all healthy communities the one thing sacred and supreme. If the course of things is guided by some unseen intelligent person, then this instinct is his highest and clearest voice, and because of it we may call him good. But if the course of things is not so guided, that voice loses nothing of its sacredness, nothing of its clearness, nothing of its obligation.

In the second place it may be said that Science ought not to deal with these questions at all; that while scientific men are concerned with physical facts, they are *dans leur droit*, but that in treating of such subjects as these they are going out of their domain, and must do harm.

What is the domain of Science? It is all possible human knowledge which can rightly be used to guide human conduct.

In many parts of Europe it is customary to leave a part of the field untilled for the Brownie to live in, because he cannot live in cultivated ground. And if you grant him this grace, he will do a great deal of your household work for you in the night while you sleep. In Scotland the piece of ground which is left wild for him to live in is called 'the good man's croft.' Now there are people who indulge a hope that the plough-share of Science will leave a sort of good man's croft around the field of reasoned truth; and they promise that in that case a good deal of our civilising work shall be done for us in the dark, by means we know nothing of. I do not share this hope; and I feel very sure that it will not be realised: I think that we should do our work with our own hands in a healthy straightforward way. It is idle to set bounds to the purifying and organising work of Science. Without mercy and without resentment she ploughs up weed and briar; from her footsteps behind her grow up corn and healing flowers; and no corner is far enough to escape her furrow. Provided only that we take as our motto and our rule of action, Man speed the plough.

From W. K. Clifford, 'Body and Mind', delivered to the Sunday Lecture Society, 1 November 1874; printed in 'Fortnightly Review', December 1874.

Limits of Religious Thought

H. L. Mansel (1820–71)

Henry Longueville Mansel was fellow of St John's College, Oxford, and later Dean of St Paul's. He was notable in his time as a philosopher and theologian, and in Oxford as an astute political organiser and deft satirist.

J 3

Religious thought, if it is to exist at all, can only exist as representative of some fact of religious intuition, — of some individual state of mind, in which is presented, as an immediate fact, that relation of man to God, of which man, by reflection, may become distinctly and definitely conscious.

Two such states may be specified, as dividing between them the rude materials out of which Reflection builds up the edifice of Religious Consciousness. These are the *Feeling of Dependence* and the *Conviction of Moral Obligation*. To these two facts of the inner consciousness may be traced, as to their sources, the two great outward acts by which religion in various forms has been manifested among men; — *Prayer*, by which they seek to win God's blessing upon the future, and *Expiation*, by which they strive to atone for the offences of the past. The Feeling of Dependence is the instinct which urges us to pray. It is the feeling that our existence and welfare are in the hands of a superior Power; — not of an inexorable Fate or immutable Law; but of a Being having at least so far the attributes of Personality, that He can shew favour or severity to those dependent upon Him, and can be regarded by them with the feelings of hope, and fear, and reverence, and gratitude. It is a feeling similar in kind, though higher in degree, to that which is awakened in the mind of the child towards his parent, who is first manifested to his mind as the giver of such things as are needful, and to whom the first language he addresses is that of entreaty. It is the feeling so fully and intensely expressed in the language of the Psalmist: 'Thou art he that took me out of my mother's womb: thou wast my hope, when I hanged yet upon my mother's breasts. I have been left unto thee ever since I was born: thou art my God even from my mother's womb. Be not thou far from me, O Lord: thou art my succour, haste thee to help me. I will declare thy Name unto my brethren: in the midst of the congregation will I praise thee (Psalm xxii. 9, 10, 19, 22).' With the first development of consciousness, there grows up, as a part of it, the innate feeling that our life, natural and spiritual, is not in our power to sustain or to prolong; — that there is One above us, on whom we are dependent, whose existence we learn, and whose presence we realize, by the sure instinct of Prayer. We have thus, in the Sense of Dependence, the foundation of one great element of Religion, — the Fear of God.

But the mere consciousness of dependence does not of itself exhibit the character of the Being on whom we depend. It is as consistent with superstition as with religion; — with the belief in a malevolent, as in a benevolent Deity: it is as much called into existence by the severities, as by the mercies of God; by the suffering which we are unable to avert, as by the benefits which we did not ourselves procure. The Being on whom we depend is, in that single relation, manifested in the infliction of pain, as well as in the bestowal of happiness. But in order to make suffering, as well as enjoyment, contribute to the religious education of man, it is necessary that he should be conscious, not merely of *suffering*, but of *sin*; — that he should look upon pain not merely as *inflicted*, as *deserved*; and should recognise in its Author the justice that punishes, not merely the anger that harms. In the feeling of dependence, we are conscious of the Power of God, but not necessarily of His Goodness. This deficiency, however, is supplied by the other element of religion, — the Consciousness of Moral Obligation, — carrying with it, as it necessarily does, the Conviction of Sin. It is impossible to establish, as a great modern philosopher has attempted to do, the theory of an absolute Autonomy of the Will; that is to say, of an obligatory law,

H

resting on no basis but that of its own imperative character. Considered solely in itself, with no relation to any higher authority, the consciousness of a law of obligation is a fact of our mental constitution, and it is no more. The fiction of an absolute law, binding on all rational beings, has only an apparent universality; because we can only conceive other rational beings by identifying their constitution with our own, and making human reason the measure and representative of reason in general. Why then has one part of our constitution, merely as such, an imperative authority over the remainder? What right has one portion of the human consciousness to represent itself as *duty*, and another merely as *inclination?* There is but one answer possible. The Moral Reason, or Will, or Conscience, of Man, call it by what name we please, can have no authority, save as implanted in him by some higher Spiritual Being, as a *Law* emanating from a *Lawgiver*. Man can be a law unto himself, only on the supposition that he reflects in himself the Law of God; – that he shews, as the Apostle tells us, the works of that law written in his heart (Romans ii. 15). If he is absolutely a law unto himself, his duty and his pleasure are undistinguishable from each other; for he is subject to no one, and accountable to no one. Duty, in this case, becomes only a higher kind of pleasure, – a balance between the present and the future, between the larger and the smaller gratification. We are thus compelled, by the consciousness of moral obligation, to assume the existence of a moral Deity, and to regard the absolute standard of right and wrong as constituted by the nature of that Deity. The conception of this standard, in the human mind, may indeed be faint and fluctuating, and must be imperfect: it may vary with the intellectual and moral culture of the nation or the individual: and in its highest human representation, it must fall far short of the reality. But it is present to all mankind, as a basis of moral obligation and an inducement to moral progress: it is present in the universal consciousness of sin; in the conviction that we are offenders against God; in the expiatory rites by which, whether inspired by some natural instinct, or inherited from some primeval tradition, divers nations have, in their various modes, striven to atone for their transgressions, and to satisfy the wrath of their righteous Judge. However erroneously the particular acts of religious service may have been understood by men; yet, in the

universal consciousness of innocence and guilt, of duty and dis-
obedience, of an appeased and offended God, there is exhibited the
instinctive confession of all mankind, that the moral nature of man, as
subject to a law of obligation, reflects and represents, in some degree,
the moral nature of a Deity by whom that obligation is imposed.

From H. L. Mansel, 'Limits of Religious Thought:
The Bampton Lectures of 1858', pp. 108-13.

Religion as a Fine Art
Leslie Stephen (1832–1904)

Sir Leslie Stephen, critic, biographer and editor, became an Anglican clergyman after graduating from Cambridge. Subsequently he lost his faith and became a leading advocate of free thought. He was first editor of the 'Dictionary of National Biography' and the father of the novelist Virginia Woolf.

J 4

If the Bible states that something is a fact which is not a fact, it makes no difference to call it a 'scientific fact.' It can hardly be seriously urged, that an inspired book is at liberty to make erroneous statements on all matters which may become the subjects of accurate investigation — the only sense which can be made of the words. A reconciliation is required, founded on some deeper principle. The sacred images must be once and for all carried fairly beyond the reach of the spreading conflagration, not moved back step by step, suffering fresh shocks at every fresh operation. The radical remedy would be to convey them at once into the unassailable ground of the imagination. Admit that the Bible has nothing to do with facts of any kind, that theology and science have no common basis, because one deals with poetry and the other with prose; the sceptic's standing ground will be cut away from beneath his feet. . . .

The division between faith and reason is a half-measure, till it is frankly admitted that faith has to do with fiction, and reason with fact. Then the two spheres of thought may be divided by so profound a gulf that each of the rival methods may be allowed its full scope without interfering with the other. There will be, for example, an ecclesiastical and a secular solar system; the earth may in one system revolve round the sun, and in the other the sun may revolve round the earth, without the smallest possibility of a collision. The only meaning of accepting a doctrine on authority to the exclusion of reason, when the words are fearlessly examined, is accepting it whether it is true or not. The Virgin Mother is a lovely symbol in the region of the true poetry; but once admit that historical criticism is to be permitted to enquire into the truth of the legends about her life or into the competency of the authority on which they are to be accepted, and no one can answer for the results. Sooner or later that 'inexorable logic,' of which we sometimes hear, must either commit suicide by admitting the extreme sceptical conclusion that all reason is fallacious, or must regard religious truth as merely a variety of what is known as artistic truth. Doctrines must be subjected to the test of their imaginative harmony, instead of the scrutiny of the verifying faculty. . . .

And yet, attractive as the vision may be, there is still a difficulty or two in the way of its realisation. The old Puritan leaven is working yet in various forms, in spite of the ridicule of artistic minds and the contempt of philosophers. A religion to be of any value must retain a grasp upon the great mass of mankind, and the mass are hopelessly vulgar and prosaic. The ordinary Briton persists in thinking that the words 'I believe' are to be interpreted in the same sense in a creed or a scientific statement. His appetite wants something more than 'theosophic moonshine.' He expects that messages from that undiscovered country, whence no traveller returns, should be as authentic as those which Columbus brought from America. He wants to draw aside the mystery by which our little lives are bounded, and to know whether there is, in fact, a beyond and a hereafter. He fancies that it is a matter of practical importance to know whether there is a heaven where he will be eternally rewarded, or a hell where he will be eternally tortured. He does not see that it really makes no difference whether those places have an objective existence or are merely the projections upon the external world of certain inward emotions. He is so inquisitive that he insists upon knowing whether the word God is to be applied to a being who will interfere, more or less, with his life, or is merely a philosophical circumlocution for the unvarying order of nature. One fiction may do as well as another in poetry, and may be taken up or laid down as the artist pleases; but he supposes that his readiness to pick pockets or cut throats will, more or less, depend upon whether he believes that God or humanity is the centre of the universe; that priests are licensed manufacturers of myths, or ambassadors revealing supernatural secrets; that the approval of men or the prospect of future reward is to be the mainspring of his conduct here. He imagines, in short, that, though certain commonplaces are common to all systems of morality, his character and the general tendency of his actions will be profoundly influenced by the view of his position on earth placed before him by his instructors. . . .

And yet, even when our prosaic friends are thoroughly suppressed, and made properly ashamed of themselves, we are not quite at the end of the question. Let us give up the question of fact, and admit that the demand for truth in a creed is utterly unreasonable, so far as its influence upon our lives is concerned. Still there remains an aesthetic perplexity. Can even an art — if religion is to be definitely an art — be noble and genuine when entirely divorced from reality? That desired separation between the two lobes of the brain is not so easily managed as might be wished. A sort of chemical reaction is set up in spite of all walls of division. You cannot combine the mythology which is the spontaneous growth of one stage of intellectual development, with the scientific knowledge characteristic of another. Even the poetical imagination requires some stronger sustenance than can be derived from mere arbitrary fancies or the relics of exploded traditions. . . .

A God who is not allowed even to make a fly or launch a thunderbolt will be worshipped in strains widely different from those which celebrated the Ruler who clothed the horse's neck with thunder, and whose voice shook the wilderness. The prevalent conceptions of the day will somehow permeate its poetry — if it has any — in spite of all that can be done to keep them out.

From Leslie Stephen, 'Religion as a Fine Art',
in 'Essays in Free Thinking and Plain Speaking', 1873.

Part Three

Part Three

Section K

The Great Exhibition

George Cruikshank, 'The Queen Opening the Great Exhibition at the Crystal Palace, 1851'.

Prince Albert's Opening Speech

Report of the Proceedings of the Royal Commission Read by His Royal Highness Prince Albert on the Occasion of the Opening of the Great Exhibition, 1 May 1851, and Her Majesty's Reply. Published in the Official Catalogue of the Great Exhibition, 1851.

K 2

May it please Your Majesty,

We, the Commissioners appointed by Your Majesty's Royal Warrant of the 3rd of January, 1850, for the Promotion of the Exhibition of the Works of Industry of all Nations, and subsequently incorporated by Your Majesty's Royal Charter of the 15th of August in the same year, humbly beg leave, on the occasion of Your Majesty's auspicious visit at the opening of the Exhibition, to lay before you a brief statement of our proceedings to the present time.

By virtue of the authority graciously committed to us by Your Majesty, we have made diligent inquiry into the matters which Your Majesty was pleased to refer to us, namely, into the best mode of introducing the productions of Your Majesty's Colonies and of Foreign Countries into this Kingdom, the selection of the most suitable site for the Exhibition, the general conduct of the undertaking, and the proper method of determining the nature of the Prizes, and of securing the most impartial distribution of them.

In the prosecution of these inquiries, and in the discharge of the duties assigned to us by Your Majesty's Royal Charter of Incorporation, we have held constant meetings of our whole body, and have, moreover, referred numerous questions connected with a great variety of subjects to Committees, composed partly of our own members and partly of individuals distinguished in the several departments of science and the arts, who have cordially responded to our applications for their assistance at a great sacrifice of their valuable time.

Among the earliest questions brought before us was the important one as to the terms upon which articles offered for exhibition should be admitted into the Building. We considered that it was a main characteristic of the national undertaking in which we were engaged that it should depend wholly upon the voluntary contributions of this country for its success; and we therefore decided, without hesitation, that no charge whatever should be made on the admission of such goods. We considered, also, that the office of selecting the articles to be sent should be intrusted in the first instance to Local Committees, to be established in every foreign country, and in various districts of Your Majesty's dominions, a general power of control being reserved to the Commission.

We have now the gratification of stating that our anticipations of support in this course have in all respects been fully realized. Your Majesty's most gracious donation to the funds of the Exhibition was the signal for voluntary contributions from all, even the humblest classes of your subjects, and the funds which have thus been placed at our disposal amount at present to about £65,000. Local Committees, from which we have uniformly received the most zealous co-operation, were formed in all parts of the United Kingdom, in many of Your Majesty's colonies, and in the territories of the Hon. East India Company. The most energetic reports have also been received from the Governments of nearly all the countries of the world, in most of which Commissions have been appointed for the special purpose of promoting the objects of an Exhibition justly characterised in Your Majesty's Royal Warrant as an Exhibition of the Works of Industry of all Nations.

We have also to acknowledge the great readiness with which persons of all classes have come forward as Exhibitors. And here again it becomes our duty to return our humble thanks to Your Majesty for the most gracious manner in which Your Majesty has condescended to associate yourself with your subjects, by yourself contributing some most valuable and interesting articles to the Exhibition.

The number of Exhibitors whose productions it has been found possible to accommodate is about 15,000 of whom nearly one-half are British. The remainder represent the productions of more than forty foreign countries, comprising almost the whole of the civilized nations of the globe. In arranging the space to be allotted to each, we have taken into consideration both the nature of its productions and the facility of access to this country afforded by its geographical position. Your Majesty will find the productions of Your Majesty's dominions arranged in the western portion of the Building, and those of foreign countries in the eastern. The Exhibition is divided into the four great classes of — 1. Raw materials; 2. Machinery; 3. Manufactures; and 4. Sculpture and the Fine Arts. A further division has been made according to the geographical position of the countries represented; those which lie within the warmer latitudes being placed near the centre of the Building, and the colder countries at the extremities.

Your Majesty having been graciously pleased to grant a site in this your Royal park for the purposes of the Exhibition, the first column of the structure now honoured by Your Majesty's presence was fixed on the 26th of September last. Within the short period, therefore, of seven months, owing to the energy of the Contractors, and the active industry of the workmen employed by them, a building has been erected, entirely novel in its construction, covering a space of more than 18 acres, measuring 1,851 feet in length, and 456 in extreme breadth, capable of containing 40,000 visitors, and affording a frontage for the Exhibition of Goods to the extent of more than 10 miles. For the original suggestion of the principle of this structure, the Commissioners are indebted to Mr Joseph Paxton, to whom they feel their acknowledgments to be justly due for this interesting feature of their undertaking.

With regard to the distribution of Rewards to deserving Exhibitors, we have decided that they should be given in the form of Medals, not with reference to merely individual competition, but as rewards for excellence in whatever shape it may present itself. The selection of persons to be so rewarded has been entrusted to Juries equally composed of British subjects and of Foreigners, the former having been selected by the Commission from the recommendations made by the Local Committees, and the latter by the Governments of the Foreign

Nations, the productions of which are exhibited. The names of these Jurors, comprising as they do many of European celebrity, afford the best guarantee of the impartiality with which the Rewards will be assigned.

It affords much gratification that, notwithstanding the magnitude of this undertaking, and the great distances from which many of the articles now exhibited have had to be collected, the day on which Your Majesty has been graciously pleased to be present at the inauguration of the Exhibition is the same day which was originally named for its opening, thus affording a proof of what may, under God's blessing, be accomplished by goodwill and cordial co-operation among nations, aided by the means that modern science has placed at our command.

Having thus briefly laid before Your Majesty the results of our labours, it now only remains for us to convey to Your Majesty our dutiful and loyal acknowledgments of the support and encouragement which we have derived throughout this extensive and laborious task from the gracious favour and countenance of Your Majesty. It is our heartfelt prayer that this undertaking, which has for its end the promotion of all branches of human industry, and the strengthening of the bonds of peace and friendship among all nations of the earth, may, by the blessing of Divine Providence, conduce to the welfare of Your Majesty's people, and be long remembered among the brightest circumstances of Your Majesty's peaceful and happy reign.

Her Majesty's Reply

I receive with the greatest satisfaction the address which you have presented to me on the opening of this Exhibition.

I have observed with a warm and increasing interest the progress of your proceedings in the execution of the duties intrusted to you by the Royal Commission, and it affords me sincere gratification to witness the successful results of your judicious and unremitting exertions in the splendid spectacle by which I am this day surrounded.

I cordially concur with you in the prayer, that by God's blessing this undertaking may conduce to the welfare of my people and to the common interests of the human race, by encouraging the arts of peace and industry, strengthening the bonds of union among the nations of the earth, and promoting a friendly and honourable rivalry in the useful exercise of those faculties which have been conferred by a beneficent Providence for the good and the happiness of mankind.

Mr Molony's Account of the Crystal Palace

William Makepeace Thackeray (1811–63)

K 3

With ganial foire
Thransfuse me loyre,
Ye sacred nymphs of Pindus,
The whoile I sing
That wondthrous thing,
The Palace made o' windows!

Say, Paxton, truth,
Thou wondthrous youth,
What sthroke of art celistial,
What power was lint
You to invint
This combineetion cristial.

'Tis here that roams,
As well becomes
Her dignitee and stations,
Victoria Great,
And houlds in state
The Congress of the Nations.

Her subjects pours
From distant shores,
Her Injians and Canajians;
And also we,
Her kingdoms three,
Attind with our allagiance.

Here come likewise
Her bould allies,
Both Asian and Europian;
From East and West
They send their best
To fill her Coornucopean.

With conscious proide
I stud insoide
And look'd the World's Great Fair in,
Until me sight
Was dazzled quite,
And couldn't see for staring.

There's fountains there
And crosses fair;
There's water-gods with urrns;
There's organs three,
To play, d'ye see?
'God save the Queen,' by turrns.

There's statues bright
Of marble white
Of silver and of copper;
And some in zinc,
And some, I think,
That isn't over proper.

There's carts and gigs,
And pins for pigs;
There's dibblers and there's harrows,
And ploughs like toys
For little boys,
And elegant wheel-barrows.

For thim genteels
Who ride on wheels,
There's plenty to indulge 'em;
There's Droskys snug
From Paytersbug,
And vayhycles from Bulgium.

Amazed I pass
From glass to glass,
Deloighted I survey 'em;
Fresh wondthers grows
Before me nose
In this sublime Musayum!

There's granite flints
That's quite imminse,
There's sacks of coals and fuels,
There's swords and guns,
And soap in tuns,
And Ginger-bread and Jewels.

There's taypots there,
And cannons rare;
There's coffins filled with roses;
There's canvas tints,
Teeth insthrumints,
And shuits of clothes by Moses.

There's lashins more
Of things in store,
But thim I don't remimber;
Nor could disclose
Did I compose
From May time to Novimber.

So let us raise
Victoria's praise,
And Albert's proud condition,
That takes his ayse
As he surveys
This Cristial Exhibition.

K 4

London in 1851. One of George Cruikshank's illustrations for Mayhew's '1851', showing crowds in Regent Circus (now Piccadilly Circus) heading for the Crystal Palace in Hyde Park.

1851; or the Adventures of Mr and Mrs Sandboys

Henry Mayhew

The full title of Mayhew's book is '1851; or the Adventures of Mr and Mrs Cursty Sandboys and family, who came up to London to "enjoy themselves", and see the Great Exhibition'. The illustrations, by George Cruikshank, make much of a crammed London and the opening of the 'Great Bee-hive'. But the 'rush' expected on the first 'shilling day' was a disappointment both to Cruikshank, who had anticipated it in a drawing made for the book, and to Mayhew, who had faith that the working class would see the advantages to them of such an exhibition.

As it turned out, at the close of the exhibition in October almost 4½ million visitors had come on shilling days, another 1½ million paying 2s. 6d. to £1 entrance fees or using season tickets.

Cruikshank's illustrations include 'drolleries' of stuffed animals sent from Stuttgart acting out day-to-day human affairs. Everyone talked about them 'with a smile and a pleasing recollection', but the 'shilling folk', as Mayhew took pleasure in observing, were more keenly interested in the machines. This sensitive document, by the author of 'London Labour and the London Poor' (1851), ranks as one of the earliest sociological studies of the working class in Great Britain.

K 5

At last, the long looked-for shilling day had arrived. Barriers had been placed up outside the building, so as to stem the expected crush, and a double force of police had been 'laid on' from Scotland-yard, and the whole of the officials had been ordered to be at their posts an hour or two earlier than usual, so that by opening the door before the appointed time, the 'rush' might be prevented. Even George Cruikshank himself, confident that a moiety of the metropolis, at least, would be congregated outside the building, had prepared a most vivid delineation of the probable consequences of the rush and crush – the cram and the jam – that every one expected to take place on the eventful occasion. If twenty thousand people attend at five shillings, surely, according to Cocker, said the Executive Committee, five times as many more will come when the charge of admission is five times less.

But alas for the vain hopes of this vain world! as all the speakers at all the 'May meetings' invariably exclaim; for, on the eventful day, the hundred thousand visitors *'in posse,'* dwindled down to twenty thousand *'in esse.'* The two policemen who had been placed outside the gilt cage of the Mountain of Light, the extra 'force' that was stationed beside the Queen of Spain's jewels, the additional 'Peelites' who had been quartered at every point and turn of the interior to direct the crowd which way to move, stared and grinned at one another as they saw the people saunter, one by one, into the building, instead of pouring in by tens of thousands, as had been anticipated. The Executive Committee knit their brows, and bit their thumbs, and then suddenly discovered the cause of the absence of the people. The masses are busy working for their bread, and are waiting for their holiday-time, when they always spend a large amount of their earnings in recreation and enjoyment; and if they come even by twenty thousands now, surely they will come by hundreds of thousands then.

Accordingly, the same farce, of barriers and police, is enacted again, and the same disappointment; for, to the inscrutable wonder of the Executive Committee, the number of visitors during the Whitsun holidays is even less than the week before, and then ensue various speculations as to the cause, and the following reason is, after much cogitation, gravely propounded in explanation of the anomaly:– 'The self-denying patience of the people, their habitual tendency to postpone pleasure to business, and their little inclination to rush madly forward in quest of what can be seen as well, or better, a week or a month hence – these seem to be the natural and truest solutions of the result.'

Now, unfortunately for this pretty compliment, a trip to Greenwich Fair or Hampton Court, on this same Whit-Monday, would soon have convinced the Executive Committee that 'the shilling folk' were neither remarkable for self-denial nor extreme patience in their enjoyments;

while the general observance of 'Saint Monday' by the operatives might have assured any one in the least acquainted with their characters, that, far from being distinguished by any habitual tendency to postpone pleasure to business, they are peculiarly prone to make business give way to pleasure.

None admire the simple sturdy honesty of the working men of England more than ourselves; but to say that they like work better than pleasure, would be to chime in with the rhodomontade of the time, and make out that there is an especial delight in industry, — that is to say, in continuous labour; whereas this is precisely what is repulsive to human nature, and what all men are striving, and, indeed, paying large sums of money to avoid. If industry be such a supreme enjoyment, as the idle rich ever rejoice in declaring, then where is the virtue of it? where the merit of doing that which we have a natural bias to do? Let those who think work a pleasure try a week's mental or manual labour, and then, feeling what a negative bliss there is in mere rest, get to know what it is to yearn, like a schoolboy, for a day's leisure, ease, and amusement. It is well for fat and phlegmatic citizens to call people 'lazy scoundrels,' and bid them 'go and work;' but let these gentlemen themselves try their soft hands at labour, even for a day, and then they will feel how much easier, and, as the world goes, how much more profitable, it is to trade on others' labour than to labour for oneself. . . .

But the reason why the shilling folk absented themselves from the Great Exhibition at first was, because none of their own class had seen it, and they had not yet heard of its wonders, one from the other. But once seen, and once talked about in their workshops, their factories, and — it must be said — their tap-rooms, each gradually became curious to see what had astonished and delighted his fellows.

They soon began to see that the Great Exhibition, rightly considered, is a huge academy for teaching the nobility of labour, and demonstrating the various triumphs of the useful arts over external nature. . . .

Far be it from us to assert that manual dexterity or muscular labour is the *summum bonum* of human existence; but what we wish to say is, that, owing so much of our comfort and happiness to both, we should honour them more than we do; and that, above all, if society would really have the world progress, it should do away with the cheat, which makes those men the most *'respectable'* who do the least for the bread they eat. If we wish to make gentlemen of our working men (we use the word 'gentleman' in its highest Dekkerian sense, and certainly not in its mere conventional signification), our first step must be to assert the natural dignity of labour. So long as we look upon work or to it as a meanness, so long will our workers and toilers remain mean. Let industry be with us 'respectable' — as it is really in the natural arrangement of things — and the industrious poor instead of the idle rich will then be the really respectable men of this country. . . .

Is there any more skill to put words together than to manufacture a razor out of a lump of iron-stone? *We* know which seems to us by far the easier occupation of the two. Nevertheless, without any wish to indulge in that mock humility which seeks to disparage our own productions, when, if there be an innate propensity, it is to value our own work immeasurably beyond its true worth, we must confess that the one craft appears no more worthy of respect than the other; so, we say again, the Great Exhibition, where all these matters are forced upon the mind, rightly considered, is a huge academy for teaching men the true dignity of even what are thought the inferior grades of labour.

One great good the Exhibition assuredly must do, and that is to decrease the large amount of slop or inferior productions that are flooding the country, and which, in the rage for cheapness, are palmed off as equal to the handiwork of the most dexterous operatives. Were the public judges of workmanship — had they been made acquainted with the best work of the best workmen, and so possessed some standard of excellence by which to test the various kinds of labour, it would be impossible for the productions of the unskilful artisan to be brought into competition with those of the most skilful. Owing to the utter ignorance of the public, however, upon all such matters, the tricky employer is now enabled to undersell the honourable master by engaging inferior workmen, while the honourable master, in order to keep pace with the tricky employer, is obliged to reduce the wages of the more dexterous 'hands.' Hence, we see the tendency of affairs at present is, for the worse to drag the better handicraftsmen down to their degradation, instead of the better raising the worse up to their pre-eminence.

The sole remedy for this state of things is greater knowledge on the part of the public. Accustom the people continually to the sight of the best works, and they will no longer submit to have bad workmanship foisted upon them as equal to good.

To those unversed in the 'labour question,' this may appear but a small benefit, but to those who know what it is to inculcate a pride of art — to make the labourer find delight in his labour — to change him from a muscular machine into an intellectual artist, it will seem perhaps as great a boon as can be offered to working men. At present, workmen are beginning to feel that skill — the 'art of industrial occupations' — is useless, seeing that want of skill is now beating them out of the market. One of the most eminent of the master shoemakers in London assured us that the skilled workmen in his business were fast disappearing before the children-workers in Northampton; and, indeed, we heard the same story from almost every trade in the metropolis. The bad are destroying the good, instead of the good improving the bad. . . .

The antidote for this special evil is a periodical exhibition of the works of industry and art. Make the public critics of industrial art, and they will be sure to call into existence a new race of industrial artists. . . .

But if the other parts of the Great Exhibition are curious and instructive, the machinery, which has been from the first the grand focus of attraction, is, on the 'shilling days,' the most peculiar sight of the whole. Here every other man you rub against is habited in a corduroy jacket, or a blouse, or leathern gaiters; and round every object more wonderful than the rest, the people press, two and three deep, with their heads stretched out, watching intently the operations of the moving mechanism. You see the farmers, their dusty hats telling of the distance they have come, with their mouths wide agape, leaning over the bars to see the self-acting mills at work, and smiling as they behold the frame spontaneously draw itself out, and then spontaneously run back again. Some, with great smockfrocks, were gazing at the girls in their long pinafores engaged at the doubling-machines.

But the chief centres of curiosity are the power-looms, and in front of these are gathered small groups of artisans, and labourers, and young men whose red coarse hands tell you they do something for their living, all eagerly listening to the attendant, as he explains the operations, after stopping the loom. Here, too, as you pass along, you meet, now a member of the National Guard, in his peculiar conical hat, with its little ball on top, and horizontal peak, and his red worsted epaulettes and full-plaited trowsers; then you come to a long, thin, and bilious-looking Quaker, with his tidy and clean-looking Quakeress by his side; and the next minute, may be, you encounter a school of charity-girls, in their large white collars and straw bonnets, with the mistress at their head, instructing the children as she goes. Round the electro-plating and the model diving-bell are crowds jostling one another for a foremost place. At the steam brewery, crowds of men and woman are continually ascending and descending the stairs; youths are watching the model carriages moving along the new pneumatic railway; young girls are waiting to see the hemispherical lamp-shades made out of a flat sheet of paper; indeed, whether it be the noisy flax-crushing machine, or the splashing centrifugal pump, or the clatter of the Jacquard lace machine, or the bewildering whirling of the cylindrical steam-press, – round each and all these are anxious, intelligent, and simple-minded artisans, and farmers, and servants, and youths, and children clustered, endeavouring to solve the mystery of its complex operations.

For many days before the 'shilling people' were admitted to the building, the great topic of conversation was the probable behaviour of the people. Would they come sober? will they destroy the things? will they want to cut their initials, or scratch their names on the panes of the glass lighthouses? But they have surpassed in decorum the hopes of their well-wishers. The fact is, the Great Exhibition is to them more of a school than a show. The working-man has often little book-learning, but of such knowledge as constitutes the education of life – viz., the understanding of human motives, and the acquisition of power over natural forces, so as to render them subservient to human happiness – of such knowledge as this, we repeat, the working-man has generally a greater share than those who are said to belong to the 'superior classes'. Hence it is, that what was a matter of tedium, and became ultimately a mere lounge, for gentlefolks, is used as a place of instruction by the people.

We have been thus prolix on the classes attending the Great Exhibition, because it is the influence that this institution is likely to exercise upon labour which constitutes its most interesting and valuable feature. If we really desire the improvement of our social state, (and surely we are far from perfection yet,) we must address ourselves to the elevation of the people; and it is because the Great Exhibition is fitted to become a special instrument towards this end, that it forms one of the most remarkable and hopeful characteristics of our time.

Mr and Mrs John Brown's Visit to London to See the Grand Exposition of all Nations
Thomas B. Onwhyn

The xenophobia released by the Great Exhibition dominates this unusual comic-strip document published in 1851. Antagonists of free trade saw the Exhibition as its fountainhead and with it the inevitability of greater intercourse with foreigners. The most extravagant denunciations, not without echoes to this very day, warned of a coming invasion of aliens who would foment revolution, commit robbery, perpretrate murder and bequeath Britain a piebald generation.

Price 1/6 plain

Mr & Mrs JOHN BROWN'S.

VISIT to LONDON

to see

THE

GRAND EXPOSITION

OF ALL NATIONS.

How they were astonished at its Wonders!!
Inconvenienced by the Crowds,& frightened
out of their Wits by the Foreigners.

Mr & Mrs John Brown, arrive at the Exhibition . Mr B. had no idea they could have
carried it, to such a length. She despairs of ever getting through it .

In the terrific rush to get in a desperate row ensues. Grand   They are carried in by
melée of all Nations . The Browns, barely escape with their lives.   the crowd.

Mrs B gets her bonnet dreadfully out of shape. Mr B looses his hat, and great coat tail. The little Bs escape wonderfully.

They soon set themselves to rights and begin to look about them. Mr B purchases a Catalogue!

A Chinese explains, only they can't understand, some of the wonderful productions of the Celestial Empire.

A good natured Don Cossack takes notice of Anna Maria, much to her terror. Some Negroes exhibit their ivories to little Johnny.

Mrs B takes a fancy to some Bedouins, for some dark Gent^n in their Bed Clothes & is quite shocked.

After viewing the productions of Germany they ascend to the Gallery to see the Transept. Johnny will climb up the railing and the consequence is he pitches over.

Fortunately he is caught on the branch of one of the Trees he is rescued from his perilous situation by a Bosjeman.

They quite have some refreshment ...a party from the Cannibal Islands,
after eyeing little Johnny, in a mysterious manner, offer a price
for him.

A party of Esquimaux Indians &c.
seize a Tub of Tallow, and have
a great feast!

The Browns accosted by some of the most polite Gent". lived ever,
viz". Chevaliers d'Industrie who go upon the principles of Liberté Egalité &c.

M". Bab so alarmed at the impudent way the
foreigners look at her, that M". B indignantly puts
on "Hare"

On leaving the Exhibition they are nearly suffocated by clouds of tobacco smoke, the Foreigners are
puffing in all directions. M". B cant stand the smoke, so they retire to a remote part of the Park.

Being oppressed with the heat, they erect an Impromptu Wigwam in imitation of those they see about the Park.

They are surprised by a party of American Indians who throw them into a state of extreme terror.

Returning from the Park, they take a turn in Regent St. & see a little Fashionable life.

Mr & Mrs B. and family, visit a Theatre.

Not being able to find sleeping accommodation at the Hotels, or Lodging Houses, they make themselves as comfortable as they can, in a Cab for the night, with orders to be driven to the Station, for the first Train in the morning, having had enough of LONDON & the EXH.

Section L

Art and Design

The Building of Paddington Station

Brunel's Letter to Digby Wyatt,
13 January 1851

L 1

13 Jan. 1851.

My dear Sir,

I am going to design, in a great hurry, and I believe to build a station after my own fancy; that is, with engineering roofs, etc. etc. It is at Paddington, in a cutting. . . . Now, such a thing will be entirely *metal* as to all the general forms, arrangements, and design: it almost of necessity becomes an Engineering Work, but, to be honest, even if it were not, it is a branch of architecture of which I am fond, and, *of course* believe myself fully competent for; but for *detail* of ornamentation I neither have time nor knowledge, and with all my confidence in my own ability I have never any objection to advice and assistance even in the department which I keep to myself, namely the general design.

Now, in this building which, *entre nous* will be one of the largest of its class, I want to carry out, strictly and fully, all those correct notions of the use of metal which I believe you and I share (except that I shall carry them still farther than you) and I think it will be a nice opportunity.

Are you willing to enter upon the work *professionally* in the subordinate capacity (I put it in the least attractive form at first) as my *assistant* for the ornamental details? Having put the question in its least elegant form, I would add that I should wish it very much, that I trust your knowledge of me would lead you to expect anything but a disagreeable mode of consulting you, and of using and acknowledging your assistance; and I would remind you that it may prove as good an opportunity as you are likely to have (unless it leads to others, and I hope better) of applying that principle you have lately advocated.

If you are disposed to accept my offer, can you be with me this evening at 9½ pm? It is the only time this week I can appoint, and the matter presses *very much*, the building must be half finished by the summer. Do not let your work for the Exhibition prevent you. You are an industrious man, and night work will suit me best.

I want to show the public also that *colours* ought to be used.*

I shall expect you at 9½ this evening.

Yours truly,
I. K. Brunel

M. D. Wyatt

* The metal framework and decorative ornament of the Crystal Palace were also painted in a carefully conceived pattern of colours (editor's note).

L 2

William Powell Frith, 'Paddington Station', 1862.

Few pictures are better known or liked than Frith's Paddington Station; certainly I should be the last to grudge it its popularity. Many a weary forty minutes have I whiled away disentangling its fascinating incidents and forging for each an imaginary past and an improbable future. . . . 'Paddington Station' is not a work of art; it is an interesting and amusing document. . . . But, with the perfection of photographic processes and of the cinematograph, pictures of this sort are becoming otiose. Who doubts that one of those 'Daily Mirror' photographers in collaboration with a 'Daily Mail' reporter can tell us far more about 'London day by day' than any Royal Academician? For an account of manners and fashions we shall go, in future, to photographs, supported by a little bright journalism, rather than to descriptive paintings. . . . Therefore it must be confessed that pictures in the Frith tradition are grown superfluous; they merely waste the hours of able men who might be more profitably employed in works of a wider beneficence.

Clive Bell, 'The Aesthetic Hypothesis', in 'Art' 1914.

Art and Manufacture
W. Cooke Taylor

The appearance of the journal 'Art-Union' in 1839 coincides with a newly awakened interest in British design and manufacture. It was dedicated in the 1840s to Prince Albert, then President of the Commission on the Fine Arts, and as its title suggests, to the union of art and industry (later the title was changed to the 'Art-Journal'). Though a few other magazines in the years around the Great Exhibition concerned themselves with industrial design (principally, the 'Journal of Design and Manufactures', 1849-52), the 'Art-Union' was the only major periodical in the nineteenth century to devote itself both to design and the fine arts. Its circulation rose from less than 1,000 in the first year to 7,000 in 1846, and by 1847 to 15,000, a substantial figure for those days. The increase probably was due to the improved character of the publication, to the greater number and better engravings with which it was illustrated. But principally the enhanced popularity of the 'Art-Union' was most likely the result of a greater interest of the public in both fine arts and design. The extract printed here is about one-sixth the length of the entire article, which was entitled 'The Mutual Interests of Artists and Manufacturers'.

L 3

There appears to us, then, a natural and early connection between the pursuits of the Artist and the Manufacturer. In the primary ages both were combined in one person; through periods of progress they advanced concurrently; and to ensure the perfection of both, the bonds by which they are united, instead of being relaxed, should be drawn closer together in mutual alliance. The Artist offers to the Manufacturer the conception which is sure to command the homage of the public; the manufacturer enables the artist to give his conception not merely a local habitation in material reality, but an existence which admits of its being known, appreciated, admired and applauded. We have abundant evidence that the greatest artists of their day furnished designs for the vases and bronzes of Greece, Etruria, and southern Italy. The Cartoons of Raffaelle testify that the greatest of modern painters did not disdain to become a designer for the workers at the loom and the embroidery frame; Benvenuto Cellini developed the purest conceptions of statuary with the chasing tool; and the revolution which our Wedgwood worked in the English potteries, was most effectually aided by Fuseli and Flaxman.

There is, then, nothing derogatory to the highest Art in lending its aid to decorate objects of utility. The sculptor does not lower his position when he supplies a model for the moulder in iron, brass, statuary-porcelain, or any other substance in which casts may be taken. The painter no way derogates from his dignity when he furnishes beautiful patterns to the manufacturer of furniture cottons, of muslins, of chintzes, or of paper hangings. Artists are public teachers; and it is their duty, as well as their interest, to aim at giving the greatest possible extent and publicity to their instructions.

Now a great but silent revolution has been taking place in the production and reproduction of works of Art for more than a century. The whole tendency of modern invention is to facilitate the multiplication of copies, and to perfect accuracy in copying. Even within our own memory these inventions and discoveries have wrought a wondrous change in the tastes and habits of the people; in their power of appreciating works of Art, and their readiness to concur in securing adequate remuneration to artists. . . .

The multiplication of the copies of a work of Art is an extension of the fame of the artists, from the applause of some score of amateurs, to the honest appreciation of some thousands, and perhaps millions of his countrymen. While the noble and wealthy possess the splendid original in marble, alabaster, or bronze, the value of that original is not deteriorated to the possessor by the multiplication of statuette copies; while the fame of the artist is infinitely extended, and his share in the education of his countrymen proportionately increased. His chances of future gain are equally enlarged; in a country like England, where skill, education, and intelligence, are constantly raising men from the ranks to social position and fortune, a future patron of Art, and perhaps of the artist, is in course of training, when the aspiring operative is enabled to purchase a copy of some of the rising artist's early productions at a moderate rate. . . .

Let us not be misunderstood; we do not wish artists to become the servants of manufacturers; we do wish them to become their friends and allies; their partners in educating the people; in improving the tastes, and consequently, the morals, of the community; in developing the intellectual strength and the intellectual resources of the United Empire.

Art has its high and holy mission; genius and talents, whatever may be their form, are given to the favoured few, that they may work out the sublime purpose of Divine Providence — the advancement of 'Glory to God in the Highest,' by the promotion of 'Peace upon Earth, Good Will towards Men.' Community in the admiration of any excellence is a strong bond of peace; union in the love of any ennobling exertion of the human faculties is, above all things, efficacious in developing and fostering good will.

From 'Art-Union', 1 March 1848.

European Revolution and British Art

Three long articles were devoted by the 'Art-Union' to the French Revolution of 1848 and its possible consequences for British manufacturing and the distribution of design products. They upheld the efficacy of competition and the middleman. The artisan, who was called a 'capitalist-labourer', was placed well up in the hierarchy of the working classes. The wealth of the manufacturer was not the cause of the poverty of the 'operative' (but see Ruskin, 'Unto This Last'). All capitalists, manufacturers and labourers had 'an educational mission'. Anything that enhanced the profits of capital necessarily profited labour too. The extract given here, from 'Effects of the European Revolutions on British Industry and Art', suggests another reason for the advocacy of free trade and the organisation of the Great Exhibition.

L 4

Whatever may have been the purpose of its leaders, the course of the French Revolution has been social rather than political. We are witnessing the triumph of Communism rather than Republicanism; a Provisional Government holds nominal sway, but France is in reality ruled by an immense Trades'-Union. Louis Blanc and Albert *Ouvrier* sat at the Luxembourg to devise a new organisation of labour, by which the employed are to be masters and the employers to be servants; laws are devised for giving operatives a share in the profits of capital, and depriving capitalists of the returns on their own investments; and finally, the French Government itself proposes to add to all its other functions, that of Manufacturer-General to the entire community.

The capital that is being banished from France will, in all human probability, locate itself on the banks of the Thames; the Industry and the Art which that capital employed must follow in its train. But this great national advantage must be purchased by some temporary inconvenience; we must expect a glut of the finer textile fabris, and of various articles of luxury, for the wholesale houses of France are driven to make ruinous sacrifices, which will produce a violent perturbation of the regular trade all over the world. Our English silks, for instance, may for a time be much injured by the unnatural competition of French silks forced into the market, at a price below the cost of production. This is an unavoidable evil, but it can only be of temporary duration; the French stock is limited, and when it is sold, the exhausted capitals of the French manufacturers will effectually prevent them from producing a fresh supply, and then the English manufacturers will have undisputed command of the world's markets. The same reasoning applies not merely to textile fabrics, but to clocks, bronzes, and other articles of *vertu*; for a time they may be expected to be unnaturally cheap, but so soon is the existing stock is exhausted, England will be ready for triumphant competition in production, while France will be too exhausted to maintain the struggle.

From 'Art-Union', 1 May 1848.

Science and the Arts

Robert Hunt

A dozen articles on this subject were published by Hund in 1848 in the 'Art-Union'. This extract, from 'The Applications of Science to the Fine and Useful Arts', is a kind of index to their contents.

L 5

The present is essentially the
age of useful applications; the
stream of thought appears to
flow almost undividedly in that
particular direction; the energies
of the intelligent are employed
in making the knowledge we possess
available to the purposes of Art
and Manufacture. The business of
the thoughtful among us is, not
to add to the amount of known truth,
so much as to render merchantable
the truths we possess, and to add
by this means to the luxuries and
the comforts of mankind.

The physical inquirer halts in his
progress, and instead of tracing up
his facts to a law, is delighted to
find that he can teach the manufacturer
to employ electricity in moulding

objects of beauty, and the artist to
use the sun-beam for delineating
nature with unerring outline, and the
most delicate gradations of light and
shadow. The chemist pauses in his
investigation to give the painter a
new pigment, and the dyer a colour of
greater permanency; to aid the potter
in the mixture of his clay, and to
assist the glass-maker in producing
articles of purer transparency or of
richer colour. The geologist, studying
the great changes which the crust of the
earth has undergone, stops to show the
economic value of its minerals, its
rocks, and its clays. The naturalist
quits his studies of the Fauna and the
Flora of the world in their great
arrangements, to learn the peculiarities
of some individual species which may
promise to be either useful or ornamental
to mankind. Indeed, the great tendency
of 'our philosophy' is to lend its
powers to the advancement of Art, to
facilitate every branch of Manufacture;
and thus, at the same time that it
assists in the refinement of taste,
it seeks to diffuse over the length
and breadth of the land specimens of
that refinement, and by placing within
the reach of the industrious, but
humble man, objects of pure and simple
beauty, to elevate him in the scale of
intelligence, and give a better and more
ennobling character to all his aspirations.

From 'Art-Union', 1 January 1848.

Signs of the Times: Household Patents in the 1890s
Opper

L 6

He will be shaved by clock-work

He will eat his breakfast with clock-work and comfort.

" Mama, Mama, oome quick ! Papa 's got all twisted up in his Patent Adjustable Reading Chair, and can't get out ! "

Appalling effect of setting the clock-work of the Patent Self-Rocking Cradle at too high a speed.

A Couple of Mistakes in Candlesticks

Much has been said about how bad Victorian design was and how low its standards of taste. That exaggeration may be somewhat dispelled by the examples which follow of contemporary criticism not altogether lacking in sensitivity.

L 7

Of the many hundred designs we have at different times examined in which a single figure does duty as Caryatid, we have scarcely ever seen one in which the great difficulties such a treatment entails have been successfully met and overcome. Sometimes the figure has to be grasped; sometimes a Hercules carries, with infinite muscular exertion, a load at the weight of which a school-boy would laugh; and sometimes a delicate female carries on her devoted head quite enough to break the back of a Samson. To the last of these anomalous classes the specimen in question belongs, and neither the grace of the figure, nor the light and pretty treatment of the cornucopia she is supporting, can reconcile us to the discrepancy between her proportions and those of the burden she is doomed to bear *in perpetuo*. The basket at the top is extremely elegant, and the execution of the whole tasteful and pretty. The base is a decided failure, being not only too heavy in mass for the rest of the design, but compounded of uncomfortable conventional shell-work, and directly imitative foliage. A little piercing would have rendered it much more pleasing.

We cannot say anything more favourable of the accompanying Or-molu Candlestick, which is a brilliant piece of tastelessness, and may be assumed as an indication of genuine *manufacture*, without one grain of thought or knowledge. Of idea it is absolutely devoid: what dolphins and tridents have to do with a candlestick we cannot imagine. Of proportion it is perfectly destitute. The base is too heavy, the stem too fat, and the socket too small. With form it is most scantily endowed, since nothing can be imagined more ugly than the junction of the inverted baluster stem and the trilobate base. What then is left of it? Nothing but the glitter of material and over-elaborated manipulation.

From 'Journal of Design and Manufactures',
March-August 1851.

Standards of Design, 1846

The editors of the 'Art-Union' also make clear their standards of design in 1846.

L 8

We append a scent jar, a good idea, well executed. Not intended to be moved very often, we presume, as it is rather prickly to the touch. The flowers on this jar are painted, and the general effect is thereby impaired. Many pieces in this style are left in the bisque, in which state they are singularly chaste and elegant. This kind of decoration is becoming rather prevalent; we trust it will not be carried too far, as the notion is curious rather than beautiful.

Our next example is of simpler form, and has not the well-defined purpose for which the first is remarkable, yet it is of excellent character. There is a slight want of congruity, however, in the ornamentation — the vine being used freely (and, so far, effectually) on the handle, while the body of the jug is covered with rather elegantly disposed but nondescript plants. Anomalies of this kind are, nevertheless, of rare occurrence.

The hat-stand which follows is, we consider, successful: in the first place, because it is better than usual in ornament; and in the second, that it is a cheap article. It is an immense improvement on the old abominable hat pegs, which, ranging in rows in lobbies, were painful to the eye, from their inelegant shapes. In this case, beauty and utility go hand in hand, as they should do.

Nature is continually supplying 'examples', so to speak, of which the designer takes too little heed; sometimes she is made to work in union with hostile matter, as in the instance referred to in the appended group, where elegantly wreathed vine branches ascend from an awkward and ungainly scrolled base.

K

Which Direction for Ornamental Art?

'Which Direction is Ornamental Art Likely to Take in this Country, toward Elaboration or Simplicity?' This prophetic article appeared fifty years before its time, in January 1852, in the 'Journal of Design and Manufactures'; the first half of the article follows.

L 9

This is a question that now naturally suggests itself. Our answer is, *toward simplicity*. And this opinion is founded on the close alliance of *utility* and *simplicity*, and the character of our race. This character may be overlaid at times by periodical fashions and temporary influences. There is, however, the strong sub-current beneath, that shews itself partially and occasionally, and asserts its power by its onward progress.

Some fifteen years ago Britain began to open her eyes to the fact, that her industrial productions of various kinds, so good in material and fabric, were inferior in appearance. She rubbed her eyes, like a 'sleeper awakened,' but did not see clearly. Objects were, however, sufficiently distinct for her to perceive the necessity of taking means to make up the deficiency. She had been, and might continue to be, assisted by foreigners, but why might not her own sons help her? The question was launched and set afloat on public opinion. Speeches were made in divers places, and in the end the Schools of Design were established. There was a deal of ignorance and cant, and proportional disagreements to wade through. The child was ricketty, at first, from bad management, and it had its teething to experience. But all this awakened, but the more thoroughly, the maternal Britain. Within the last few years, consequent on this movement, and parallel with its course, individual speculations arose. Manufacturers and artists thought it was their vocation to assist in its onward progress, and that it would be for their own good and that of the public to do so. Both floundered about in ignorance. They had not yet learnt how to swim; but each was pertinacious of his own scheme of keeping afloat, and of raising art ornamentation to its proper altitude and position. Various were the dogmas put forward and vigorously asserted. One set of schemes were for reproduction, and individuals took up respectively this or that style of ornamentation, and each was devoted to some by-gone precedent, 'aut Caesar aut mullus.' Another plan was, that each article of furniture should 'tell its own story,' from a coal-scuttle to a piano! That the one should be decorated with a scene from a coal-mine, and the other with the Muse of Harmony and singing birds! One disciple averred that to drink beer out of a jug ornamented with vine-leaves, or wine from a glass decorated with the hop, was rank heresy! Neither of these theories was recognised by the public — and rightly. The styles of former times were not suited to the familiar uses of the present; and the latter scheme, although there was something of vitality about it, was carried to excess, and became in some cases ludicrous.

Both, however, had their use. They were part of the flounderings that were to teach us eventually to swim. They had both also their truths, and their dogmas were wrong only, inasmuch as they were enforced as principal and not as subsidiary. All the fanciful and mythic principles of ornamentation in the world would not induce a lady of good taste, to array herself in a dress that was not becoming; for utility, in the wide sense we use it, comprehends this quality as well as 'washing and wearing;' nor would all the dogmas in the world force upon the public the use of a tea-urn that was ugly and inconvenient, merely because there was much to be said about its propriety, aesthetically and theoretically!

These sects, however, were not the only ones. The masses only saw their own crudity, and thought that the farther and the sooner they fled from it the better. Thus many rushed into the opposite extreme of over-elaboration. This was unfortunate, for a slight knowledge of these matters serves to inform us that *elegant simplicity* is a far more effective object to obtain, than mere multitude and confusion of parts which some call *richness*. Thus many avoided a difficulty, by rushing at once into French luxuriance. With the usual blindness of copyists, they grappled the faults, and the finer parts escaped them. We believe, however, that the mistake is now pretty generally admitted. The Exhibition is a good exponent of it.

Art and Socialism
Roger Fry (1866–1934)

This article was first published as 'The Great State' in 1912, and republished in 'Vision and Design' (1920, etc.). This extract, from the 1929 edition, provides us with an unusual inventory of the art and design that went into the furnishing of a railway restaurant at the beginning of the century. Fry, a painter and critic, had become, at the time of writing, England's most distinguished aesthetician. His theories of 'pure' and 'impure' art and his encouragement of Post-Impressionism made a significant impact on artistic styles of the period. In essays like 'Art and Socialism', the reverberations from Ruskin and Morris (q.v.) are still loud and clear, though Fry's exclusive and rarefied concepts would have been anathema to them.

L 10

We are so far obliged to protect ourselves from the implications of modern life that without a special effort it is hard to conceive the enormous quantity of 'art' that is annually produced and consumed. For the special purpose of realising it I take the pains to write the succeeding paragraphs in a railway refreshment-room, where I am actually looking at those terribly familiar but fortunately fleeting images which such places afford. And one must remember that public places of this kind merely reflect the average citizen's soul, as expressed in his home.

The space my eye travels over is a small one, but I am appalled at the amount of 'art' that it harbours. The window towards which I look is filled in its lower part by stained glass; within a highly elaborate border, designed by some one who knew the conventions of thirteenth-century glass, is a pattern of yellow and purple vine leaves with bunches of grapes, and flitting about among these many small birds. In front is a lace curtain with patterns taken from at least four centuries and as many countries. On the walls, up to a height of four feet, is a covering of lincrusta walton stamped with a complicated pattern in two colours, with sham silver medallions. Above that a moulding but an inch wide, and yet creeping throughout its whole with a degenerate descendant of a Graeco-Roman carved guilloche pattern; this has evidently been cut out of the wood by machine or stamped out of some composition – its nature is so perfectly concealed that it is hard to say which. Above this is a wall-paper in which an effect of eighteenth-century satin brocade is imitated by shaded staining of the paper. Each of the little refreshment-tables has two cloths, one arranged symmetrically with the table, the other a highly ornate printed cotton arranged 'artistically' in a diagonal position. In the centre of each table is a large pot in which every beautiful quality in the material and making of pots has been carefully obliterated by methods each of which implies profound scientific knowledge and great inventive talent. Within each pot is a plant with large dark green leaves, apparently made of india-rubber. This painful catalogue makes up only a small part of the inventory of the 'art' of the restaurant. If I were to go on to tell of the legs of the tables, of the electric-light fittings, of the chairs into the wooden seats of which some tremendous mechanical force has deeply impressed a large distorted anthemion – if I were to tell of all these things, my reader and I might both begin to realise with painful acuteness something of the horrible toil involved in all this display. Display is indeed the end and explanation of it all. Not one of these things has been made because the maker enjoyed the making; not one has been bought because its contemplation would give any one any pleasure, but solely because each of these things is accepted as a symbol of a particular social status. I say their contemplation can give no one pleasure; they are there because their absence would be resented by the average man who regards a large amount of futile display as in some way inseparable from the conditions of that well-to-do life to which he belongs or aspires to belong.

The Ornament of the Future

Lewis Foreman Day (1845–1910)

Day, an industrial designer, had an extraordinarily subtle capacity for describing the conjunction of art and the machine. His writings in the last two decades of the nineteenth century anticipate to a remarkable degree the ideology of art and design in the twentieth.

L 11

There were times when ornament was produced without a thought of the traffic in it. Now it is the traffic that gives rise to ornament. We cannot, therefore, leave commerce out of the account, since trade is no longer simply the outlet for the arts applied, but in a great measure the origin of them. It is a pity that there should ever be antagonism between artist and manufacturer. Each is only too ready to make use of the other, and to form an alliance with that personal end in view. But while each party to the bargain looks only to his own interest, the cause of neither is likely to prosper. Since they are dependent one upon the other, since for good or ill their fate is knit together, and divorce between them is impossible, they had best come to a clear understanding, and working together for the common good.

The conditions of other days may have been more favourable to art than the present state of things. We who live in the present and know so well where it pinches, are inclined to look back longingly to a past of whose hardships we have had no experience. But it is with the present that we have to do. Nor can we long maintain an attitude of opposition to its spirit. Strong men may to some extent direct the age they live in; but to resist it is idle, and to wail is foolish. Whether we like it or no, machinery and steam-power, and electricity for all we know, will have something to say concerning the ornament of the future.

No artist will think of denying that the highest art is of necessity hand-work. No machine can approach the best work of men's hands. And even in the arts of every-day there must always be room for actual handicraftsmen. But they will inevitably be in that minority in which the most accomplished find themselves always. The popular demand is for machine work. Its smoother and cleaner finish, its cheapness, and the certainty with which it can be produced, more than outweigh in public opinion the artistic merits of rougher, costlier, and less certain results. The practical and commercial mind of those in whose hands the matter mainly rests, is not likely to be swayed by our sentimental regrets; and the discussion of the relative merits of art and manufacture is, therefore, to little purpose. It has been practically settled by the public that they want machine-work, and they mean to have it. We may protest that they have chosen unwisely, but they will not pay much heed to us. We may shrug our shoulders and retire, if we can afford that luxury, to the select and solitary enjoyment of our own ideas; but in so doing we leave our art at the mercy of those who neither know nor care about it, and the last state of ugliness to which they deliver it up will be worse than the first. It is a question whether the perfect precision now possible by means of modern mechanical contrivances might not, rightly applied, be as valuable in ornament as it is actually pernicious.

We cannot do without common-sense, even though at times it be so common as not greatly to commend itself to us. Men who live by their art have as little right to despise the pecuniary considerations attaching to its connection with manufacture and commerce as to pander to what they believe to be vulgarity, or prostitute their art to money-getting. The profit that an artist derives from commerce puts him in a better position to carry out his own idea of what is best in art, and to insist upon a higher and still higher standard of excellence in the manufacture for which he designs. There is scarcely a branch of manufacture that is beneath the consideration of the designer, provided only he be allowed to do his best. The work that degrades is that in which he is forced to work under his strength, placing himself upon the level of an ignorant or stupid employer. The producer who has some knowledge of art and believes thoroughly in its commercial value, is its best patron. The worst is the Mr Brooke of commerce, who has faith in its efficacy only 'up to a certain point.' His instructions to the artist are always, 'Something saleable, now!' He doctors the designs he has purchased, purges them of all that had any value as art in them, and then, when the enfeebled result of his experiment appeals to no one, he complains that 'Art may be all very well in its way, you know, but the public do not appreciate it; they want something attractive, something showy now!' He has a long list of epithets at the tip of his tongue, all of which, being interpreted, mean 'vulgar.'

'Thirty millions, mostly fools,' was the cry of the Jeremiah of our own time. The manufacturer appears to think that the millions are mostly vulgar. He may be right or wrong; but it is to be hoped that there is a public also for the taste that is not loud. The fit audience is always few. For all that, the highest wisdom may not consist in lowering our standard to the imagined level of the many. The fact that the public accepts a poor bait, is no proof that it would not more greedily seize a richer one.

There is no compromise possible with vulgarity. Those who like it prefer it undiluted, and those who have taste are disgusted by the least taint of it. You cannot well catch two publics with one bait, but you may easily miss them both.

> From L. F. Day, 'Everyday Art: Short Essays on
> the Arts Not-Fine', 1882.

David Octavius Hill (left). Calotype photograph made from paper negative, 1846 or earlier.

Photography

Elizabeth, Lady Eastlake

No finer, more sensitive, exploration of the visual character of photography and its significance for art has been made than by Lady Eastlake. She was advantageously placed to comment on photography and art. Her husband, Sir Charles Eastlake, was in the early 1850s President of the Royal Academy, Director of the National Gallery and first President of the London Photographic Society — all three! Here is an extract from her article, 'Photography', published in 1857 by the London 'Quarterly Review'.

L 13

Thus the whole question of success and failure resolves itself into an investigation of the capacities of the machine, and well may we be satisfied with the rich gifts it bestows, without straining it into a competition with art. For everything for which art, so-called, has hitherto been the means but not the end, photography is the allotted agent — for all that requires mere manual correctness, and mere manual slavery, without any employment of the artistic feeling, she is the proper and therefore the perfect medium. She is made for the present age, in which the desire for art resides in a small minority, but the craving, or rather necessity for cheap, prompt, and correct facts in the public at large. Photography is the purveyor of such knowledge to the world. She is the sworn witness of everything presented to her view. What are her unerring records in the service of mechanics, engineering, geology, and natural history, but facts of the most sterling and stubborn kind? What are her studies of the various stages of insanity — pictures of life unsurpassable in pathetic truth — but facts as well as lessons of the deepest physiological interest? What are her representations of the bed of the ocean, and the surface of the moon – of the launch of the Marlborough, and of the contents of the Great Exhibition – of Charles Kean's now destroyed scenery of the 'Winter's Tale,' and of Prince Albert's now slaughtered prize ox – but facts which are neither the province of art nor of description, but of that new form of communication between man and man – neither letter, message, nor picture – which now happily fills up the space between them? What indeed are nine-tenths of those facial maps called photographic portraits, but accurate landmarks and measurements for loving eyes and memories to deck with beauty and animate with expression, in perfect certainty that the ground plan is founded upon fact?

In this sense no photographic picture that ever was taken, in heaven, or earth, or in the waters underneath the earth, of any thing, or scene, however defective when measured by an artistic scale, is destitute of a special, and what we may call an historic interest. Every form which is traced by light is the impress of one moment, or one hour, or one age in the great passage of time. Though the faces of our children may not be modelled and rounded with that truth and beauty which art attains, yet minor things – the very shoes of the one, the inseparable toy of the other – are given with a strength of identity which art does not even seek. Though the view of a city be deficient in those niceties of reflected lights and harmonious gradations which belong to the facts of which Art takes account, yet the facts of the age and of the hour are there, for we count the lines in that keen perspective of telegraphic wire, and read the characters on the playbill or manifesto, destined to be torn down on the morrow.

Here, therefore, the much-lauded and much-abused agent called Photography takes her legitimate stand. Her business is to give evidence of facts, as minutely and as impartially as, to our shame, only an unreasoning machine can give. In this vocation we can as little overwork her as tamper with her. The millions and millions of hieroglyphics mentioned by M. Arago may be multiplied by millions and millions more, – she will render all as easily and as accurately as one. When people, therefore, talk of photography, as being intended to supersede art, they utter what, if true, is not so in the sense they mean. Photography is intended to supersede much that art has hitherto done, but only that which it was both a misappropriation and a deterioration of Art to do. The field of delineation, having two distinct spheres, requires two distinct labourers; but though hitherto the freewoman has done the work of the bondwoman, there is no fear that the position should be in future reversed. Correctness of drawing, truth of detail, and absence of convention, the best artistic characteristics of photography, are qualities of no common kind, but the student who issues from the academy with these in his grasp stands, nevertheless, but on the threshold of art. The power of selection and rejection, the living application of that language which lies dead in his paint-box, the marriage of his own mind with the object before him, and the offspring, half stamped with his own features, half with those of Nature, which is born of the union — whatever appertains to the free-will of the intelligent being, as opposed to the obedience of the machine, — this, and much more than this, constitutes that mystery called Art, in the elucidation of which photography can give valuable help, simply by showing what it is not. There is, in truth, nothing in that power of literal, unreasoning imitation, which she claims as her own, in which, rightly viewed, she does not relieve the artist of a burden rather than supplant him in an office. We do not even except her most pictorial feats — those splendid architectural representations — from this rule. Exquisite as they are, and fitted to teach the young, and assist the experienced in art, yet the hand of the artist is but ignobly employed in closely imitating the texture of stone, or in servilely following the intricacies of the zigzag ornament. And it is not only in what she can do to relieve the sphere of art, but in what she can sweep away from it altogether, that we have reason to congratulate ourselves. Henceforth it may be hoped that we shall hear nothing further of that miserable contradiction in terms 'bad art' — and see nothing more of that still more miserable mistake in life 'a bad artist.' Photography at once does away with anomalies with which the good sense of society has always been more or less at variance. As what she does best is beneath the doing of a real artist at all, so even what she does worst she is a better machine than the man who is nothing but a machine.

Let us, therefore, dismiss all mistaken ideas about the harm which photography does to art. As in all great and sudden improvements in the material comforts and pleasures of the public, numbers, it is true, have found their occupation gone, simply because it is done cheaper and better in another way. But such improvements always give more than they take. Where ten self-styled artists eked out a precarious living by painting inferior miniatures, ten times that number now earn their bread by supplying photographic portraits. Nor is even such manual skill as they possessed thrown out of the market. There is no photographic establishment of any note that does not employ artists at high salaries — we understand not less than £1 a day — in touching, and colouring, and finishing from nature those portraits for which the camera may be said to have laid the foundation. And it must be remembered that those who complain of the encroachments of photography in this department could not even supply the demand. Portraits, as is evident to any thinking mind, and as photography now proves, belong to that class of facts wanted by numbers who know and care nothing about their value as works of art. For this want, art, even of the most abject kind, was, whether as regards correctness, promptitude, or price, utterly inadequate. These ends are not only now attained, but, even in an artistic sense, attained far better than before. The coloured portraits to which we have alluded are a most satisfactory coalition between the artist and the machine. Many an inferior miniature-painter who understood the mixing and applying of pleasing tints was wholly unskilled in the true drawing of the human head. With this deficiency supplied, their present productions, therefore, are far superior to anything they accomplished single-handed, before. Photographs taken on ivory, or on substances invented in imitation of ivory, and coloured by hand from nature, such as are seen at the rooms of Messrs Dickinson, Claudet, Mayall, Kilburn, &c., are all that can be needed to satisfy the mere portrait want, and in some instances may be called artistic productions of no common kind besides. If, as we understand, the higher professors of miniature-painting — and the art never attained greater excellence in England than now — have found their studios less thronged of late, we believe that the desertion can be but temporary. At all events, those who in future desire their exquisite productions will be more worthy of them. The broader the ground which the machine may occupy, the higher will that of the intelligent agent be found to stand. If, therefore, the time should ever come when art is sought, as it ought to be, mainly for its own sake, our artists and our patrons will be of a far more elevated order than now: and if anything can bring about so desirable a climax, it will be the introduction of Photography.

William Henry Fox Talbot's calotype printing establishment at Reading (1844-7).

The Kodak Camera

*"You press the button,   -
- - - we do the rest."*

The only camera that anybody can use without instructions.   Send for the Primer free.

_____

A Transparent Film

For Roll Holders.

The announcement is hereby made that the undersigned have perfected a process for making transparent flexible films for use in roll holders and Kodak Cameras.

The new film is as thin, light and flexible as paper and as transparent as glass.   It requires *no stripping*, and it is wound on spools for roll holders.

It will be known as *Eastman's Transparent Film*.   Circulars and samples will be sent to any address on receipt of 4 cents in stamps.

Price $25.00—Loaded for 100 Pictures.

The Eastman Dry Plate and Film Co.

ROCHESTER, N. Y.

An early advertisement for the Number One Kodak Camera. The Kodak first appeared in 1888, the first 'Brownie' in 1900. In that year, at the Exposition Universelle in Paris, 17 of every 100 persons attending carried portable cameras. It is estimated that on certain days as many as 51,000 cameras were being used inside the exhibition grounds.

A demonstration of industrial 'know-how': a monster American camera shown at the 1900 exhibition in Paris. Glass plates used to make the negatives measured 6½ X 9 ft. The camera was employed by the Chicago and Alton Railroad Company to photograph their trains. It took fifteen men to make a photograph.

W. K. L. Dickson filming the Boer War for the Biograph Company in 1899. The emerging newsreel industry accounted for a large number of films recording newsworthy events at the turn of the century. Pathé also filmed the war in the Transvaal in 1900, and in 1904 their cameraman covered the Russo-Japanese War. Visits by State dignitaries, like that of Tsar Nicholas II to Paris, were easy pickings for the cameramen. But situations like the Spanish-American War, the Boxer Rebellion and the mutiny on the battleship 'Potemkin', or the Dreyfus retrial, were 'reconstituted' or faked without the slightest hesitation.

Section M

John Ruskin

John Ruskin

The barometer of Ruskin's influence can be read by the eulogies made of the man in his own time and after his death. It is little known that the great Impressionist painter, Claude Monet, paid a remarkable tribute in 1900 (the year of Ruskin's death) when he said that '90 per cent of the theory of impressionist painting is . . . in [Ruskin's book] "Elements of Drawing" '. Monet may have been reminded of his debt to Ruskin when, a year earlier, in Paul Signac's important 'From Eugène Delacroix to Neo-Impressionism', a prominent place was given to 'Elements of Drawing'. And, indeed, among Ruskin's voluminous writings on art will be found brilliant and cogent discussions on perception and aesthetic theory of a remarkably prophetic character. Even the irascible Wyndham Lewis, in 'The Demon of Progress in the Arts' (1954), praised Ruskin as the only 'word man' the artist could trust.

Despite such praise, it has taken half a century since Ruskin's death to dispel the misdemeanours attributed to that evangelical guardian of the naturalist tradition. His reputation had been passed over without discrimination along with other legacies of Victorian life and thought which were unacceptable in the early part of the twentieth century. Only recently has interest in his work been sufficiently revived to demonstrate what significance he still holds for the present.

Ruskin is no less honoured for his political and moral philosophy. His 'Sesame and Lilies' first appeared in 1865 running into several editions. By 1905 this moral essay had sold 76,000 copies. By 1907, together with his lecture, 'The Mystery of Life and its Arts', the book in that form reached a figure of 108,000. And with 'The Ethics of the Dust' (which itself topped the 56,000 mark) it accounted by 1907 for 162,000 issues — a grand total for 'Sesame and Lilies' of 346,000, surpassing most best-sellers today.

Herbert Read considered Ruskin to have been the prime galvanising force in the advocacy of a kind of political morality which, even in the pursuit of a new society, renounces political action. He saw Ruskin as the progenitor in a lineage which includes William Morris, Tolstoy and Mahatma Gandhi. Morris's biographer J. W. Mackail points to Ruskin's 'Unto This Last' as the inspirational source of Morris's socialism. And Gandhi, too, acknowledged his indebtedness to the same work as 'The one book that brought about an instantaneous and practical transformation in my life'.

Ruskin (centre) with William Bell Scott (left) and Dante Gabriel Rossetti (right), taken in 1863.

The Opening of the Crystal Palace

Ruskin's invective, written in 1854, is provoked not only by the Great Exhibition of 1851, but by an even grander apotheosis of the iron and glass structure removed from Hyde Park and set on the imposing heights of Sydenham Hill in the south of London. (It was there gutted by fire in 1936 and never rebuilt.) Ruskin showed considerable pique at the great mobilisation of money and manpower for that monumental congeries of manufacturing trivia while the really magnificent architectural tributes to the human spirit were falling into decay. His beloved Turner, too, died in December 1851 while an uninterested public was resuscitating itself from the binge of the previous summer.

M 2

I read the account in the 'Times' newspaper of the opening of the Crystal Palace at Sydenham, as I ascended the hill between Vevay and Chatel St Denis, and the thoughts which it called up haunted me all day long, as my road wound among the grassy slopes of the Simmenthal. There was a strange contrast between the image of that mighty palace, raised so high above the hills on which it is built as to make them seem little else than a basement for its glittering stateliness, and those low larch huts, half hidden beneath their coverts of forest, and scattered like grey stones along the masses of far away mountain. Here, man contending with the power of Nature for his existence; there, commanding them for his recreation: here a feeble folk nested among the rocks with the wild goat and the coney, and retaining the same quiet thoughts from generation to generation; there, a great multitude triumphing in the splendour of immeasurable habitation, and haughty with hope of endless progress and irresistible power.

It is indeed impossible to limit, in imagination, the beneficent results which may follow from the undertaking thus happily begun. For the first time in the history of the world, a national museum is formed in which a whole nation is interested; formed on a scale which permits the exhibition of monuments of art in unbroken symmetry, and of the productions of nature in unthwarted growth, — formed under the auspices of science which can hardly err, and of wealth which can hardly be exhausted; and placed in the close neighbourhood of a metropolis overflowing with a population weary of labour, yet thirsting for knowledge, where contemplation may be consistent with rest, and instruction with enjoyment. It is impossible, I repeat, to estimate the influence of such an institution on the minds of the working-classes. How many hours once wasted may now be profitably dedicated to pursuits in which interest was first awakened by some accidental display in the Norwood palace; how many constitutions, almost broken, may be restored by the healthy temptation into the country air, — how many intellects, once dormant, may be roused into activity within the crystal walls, and how these noble results may go on multiplying and increasing and bearing fruit seventy times sevenfold, as the nation pursues its career, — are questions as full of hope as incapable of calculation. But with all these grounds for hope there are others for despondency, giving rise to a group of melancholy thoughts, of which I can neither repress the importunity nor forbear the expression.

For three hundred years, the art of architecture has been the subject of the most curious investigation; its principles have been discussed with all earnestness and acuteness; its models in all countries and of all ages have been examined with scrupulous care, and imitated with unsparing expenditure. And of all this refinement of enquiry, — this lofty search after the ideal, — this subtlety of investigation and sumptuousness of practice, — the great result, the admirable and long-expected conclusion is, that in the centre of the nineteenth century, we suppose ourselves to have invented a new style of architecture, when we have magnified a conservatory!

In Mr Laing's speech, at the opening of the palace, he declares that 'an entirely novel order of architecture, producing, by means of unrivalled mechanical ingenuity, the most marvellous and beautiful effects, sprang into existence to provide a building.' In these words, the speaker is not merely giving utterance to his own feelings. He is expressing the popular view of the facts, nor that a view merely popular, but one which has been encouraged by nearly all the professors of art of our time.

It is to this, then, that our Doric and Palladian pride is at last reduced! We have vaunted the divinity of the Greek ideal — we have plumed ourselves on the purity of our Italian taste — we have cast our whole souls into the proportions of pillars, and the relations of orders — and behold the end! Our taste, thus exalted and disciplined, is dazzled by the lustre of a few rows of panes of glass; and the first principles of architectural sublimity, so far sought, are found all the while to have consisted merely in sparkling and in space.

Let it not be thought that I would depreciate (were it possible to depreciate) the mechanical ingenuity which has been displayed in the erection of the Crystal Palace, or that I underrate the effect which its vastness may continue to produce on the popular imagination. But mechanical ingenuity is *not* the essence either of painting or architecture: and largeness of dimension does not necessarily involve nobleness of design. There is assuredly as much ingenuity required to build a screw frigate, or a tubular bridge as a hall of glass; — all these are works characteristic of the age; and all, in their several ways, deserve our highest admiration; but not admiration of the kind that is rendered to poetry or to art. We may cover the German Ocean with frigates, and bridge the Bristol Channel with iron, and roof the county of Middlesex with crystal, and yet not possess one Milton, or Michael Angelo.

Well, it may be replied, we need our bridges, and have pleasure in our palaces; but we do not want Miltons, nor Michael Angelos.

Truly, it seems so; for, in the year in which the first Crystal Palace was built, there died among us a man whose name, in after ages, will stand with those of the great of all time [i.e. J. M. W. Turner (1775-1851)]. Dying, he bequeathed to the nation the whole mass of his most cherished works: and for these three years, while we have been building this colossal receptacle for casts and copies of the art of other nations, these works of our own greatest painter have been left to decay in a dark room near Cavendish Square, under the custody of an aged servant.

This is quite natural. But it is also memorable.

There is another interesting fact connected with the history of the Crystal Palace as it bears on that of the art of Europe, namely, that in the year 1851, when all that glittering roof was built, in order to exhibit the petty arts of our fashionable luxury – the carved bedsteads of Vienna, and glued toys of Switzerland, and gay jewellery of France – in that very year, I say, the greatest pictures of the Venetian masters were rotting at Venice in the rain, for want of roof to cover them, with holes made by cannon shot through their canvass.

There is another fact, however, more curious than either of these, which will hereafter be connected with the history of the palace now in building; namely, that at the very period when Europe is congratulated on the invention of a new style of architecture, because fourteen acres of ground have been covered with glass, the greatest examples in existence of true and noble Christian architecture were being resolutely destroyed; and destroyed by the effects of the very interest which was slowly beginning to be excited by them.

Under the firm and wise government of the third Napoleon, France has entered on a new epoch of prosperity, one of the signs of which is a zealous care for the preservation of her noble public buildings. Under the influence of this healthy impulse, repairs of the most extensive kind are at this moment proceeding, on the cathedrals of Rheims, Amiens, Rouen, Chartres, and Paris; (probably also in many other instances unknown to me). These repairs were, in many cases, necessary up to a certain point; and they have been executed by architects as skilful and learned as at present exist, – executed with noble disregard of expense, and sincere desire on the part of their superintendents that they should be completed in a manner honourable to the country.

They are nevertheless more fatal to the monuments they are intended to preserve, than fire, war, or revolution. For they are undertaken, in the plurality of instances, under an impression, which the efforts of all true antiquaries have as yet been unable to remove, that it is possible to reproduce the mutilated sculpture of past ages in its original beauty.

'Reproduire avec une exactitude mathématique,' are the words used, by one of the most intelligent writers on this subject, of the proposed regeneration of the statue of Ste Modeste, on the north porch of the Cathedral of Chartres.

Now, it is not the question at present, whether thirteenth century sculpture be of value, or not. Its value is assumed by the authorities who have devoted sums so large to its so-called restoration, and may therefore be assumed in my argument. The worst state of the sculptures whose restoration is demanded may be fairly represented by that of the celebrated group of the Fates, among the Elgin Marbles in the British Museum. With what favour would the guardians of those marbles, or any other persons interested in Greek art, receive a proposal from a living sculptor to 'reproduce with mathematical exactitude' the group of the Fates, in a perfect form, and to destroy the original? For with exactly such favour, those who are interested in Gothic art should receive proposals to reproduce the sculpture of Chartres or Rouen.

In like manner, the state of the architecture which it is proposed to restore, may, at its worst, be fairly represented to the British public by that of the best preserved portions of Melrose Abbey. With what encouragement would those among us who are sincerely interested in history, or in art, receive a proposal to pull down Melrose Abbey, and 'reproduce it mathematically?' There can be no doubt of the answer which, in the instances supposed, it would be proper to return. 'By all means, if you can, reproduce mathematically, elsewhere, the group of the Fates, and the Abbey of Melrose. But leave unharmed the original fragment, and the existing ruin.' And an answer of the same tenour ought to be given to every proposal to restore a Gothic sculpture or building. Carve or raise a model of it in some other part of the city: but touch not the actual edifice, except only so far as may be necessary to sustain, to protect it. I said above that repairs were in many instances necessary. These necessary operations consist in substituting new stones for decayed ones, where they are absolutely essential to the stability of the fabric; in propping, with wood or metal, the portions likely to give way; in binding or cementing into their places the sculptures which are ready to detach themselves; and in general care to remove luxuriant weeds, and obstructions of the channels for the discharge of the rain.

But no modern or imitative sculpture ought *ever*, under any circumstances, to be mingled with the ancient work.

Unfortunately, repairs thus conscientiously executed are always unsightly, and meet with little approbation from the general public; so that a strong temptation is necessarily felt by all superintendents of public works, to execute the required repairs in a manner which, though indeed fatal to the monument, may be, in appearance, seemly. But a far more cruel temptation is held out to the architect. He who should propose to a municipal body, to build in the form of a new church, to be erected in some other part of their city, models of such portions of their cathedral as were falling into decay, would be looked upon as merely asking for employment, and his offer would be rejected with disdain. But let an architect declare that the existing fabric stands in need of repairs, and offer to restore it to its original beauty, and he is instantly regarded as a lover of his country, and has a chance of obtaining a commission which will furnish him with a large and steady income, and enormous patronage, for twenty or thirty years to come.

I have great respect for human nature. But I would rather leave it to others than myself to pronounce how far such a temptation is always likely to be resisted, and how far, when repairs are once permitted to be under-taken, a fabric is likely to be spared from mere interest in its beauty, when its destruction, under the name of restoration, has become permanently remunerative to a large body of workmen.

Let us assume, however, that the architect is always conscientious — always willing, the moment he has done what is strictly necessary for the safety and decorous aspect of the building, to abandon his income, and declare his farther services unnecessary. Let us presume, also, that every one of the two or three hundred workmen who must be employed under him, is equally conscientious, and, during the course of years of labour, will never destroy in carelessness what it may be inconvenient to save, or in cunning, what is difficult to imitate. Will all this probity of purpose preserve the hand from error, and the heart from weariness? Will it give dexterity to the awkward — sagacity to the dull — and at once invest two or three hundred imperfectly educated men with feeling, intention, and information, of the freemasons of the thirteenth century? Grant that it can do all this, and that the new building is both equal to the old in beauty, and precisely correspondent to it in detail. Is it, therefore, altogether *worth* the old building? Is the stone carved to-day in their masons' yards altogether the same in value to the hearts of the French people as that which the eyes of St Louis saw lifted to its place? Would a loving daughter, in mere desire for gaudy dress, ask a jeweller for a bright facsimile of the worn cross which her mother bequeathed to her on her death-bed? — would a thoughtful nation, in mere fondness for splendour of streets, ask its architects to provide for it facsimiles of the temples which for centuries had given joy to its saints, comfort to its mourners, and strength to its chivalry?

But it may be replied, that all this is already admitted by the antiquaries of France and England; and that it is impossible that works so important should now be undertaken without due consideration and faithful superintendence.

I answer, that the men who justly feel these truths are rarely those who have much influence in public affairs. It is the poor abbé, whose little garden is sheltered by the mighty buttresses from the north wind, who knows the worth of the cathedral. It is the bustling mayor and the prosperous architect who determine its fate. . . .

It is a sad truth, that there is something in the solemn aspect of ancient architecture which, in rebuking frivolity and chastening gaiety, has become at this time literally *repulsive* to a large majority of the population of Europe. Examine the direction which is taken by all the influences of fortune and of fancy, wherever they concern themselves with art, and it will be found that the real, earnest effort of the upper classes of European society is to make every place in the world as much like the Champs Elysées of Paris as possible. Wherever the influence of that educated society is felt, the old buildings are relentlessly destroyed; vast hotels, like barracks, and rows of high, square-windowed dwelling-houses, thrust themselves forward to conceal the hated antiquities of the great cities of France and Italy. Gay promenades, with fountains and statues, prolong themselves along the quays once dedicated to commerce; ball-rooms and theatres rise upon the dust of desecrated chapels, and thrust into darkness the humility of domestic life. And when the formal street, in all its pride of perfumery and confectionary, has successfully consumed its way through the wrecks of historical monuments, and consummated its symmetry in the ruin of all that once prompted to reflection, or pleaded for regard, the whitened city is praised for its splendour, and the exulting inhabitants for their patriotism — patriotism which consists in insulting their fathers with forgetfulness, and surrounding their children with temptation. . . .

Must this little Europe — this corner of our globe, gilded with the blood of old battles, and grey with the temples of old pieties — this narrow piece of the world's pavement, worn down by so many pilgrims' feet, be utterly swept and garnished for the masque of the Future? Is America not wide enough for the elasticities of our humanity? Asia not rich enough for its pride? or among the quiet meadow-lands and solitary hills of the old land, is there not yet room enough for the spreadings of power, or the indulgences of magnificence, without founding all glory upon ruin, and prefacing all progress with obliteration?

We must answer these questions speedily, or we answer them in vain. The peculiar character of the evil which is being wrought by this age is its utter irreparableness. Its newly formed schools of art, its extending galleries, and well-ordered museums will assuredly bear some fruit in time, and give once more to the popular mind the power to discern what is great, and the disposition to protect what is precious. But it will be too late. We shall wander through our palaces of crystal, gazing sadly on copies of pictures torn by cannon-shot, and on casts of sculpture dashed to pieces long ago. We shall gradually learn to distinguish originality and sincerity from the decrepitudes of imitation and palsies of repetition; but it will be only in hopelessness to recognise the truth, that architecture and painting can be 'restored' when the dead can be raised. — and not till then.

The Nature of Gothic

William Morris (q.v.) reprinted this chapter from vol. 2 of 'The Stones of Venice' (1853) as the fourth Kelmscott Press book in 1892. The 'Nature of Gothic' fired Morris's enthusiasm and gave him a goal in life as a student at Oxford. He believed that the future would think of it as 'one of the very few necessary and inevitable utterances of the century'. In 'The Stones of Venice' Ruskin is concerned not purely with architecture as such but with the larger moral and ethical issues involved. To Ruskin, art was not merely external form or technique but a response to deeper motivations in human sensibility and social convictions and aspirations. The humour and ingenuousness of Gothic art represented to Ruskin a sign of healthy vitality compared to the cold solemnity of Renaissance art. Despite the fact that he read into the architectural decoration expressions of Protestantism, Heathenism and Papistry, the staggering intensity of his description of detail down to the minutest parts of capitals and cornices has in itself a strangely poetic quality.

M 3

§ 12. And observe, you are put to stern choice in this matter. You must either make a tool of the creature, or a man of him. You cannot make both. Men were not intended to work with the accuracy of tools, to be precise and perfect in all their actions. If you will have that precision out of them, and make their fingers measure degrees like cog-wheels, and their arms strike curves like compasses, you must unhumanize them. All the energy of their spirits must be given to make cogs and compasses of themselves. All their attention and strength must go to the accomplishment of the mean act. The eye of the soul must be bent upon the finger-point, and the soul's force must fill all the invisible nerves that guide it, ten hours a day, that it may not err from its steely precision, and so soul and sight be worn away, and the whole human being be lost at last — a heap of sawdust, so far as its intellectual work in this world is concerned: saved only by its Heart, which cannot go into the form of cogs and compasses, but expands, after the ten hours are over, into fireside humanity. On the other hand, if you will make a man of the working creature, you cannot make a tool. Let him but begin to imagine, to think, to try to do anything worth doing; and the engine-turned precision is lost at once. Out come all his roughness, all his dulness, all his incapability; shame upon shame, failure upon failure, pause after pause: but out comes the whole majesty of him also; and we know the height of it only when we see the clouds settling upon him. And, whether the clouds be bright or dark, there will be trans-figuration behind and within them.

§ 13. And now, reader, look round this English room of yours, about which you have been proud so often, because the work of it was so good and strong, and the ornaments of it so finished. Examine again all those accurate mouldings, and perfect polishings, and unerring adjust-ments of the seasoned wood and tempered steel. Many a time you have exulted over them, and thought how great England was, because her slightest work was done so thoroughly. Alas! if read rightly, these perfectnesses are signs of a slavery in our England a thousand times more bitter and more degrading than of the scourged African, or helot Greek. Men may be beaten, chained, tormented, yoked like cattle, slaughtered like summer flies, and yet remain in one sense, and the best sense, free. But to smother their souls with them, to blight and hew into rotting pollards the suckling branches of their human intelligence, to make the flesh and skin which, after the worm's work on it, is to see God, into leathern thongs to yoke machinery with, — this is to be slave-masters indeed; and there might be more freedom in England, though her feudal lords' lightest words were worth men's lives, and though the blood of the vexed husbandman dropped in the furrows of her fields, than there is while the animation of her multitudes is sent like fuel to feed the factory smoke, and the strength of them is given daily to be wasted into the fineness of a web, or racked into the exactness of a line.

§ 14. And, on the other hand, go forth again to gaze upon the old cathedral front, where you have smiled so often at the fantastic ignorance of the old sculptors: examine once more those ugly goblins, and formless monsters, and stern statues, anatomiless and rigid; but do not mock at them, for they are signs of the life and liberty of every workman who struck the stone; a freedom of thought, and rank in scale of being, such as no laws, no charters, no charities can secure; but which it must be the first aim of all Europe at this day to regain for her children.

§ 15. Let me not be thought to speak wildly or extravagantly. It is verily this degradation of the operative into a machine, which, more than any other evil of the times, is leading the mass of the nations everywhere into vain, incoherent, destructive struggling for a freedom of which they cannot explain the nature to themselves. Their universal outcry against wealth, and against nobility, is not forced from them either by the pressure of famine, or the sting of mortified pride. These do much, and have done much in all ages; but the foundations of society were never yet shaken as they are at this day. It is not that men are ill fed, but that they have no pleasure in the work by which they make their bread, and therefore look to wealth as the only means of pleasure. It is not that men are pained by the scorn of the upper classes, but they cannot endure their own; for they feel that the kind of labour to which they are condemned is verily a degrading one, and makes them less than men. Never had the upper classes so much sympathy with the lower, or charity for them, as they have at this day, and yet never were they so much hated by them: for, of old, the separation between the noble and the poor was merely a wall built by law; now it is a veritable difference in level of standing, a precipice between upper and lower grounds in the field of humanity, and there is pestilential air at the bottom of it. I know not if a day is ever to come when the nature of right freedom will be understood, and when men will see that to obey another man, to labour for him, yield reverence to him or to his place, is not slavery. It is often the often the best kind of liberty, — liberty from care. The man who says to one, Go, and he goeth, and to another, Come, and he cometh, has, in most cases, more sense of restraint and difficulty than the man who obeys him. The movements of the one are hindered by the burden on his shoulder; of the other by the bridle on his lips: there is no way by which the burden may be lightened; but we need not suffer from the bridle if we do not champ at it. To yield reverence to another, to hold ourselves and our lives at his disposal, is not slavery; often it is the noblest state in which a man can live in this world. There is, indeed, a reverence which is servile, that is to say, irrational or selfish: but there is also noble reverence, that is to say, reasonable and loving; and a man is never so noble as when he is reverent in this kind; nay, even if the feeling pass the bounds of mere reason, so that it be loving, a man is raised by it. Which had, in reality, most of the serf nature in him, — the Irish peasant who was lying in wait yesterday for his landlord, with his musket muzzle thrust through the ragged hedge; or that old mountain servant, who 200 years ago, at Inverkeithing, gave up his own life and the lives of his seven sons for his chief? — as each fell, calling forth his brother to the death, 'Another for Hector!' And therefore, in all ages and in all countries, reverence has been paid and sacrifice made by men to each other, not only without complaint, but rejoicingly; and famine, and peril, and sword, and all evil, and all shame, have been borne willingly in the causes of masters and kings; for all these gifts of the heart ennobled the men who gave, not less than the men who received them, and nature prompted, and God rewarded the sacrifice. But to feel their souls withering within them, unthanked, to find their whole being sunk into an unrecognized abyss, to be counted off into a heap of mechanism numbered with its wheels, and weighed with its hammer strokes — this, nature bade not, — this, God blesses not, — this, humanity for no long time is able to endure.

§ 16. We have much studied and much perfected, of late, the great civilized invention of the division of labour; only we give it a false name. It is not, truly speaking, the labour that is divided; but the men: — Divided into mere segments of men — broken into small fragments and crumbs of life; so that all the little piece of intelligence that is left in a man is not enough to make a pin, or a nail, but exhausts itself in making the point of a pin or the head of a nail. Now it is a good and desirable thing, truly, to make many pins in a day; but if we could only see with what crystal sand their points were polished, — sand of human soul, much to be magnified before it can be discerned for what it is — we should think there might be some loss in it also. And the great cry that rises from all our manufacturing cities, louder than their furnace blast, is all in very deed for this, — that we manufacture everything there except men; we blanch cotton, and strengthen steel, and refine sugar, and shape pottery; but to brighten, to strengthen, to refine, or to form a single living spirit, never enters into our estimate of advantages. And all the evil to which that cry is urging our myriads can be met only in one way: not by teaching nor preaching, for to teach them is but to show them their misery, and to preach to them, if we do nothing more than preach, is to mock at it, It can be met only by a right understanding, on the part of all classes, of what kinds of labour are good for men, raising them, and making them happy; by a determined sacrifice of such convenience, or beauty, or cheapness as is to be got only by the degradation of the workman; and by equally determined demand for the products and results of healthy and ennobling labour.

§ 17. And how, it will be asked, are these products to be recognized, and this demand to be regulated? Easily: by the observance of three broad and simple rules:

1. Never encourage the manufacture of any article not absolutely necessary, in the production of which *Invention* has no share.

2. Never demand an exact finish for its own sake, but only for some practical or noble end.

3. Never encourage imitation or copying of any kind, except for the sake of preserving records of great works.

Modern Manufacture and Design

An extract from 'The Two Paths' (1859), 'being lectures on art and its application to decoration and manufacture' given in Edinburgh. Students were warned that they had to choose between two paths, one leading to the Mount of Olives, and the other to the Dead Sea. Ruskin believed there were too many designers and too many design industries, though these lectures were intended 'for the advancement of taste in special branches of manufacture'. In the preface to the first edition he writes of his intention to demonstrate that all 'noble design' must depend in the first place 'on the sculpture or painting of organic form. . . . This is the vital law.' He was doubtful that design could be taught to anyone who was interested: 'all the lecturings and teachings and prizes, and principles of art, in the world, are of no use so long as you don't surround your men with happy influences and beautiful things'. Anticipating a catechism of twentieth-century design, one of Ruskin's cardinal laws was that an artist or designer must know and respect the nature of his materials. This is the subject of the second extract from 'The Two Paths': 'The Work of Iron'.

M 4

And observe in the outset, it is not so much what the present circumstances of England are, as what we wish to make them, that we have to consider. If you will tell me what you ultimately intend Bradford to be, perhaps I can tell you what Bradford can ultimately produce. But you must have your minds clearly made up, and be distinct in telling me what you do want. At present I don't know what you are aiming at, and possibly on consideration you may feel some doubt whether you know yourselves. As matters stand, all over England, as soon as one mill is at work, occupying two hundred hands, we try, by means of it, to set another mill at work, occupying four hundred. That is all simple and comprehensible enough — but what is it to come to? How many mills do we want? or do we indeed want no end of mills? Let us entirely understand each other on this point before we go any farther. Last week, I drove from Rochdale to Bolton Abbey; quietly, in order to see the country, and certainly it was well worth while. I never went over a more interesting twenty miles than those between Rochdale and Burnley. Naturally, the valley has been one of the most beautiful in the Lancashire hills; one of the far away solitudes, full of old shepherd ways of life. At this time there are not — I speak deliberately, and I believe quite literally — there are not, I think, more than a thousand yards of road to be traversed anywhere, without passing a furnace or mill.

Now, is that the kind of thing you want to come to everywhere? Because, if it be, and you tell me so distinctly, I think I can make several suggestions to-night, and could make more if you give me time, which would materially advance your object. The extent of our operations at present is more or less limited by the extent of coal and ironstone, but we have not yet learned to make proper use of our clay. Over the greater part of England, south of the manufacturing districts, there are magnificent beds of various kinds of useful clay; and I believe that it would not be difficult to point out modes of employing it which might enable us to turn nearly the whole of the south of England into a brick-field, as we have already turned nearly the whole of the north into a coal-pit. I say 'nearly' the whole, because, as you are doubtless aware, there are considerable districts in the south composed of chalk, renowned up to the present time for their downs and mutton. But, I think, by examining carefully into the conceivable uses of chalk, we might discover a quite feasible probability of turning all the chalk districts into a limekiln, as we turn the clay districts into a brickfield. There would then remain nothing but the mountain districts to be dealt with; but, as we have not yet ascertained all the uses of clay and chalk, still less have we ascertained those of stone; and I think, by draining the useless inlets of the Cumberland, Welsh, and Scotch lakes, and turning them, with their rivers, into navigable reservoirs and canals, there would be no difficulty in working the whole of our mountain districts as a gigantic quarry of slate and granite, from which all the rest of the world might be supplied with roofing and building stone.

Is this, then, what you want? You are going straight at it at present; and I have only to ask under what limitations I am to conceive or describe your final success? Or shall there be no limitations? There are none to your powers; every day puts new machinery at your disposal, and increases, with your capital, the vastness of your undertakings. The changes in the state of this country are now so rapid that it would be wholly absurd to endeavour to lay down laws of art education for it under its present aspect and circumstances; and therefore I must necessarily ask, how much of it do you seriously intend within the next fifty years to be coal-pit, brickfield, or quarry? For the sake of distinctness of conclusion, I will suppose your success absolute: that from shore to shore the whole of the island is to be set as thick with chimneys as the masts stand in the docks of Liverpool; that there shall be no meadows in it; no trees; no gardens; only a little corn grown upon the house tops, reaped and threshed by steam: that you do not leave even room for roads, but travel either over the roofs of your mills, on viaducts; or under their floors, in tunnels: that, the smoke having rendered the light of the sun unserviceable, you work always by the light of your own gas: that no acre of English ground shall be without its shaft and its engine; and therefore, no spot of English ground left on which it shall be possible to stand without a definite and calculable chance of being blown off it, at any moment, into small pieces.

Under these circumstances (if this is to be the future of England), no designing or any other development of beautiful art will be possible. Do not vex your minds nor waste your money with any thought or effort in the matter. Beautiful art can only be produced by people who have beautiful things about them, and leisure to look at them; and unless you provide some elements of beauty for your workmen to be surrounded by, you will find that no elements of beauty can be invented by them.

The Work of Iron

M 5

The reason of this second law is, that if you don't want the qualities of the substance you use, you ought to use some other substance: it can only be affectation, and desire to display your skill, that lead you to employ a refractory substance, and therefore your art will all be base. Glass, for instance, is eminently, in its nature, transparent. If you don't want transparency, let the glass alone. Do not try to make a window look like an opaque picture, but take an opaque ground to begin with. Again, marble is eminently a solid and massive substance. Unless you want mass and solidity, don't work in marble. If you wish for lightness, take wood; if for freedom, take stucco; if for ductility, take glass. Don't try to carve feathers, or trees, or nets, or foam, out of marble. Carve white limbs and broad breasts only out of that.

So again iron is eminently a ductile and tenacious substance — tenacious above all things, ductile more than most. When you want tenacity, therefore, and involved form, take iron. It is eminently made for that. It is the material given to the sculptor as the companion of marble, with a message, as plain as it can well be spoken, from the lips of the earth-mother: 'Here's for you to cut, and here's for you to hammer. Shape this and twist that. What is solid and simple, carve out; what is thin and entangled, beat out. I give you all kinds of forms to be delighted in — fluttering leaves as well as fair bodies; twisted branches as well as open brows. The leaf and the branch you may beat and drag into their imagery: the body and brow you shall reverently touch into their imagery. And if you choose rightly and work rightly, what you do shall be safe afterwards. Your slender leaves shall not break off in my tenacious iron, though they may be rusted a little with an iron autumn. Your broad surfaces shall not be un-smoothed in my pure crystalline marble — no decay shall touch them. But if you carve in the marble what will break with a touch, or mould in the metal what a stain of rust or verdigris will spoil, it is your fault — not mine.'

These are the main principles in this matter; which, like nearly all other right principles in art, we moderns delight in contradicting as directly and specially as may be. We continually look for, and praise, in our exhibitions, the sculpture of veils, and lace, and thin leaves, and all kinds of impossible things pushed as far as possible in the fragile stone, for the sake of showing the sculptor's dexterity. On the other hand, we *cast* our iron into bars — brittle, though an inch thick — sharpen them at the ends, and consider fences, and other work, made of such materials, decorative! I do not believe it would be easy to calculate the amount of mischief done to our taste in England by that fence iron-work of ours alone. If it were asked of us, by a single characteristic, to distinguish the dwellings of a country into two broad sections; and to set, on one side, the places where people were, for the most part, simple, happy, benevolent, and honest; and, on the other side, the places where at least a great number of the people were sophisticated, unkind, uncomfortable, and unprincipled, there is, I think, one feature that you could fix upon as a positive test; the uncomfortable and unprincipled parts of a country would be the parts where people lived among iron railings and the comfortable and principled parts where they had none. A broad generalisation, you will say! Perhaps a little too broad; yet, in all sobriety, it will come truer than you think. Consider every other kind of fence or defence, and you will find some virtue in it; but in the iron railing none.

Section N

William Morris

William Morris

In these times of growing fears of technological suicide, William Morris (1834-96) has a particular relevance for all of us. From amidst the physical and moral debris of the Industrial Revolution, his voice was raised in a ceaseless invective against the mindless violation of human and natural resources in the name of progress: the desecration of the landscape, the degradation of the cities, the debasement of art. Sometimes, in moods of despondency, Morris found society so hopelessly irretrievable that he longed for its decimation by a wave of barbarism so that it might start again fresh and beautiful.

But Morris's Utopia was not a return to the past. It was an attempt to restore earlier virtues, the simple life, art in harmony with life, pleasure in work, those things eaten away by an industrial Moloch. And here the machine was cast in a beneficent role. In an environment of rapid and disconcerting change, he calls his 'News from Nowhere' 'an epoch of rest', a 'utopian romance', where unexpectedly idleness was thought of as a queer disease, and history the concern of people only when times were bad and anxiety about life prevalent. This dream of a new Golden Age, 'Nowwhere', was the antipode of nineteenth century Britain. And in its warm, soporific atmosphere — too sweet perhaps for our own tastes — social values are reversed. Pleasure came in giving, not taking; work was pleasure; art was not a matter of genius but an inalienable part of life; everyman was an artist. To Morris, as to Ruskin, the cause of art was the cause of the people. Through craftsmanship came the liberation of the soul.

The irony of it all is that designers in this century, followers of Morris, disciples almost, with a subtle change of emphasis, placed faith in their ability to control the machine — not just to make labour more pleasurable but to find in its products an intrinsic beauty. But Morris too, having earlier denounced the machine as totally evil, later changed his mind. He accepted it as an instrument for mitigating the conditions of life. Men were to be masters of their machines, to save their toil for more useful and rewarding labour.

N 1

Ford Madox Brown, 'Work'.

Not very often does a painter comment on his pictures in as lengthy and detailed a way as does Ford Madox Brown, writing about this allegorical canvas, 'Work'. The crowded picture is crammed with meaning. It carries an elaborate moral message, and it is therefore not surprising that its author should want to make certain his representations and symbols were perfectly understood.

The painting means what it says. Work. But not work as the scourge of industrial society, but work as a chastening and an uplifting thing. The central figure, posed à l'antique, is the hero of the piece. He is the British navvy whose 'manly health and beauty' Madox Brown worships. The navvy of 'strong animal nature', 'who does his work and loves his beer' — who was taught the value of useful work, who knows the dignity of labour. This paragon of the labouring classes is juxtaposed with the ragged wretch on the left, an amiable idler, never taught to work, who lives restless and despairing in the forlorn hope of selling a few paltry flowers.

The two men on the right, apparently idle, but designated 'brain-workers' by the artist, sages whose impact on men's minds bring greater happiness, turn out to be Thomas Carlyle and Frederick Denison Maurice, the radical Broad Church divine and founder of the Working Men's College where Madox Brown himself taught. Carlyle's 'Past and Present' may well have stimulated Madox Brown's interest in painting a picture of this kind.

Sleeping on the verge of Hampstead's Heath Street are unemployed but stoic labourers. At the left behind the flower seller are the idle rich of Hampstead and a pastry cook with his tray, the artist's symbol for superfluity. The picture thus carries all representative types from all

Ford Madox Brown, 'Work', begun 1852. This version S. & D., 1852-65, 53 × 77 inches (Manchester City Art Gallery).

classes and social persuasions. The do-gooding rich woman dropping her tract to the navvy in the pit. 'Drink for Thirsty Souls' it says. The hump-backed beer seller, complete with black eye, becomes a story of struggle and fortitude. One of the posters on the wall at the extreme left advertises 'The Working Men's College, Great Ormond Street', and in another, Madox Brown ridicules the 'Flamstead Institute of Arts' where Professor Snoöx holds forth. Even the minute figures behind Maurice's head represent another episode in this didactic canvas: a British policeman manhandling a poor girl, an orange seller, for resting her basket on a gate-post.

To reveal such stark 'truths' in all their painful details, Madox Brown deliberately sets the scene in the severity of a hot July sunlight. The whole is a relentless genuflection to the dignity of labour and apotheosis of the working class. (The full description is in Ford Madox Hueffer, 'Ford Madox Brown: A Record of His Life and Work' (London 1896).)

A Dream of Ease.

"Chair Comfort," Catalogue C 7, Sent Free.

Convenience, comfort, and luxury are combined to a marked degree.
For Readers, Literary Workers, Students, and Invalids it is unique.

Simply press a small knob and the Back will decline to any position from upright to flat, or rise automatically. The Arms lift up and extend outwards, forming side-tables for books, papers, writing materials, &c.

'A dream of ease'

On the Lack of Incentive to Labour in a Communist Society

'News from Nowhere' (1891), translated into several languages, was widely read abroad. It was very likely influenced by Edward Bellamy's 'Looking Backward' (1888). But unlike 'Nowhere', the American Utopia rested on the exploitation of the machine and the construction of large cities for the social good cast in a matrix of science fiction. Morris took issue with Bellamy for not seeing that incentive to work could be other than fear of starvation — could be simply pleasure in work. The text given here is from chapter xv, 'On the Lack of Incentive to Labour in a Communist Society'.

N 3

'Now, this is what I want to ask you about — to wit, how you get people to work when there is no reward of labour, and especially how you get them to work strenuously?'

'No reward of labour?' said Hammond, gravely. 'The reward of labour is *life*. Is that not enough?'

'But no reward for especially good work,' quoth I.

'Plenty of reward,' said he — 'the reward of creation. The wages which God gets, as people might have said time agone. If you are going to ask to be paid for the pleasure of creation, which is what excellence in work means, the next thing we shall hear of will be a bill sent in for the begetting of children.'

'Well, but,' said I, 'the man of the nineteenth century would say there is a natural desire towards the procreation of children, and a natural desire not to work.'

'Yes, yes,' said he, 'I know the ancient platitude, — wholly untrue; indeed, to us quite meaningless. Fourier, whom all men laughed at, understood the matter better.'

'Why is it meaningless to you?' said I.

He said: 'Because it implies that all work is suffering, and we are so far from thinking that, that, as you may have noticed, whereas we are not short of wealth, there is a kind of fear growing up amongst us that we shall one day be short of work. It is a pleasure which we are afraid of losing, not a pain.'

'Yes,' said I, 'I have noticed that, and I was going to ask you about that also. But in the meantime, what do you positively mean to assert about the pleasurableness of work amongst you?'

'This, that *all* work is now pleasurable; either because of the hope of gain in honour and wealth with which the work is done, which causes pleasurable excitement, even when the actual work is not pleasant; or else because it has grown into a pleasurable *habit*, as in the case with what you may call mechanical work; and lastly (and most of our work is of this kind) because there is conscious sensuous pleasure in the work itself; it is done, that is, by artists. . . .

'The wares which we make are made because they are needed: men make for their neighbours' use as if they are making for themselves, not for a vague market of which they know nothing, and over which they have no control: as there is no buying and selling, it would be mere insanity to make goods on the chance of their being wanted; for there is no longer any one who can be *compelled* to buy them. So that whatever is made is good, and thoroughly fit for its purpose. Nothing *can* be made except for genuine use; therefore no inferior goods are made. Moreover, as aforesaid, we have now found out what we want, so we make no more than we want; and as we are not driven to make a vast quantity of useless things, we have time and resources enough to consider our pleasure in making them. All work which would be irksome to do by hand is done by immensely improved machinery; and in all work which it is a pleasure to do by hand machinery is done without. There is no difficulty in finding work which suits the special turn of mind of everybody; so that no man is sacrificed to the wants of another. From time to time, when we have found that some piece of work was too disagreeable or troublesome, we have given it up and done altogether without the thing produced by it.'

The Prospects of Architecture in Civilisation

This was first published in 'Hopes and Fears for Art', five lectures delivered in London, Birmingham and Nottingham, 1878-81.

No one of you can fail to know what neglect of art has done to this great treasure of mankind: the earth which was beautiful before man lived on it, which for many ages grew in beauty as men grew in numbers and power, is now growing uglier day by day, and there the swiftest where civilisation is the mightiest: this is quite certain; no one can deny it: are you contented that it should be so?

Surely there must be few of us to whom this degrading change has not been brought home personally. I think you will most of you understand me but too well when I ask you to remember the pang of dismay that comes on us when we revisit some spot of country which has been specially sympathetic to us in times past; which has refreshed us after toil, or soothed us after trouble; but where now as we turn the corner of the road or crown the hill's brow we can see first the inevitable blue slate roof, and then the blotched mud-coloured stucco, or ill-built wall of ill-made bricks of the new buildings; then as we come nearer, and see the arid and pretentious little gardens, and cast-iron horrors of railings, and miseries of squalid outhouses breaking through the sweet meadows and abundant hedge-rows of our old quiet hamlet, do not our hearts sink within us, and are we not troubled with a perplexity not altogether selfish, when we think what a little bit of carelessness it takes to destroy a world of pleasure and delight, which now whatever happens can never be recovered?...

You cannot be contented with it; all you can do is to try to forget it, and to say that such things are the necessary and inevitable consequences of civilisation. Is it so indeed? The loss of suchlike beauty is an undoubted evil: but civilisation cannot mean at heart to produce evils for mankind: such losses therefore must be accidents of civilisation, produced by its carelessness, not its malice: and we, if we be men and not machines, must try to amend them: or civilisation itself will be undone.

Now if the public knew anything of art, that is excellence in things made by man, they would not abide the shams of it; and if the real thing were not to be had, they would learn to do without, nor think their gentility injured by the forbearance.

Simplicity of life, even the barest, is not misery, but the very foundation of refinement: a sanded floor and whitewashed walls, and the green trees, and flowery meads, and living waters outside; or a grimy palace amid the smoke with a regiment of housemaids always working to smear the dirt together so that it may be unnoticed; which, think you, is the most refined, the most fit for a gentleman of those two dwellings?

So I say, if you cannot learn to love real art; at least learn to hate sham art and reject it. It is not so much because the wretched thing is so ugly and silly and useless that I ask you to cast it from you; it is much more because these are but the outward symbols of the poison that lies within them: look through them and see all that has gone to their fashioning, and you will see how vain labour, and sorrow, and disgrace have been their companions from the first, — and all this for trifles that nc man really needs!

Learn to do without; there is virtue in those words; a force that rightly used would choke both demand and supply of Mechanical Toil: would make it stick to its last: the making of machines.

And then from simplicity of life would rise up the longing for beauty, which cannot yet be dead in men's souls, and we know that nothing can satisfy that demand but Intelligent work rising gradually into Imaginative work; which will turn all 'operatives' into workmen, into artists, into men.

Now, I have been trying to show you how the hurry of Modern

Civilisation accompanied by the tyrannous organisation of labour which was a necessity to the full development of Competitive Commerce, has taken from the people at large, gentle and simple, the eyes to discern and the hands to fashion that popular art which was once the chief solace and joy of the world: I have asked you to think of that as no light matter but a grievous mishap: I have prayed you to strive to remedy this evil: first by guarding jealously what is left, and by trying earnestly to win back what is lost of the Fairness of the Earth; and next by rejecting luxury, that you may embrace art, if you can, or if indeed you in your short lives cannot learn what art means, that you may at least live a simple life fit for men.

The Vulgarisation of Oxford

Letter to the 'Daily News', 20 November 1885

Sir,

I have just read your too true article on the vulgarisation of Oxford, and I wish to ask if it is too late to appeal to the mercy of the 'dons' to spare the few specimens of ancient town architecture which they have not yet had time to destroy, such, for example, as the little plaster houses in front of Trinity College or the beautiful houses left on the north side of Holywell Street. These are in their way as important as the more majestic buildings to which all the world makes pilgrimage. Oxford thirty years ago, when I first knew it, was full of these treasures; but Oxford 'culture', cynically contemptuous of the knowledge which it does not know, and steeped to the lips in the commercialism of the day, has made a clean sweep of most of them; but those that are left are of infinite value, and still give some character above that of Victoria Street or Bayswater to modern Oxford. Is it impossible, Sir, to make the authorities of Oxford, town and gown, see this, and stop the destruction? The present theory of the use to which Oxford should be put appears to be that it should be used as a huge upper public school for fitting lads of the upper and middle class for their laborious future of living on other people's labour. For my part I do not think this a lofty conception of the function of a University; but if it be the only admissible one nowadays, it is at least clear that it does not need the history and art of our forefathers which Oxford still holds to develop it. London, Manchester, Birmingham, or perhaps a rising city of Australia would be a fitter place for the experiment, which it seems to me is too rough a one for Oxford. In sober truth, what speciality has Oxford if it is not the genius loci which our modern commercial dons are doing their best to destroy? One word on the subject of Dr Hornby and Eton. Is there no appeal against a brutality of which I dare not trust myself to write further? Is it impossible that the opinions of distinguished men of all kinds might move him? Surely a memorial might be got up which would express those opinions.

The Old Alhambra in the 1890s.

Art under Plutocracy

A lecture delivered at Oxford with John Ruskin in the Chair, 14 November 1883; published in 'Architecture, Industry and Wealth' (1902).

Yet civilisation, it seems to me, owes us some compensation for the loss of this romance, which now only hangs like a dream about the country life of busy lands. To keep the air pure and the rivers clean, to take some pains to keep the meadows and tillage as pleasant as reasonable use will allow them to be; to allow peaceable citizens freedom to wander where they will, so they do no hurt to garden or cornfield; nay, even to leave here and there some piece of waste or mountain sacredly free from fence or tillage as a memory of man's ruder struggles with nature in his earlier days: is it too much to ask civilisation to be so far thoughtful of man's pleasure and rest, and to help so far as this her children to whom she has most often set such heavy tasks of grinding labour? Surely not an unreasonable asking. But not a whit of it shall we get under the present system of society. That loss of the instinct for beauty which has involved us in the loss of popular art is also busy in depriving us of the only compensation possible for that loss, by surely and not slowly destroying the beauty of the very face of the earth. Not only are London and our other great commercial cities mere masses of sordidness, filth, and squalor, embroidered with patches of pompous and vulgar hideousness, no less revolting to the eye and the mind when one knows what it means: not only have whole counties of England, and the heavens that hang over them, disappeared beneath a crust of unutterable grime, but the disease, which, to a visitor coming from the times of art, reason, and order, would seem to be a love of dirt and ugliness for its own sake, spreads all over the country, and every little market town seizes the opportunity to imitate, as far as it can, the majesty of the hell of London and Manchester. Need I speak to you of the wretched suburbs that sprawl all round our fairest and most ancient cities? Must I speak to you of the degradation that has so speedily befallen this city, still the most beautiful of them all; a city which, with its surroundings, would, if we had had a grain of common sense, have been treated like a most precious jewel, whose beauty was to be preserved at any cost? I say at any cost, for it was a possession which did not belong to us, but which we were trustees of for all posterity. I am old enough to know how we have treated that jewel; as if it were any common stone kicking about on the highway, good enough to throw at a dog. When I remember the contrast between the Oxford of to-day and the Oxford which I first saw thirty years ago, I wonder I can face the misery (there is no other word for it) of visiting it, even to have the honour of addressing you to-night. But furthermore, not only are the cities a disgrace to us, and the smaller towns a laughing-stock; not only are the dwellings of man grown inexpressibly base and ugly, but the very cowsheds and cart-stables, nay, the merest piece of necessary farm engineering, are tarred with the same brush. Even if a tree is cut down or blown down, a worse one, if any, is planted in its stead, and, in short, our civilisation is passing like a blight, daily growing heavier and more poisonous, over the whole face of the country, so that every change is sure to be a change for the worse in its outward aspect. So then it comes to this, that not only are the minds of great artists narrowed and their sympathies frozen by their isolation, not only has co-operative art come to a standstill, but the very food on which both the greater and the lesser art subsists is being destroyed; the well of art is poisoned at its spring. . . .

Something must be wrong then in art, or the happiness of life is sickening in the house of civilisation. What has caused the sickness? Machine-labour will you say? Well, I have seen quoted a passage from one of the ancient Sicilian poets rejoicing in the fashioning of a water-mill, and exulting in labour being set free from the toil of the handquern in consequence; and that surely would be a type of a man's natural hope when foreseeing the invention of labour-saving machinery as 'tis called; natural surely, since though I have said that the labour of which art can form a part should be accompanied by pleasure, no one could deny that there is some necessary labour even which is not pleasant in itself, and plenty of unnecessary labour which is merely painful. If machinery had been used for minimising such labour, the utmost ingenuity would scarcely have been wasted on it; but is that the case in any way? Look round the world, and you must agree with John Stuart Mill in his doubt whether all the machinery of modern times has lightened the daily work of one labourer. And why have our natural hopes been so disappointed? Surely because in these latter days, in which as a matter of fact machinery has been invented, it was by no means invented with the aim of saving the pain of labour. The phrase labour-saving machinery is elliptical, and means machinery which saves the cost of labour, not the labour itself, which will be expended when saved on tending other machines. For a doctrine which, as I have said, began to be accepted under the workshop system, is now universally received, even though we are yet short of the complete development of the system of the Factory. Briefly, the doctrine is this, that the essential aim of manufacture is making a profit; that it is frivolous to consider whether the wares when made will be of more or less use to the world so long as any one can be found to buy them at a price which, when the workman engaged in making them has received of necessaries and comforts as little as he can be got to take, will leave something over as a reward to the capitalist who has employed him. This doctrine of the sole aim of manufacture (or indeed of life) being the profit of the capitalist and the occupation of the workman, is held, I say, by almost every one; its corollary is, that labour is necessarily unlimited, and that to attempt to limit it is not so much foolish as wicked, whatever misery may be caused to the community by the manufacture and sale of the wares made.

It is this superstition of commerce being an end in itself, of man made for commerce, not commerce for man, of which art has sickened; not of the accidental appliances which that superstition when put in practice has brought to its aid; machines and railways and the like, which do now verily control us all, might have been controlled by us, if we had not been resolute to seek profit and occupation at the cost of establishing for a time that corrupt and degrading anarchy which has usurped the name of Society. It is my business here to-night and everywhere to foster your discontent with that anarchy and its visible results; for indeed I think it would be an insult to you to suppose that you are contented with the state of things as they are; contented to see all beauty vanish from our beautiful city, for instance; contented with the squalor of the black country, with the hideousness of London, the wen of all wens, as Cobbett called it; contented with the ugliness and baseness which everywhere surround the life of civilised man; contented, lastly, to be living above that unutterable and sickening misery of which a few details are once again reaching us as if from some distant unhappy country, of which we could scarcely expect to hear, but which I tell you is the necessary foundation on which our society, our anarchy rests.

The Revival of Handicraft

Is the change from handicraft to machinery good or bad? And the answer to that question is to my mind that, as my friend Belfort Bax has put it, statically it is bad, dynamically it is good. As a condition of life, production by machinery is altogether an evil; as an instrument for forcing on us better conditions of life it has been, and for some time yet will be, indispensable.

Having thus tried to clear myself of mere reactionary pessimism, let me attempt to show why statically handicraft is to my mind desirable, and its destruction a degradation of life. Well, first I shall not shrink from saying bluntly that production by machinery necessarily results in utilitarian ugliness in everything which the labour of man deals with, and that this is a serious evil and a degradation of human life. So clearly is this the fact that though few people will venture to deny the latter part of the proposition, yet in their hearts the greater part of cultivated civilised persons do not regard it as an evil, because their degradation has already gone so far that they cannot, in what concerns the sense of seeing, discriminate between beauty and ugliness: their languid assent to the desirableness of beauty is with them only a convention, a superstitious survival from the times when beauty was a necessity to all men. The first part of the proposition (that machine industry produces ugliness) I cannot argue with these persons, because they neither know, nor care for, the difference between beauty and ugliness; and with those who do understand what beauty means I need not argue it, as they are but too familiar with the fact that the produce of all modern industrialism is ugly, and that whenever anything which is old disappears, its place is taken by something inferior to it in beauty; and that even out in the very fields and open country. The art of making beautifully all kinds of ordinary things, carts, gates, fences, boats, bowls, and so forth, let alone houses and public buildings, unconsciously and without effort has gone; when anything has to be renewed among these simple things the only question asked is how little it can be done for, so as to tide us over our responsibility and shift its mending on to the next generation.

From 'Fortnightly Review', November 1888.

The Lesser Arts of Life

From a lecture given in support of a society for the protection of ancient buildings, 1878.

Extravagances of fashion have not been lacking to us, but no one has been compelled to adopt them; every one might dress herself in the way which her own good sense told her suited her best. Now this, ladies, is the first and greatest necessity of rational and beautiful costume, that you should keep your liberty of choice; so I beg you to battle stoutly for it, or we shall all tumble into exploded follies again. Then next, your only chance of keeping that liberty is, to resist the imposition on costume of unnatural monstrosities. Garments should veil the human form, and neither caricature it, nor obliterate its lines: the body should be draped, and neither sown up in a sack, nor stuck in the middle of a box: drapery, properly managed, is not a dead thing, but a living one, expressive of the endless beauty of motion; and if this be lost, half the pleasure of the eyes in common life is lost. You must specially bear this in mind, because the fashionable milliner has chiefly one end in view, how to hide and degrade the human body in the most expensive manner. She or he would see no beauty in the Venus of Milo; she or he looks upon you as scaffolds on which to hang a bundle of cheap rags, which can be sold dear under the name of a dress. Now, ladies, if you do not resist this to the bitter end, costume is ruined again, and all we males are rendered inexpressibly unhappy. So I beg of you fervently, do not allow yourselves to be upholstered like armchairs, but drape yourselves like women. Lastly, and this is really part of the same counsel, resist change for the sake of change; this is the very bane of all the arts. I say resist this stupidity, and the care of dress, duly subordinated to other duties, is a serious duty to you; but if you do not resist it, the care of dress becomes a frivolous waste of time. It follows, from the admission of this advice, that you should insist on having materials for your dresses that are excellent of their kind, and beautiful of their kind, and that when you have a dress of even moderately costly materials you won't be in a hurry to see the end of it. This is a thing too which will help us weavers, body and soul, and in a due and natural way: not like the too good-natured way of my Lady Bective, who wants you to wear stiff alpaca, so that the Bradford capitalists may not have to change their machinery. I can't agree to that; if they will weave ugly cloth let them take the consequences.

But one good thing breeds another; and most assuredly a steadiness in fashion, when a good fashion has been attained, and a love of beautiful things for their own sakes and not because they are novelties, is both human, reasonable, and civilised, and will help the maker of wares, both master and man, and give them also time to think of beautiful things, and thus to raise their lives to a higher level.

Photo-journalism: John Thomson (1837-1921), 'The Crawlers', from 'Street Life in London' (1877). A series of booklets made with Adolphe Smith containing texts and 36 fine Woodbury type photographs. These are among the first social documents made with the camera and published as photographs.

Art and Socialism: the Aims and Ideals of the English Socialists of Today

Extracts from a lecture delivered before the Secular Society of Leicester, 23 January 1884.

My friends, I want you to look into the relation of Art to Commerce, using the latter word to express what is generally meant by it; namely, that system of competition in the market which is indeed the only form which most people nowadays suppose that Commerce can take. Now whereas there have been times in the world's history when Art held the supremacy over Commerce; when Art was a good deal, and Commerce, as we understood the word, was a very little; so now on the contrary it will be admitted by all, I fancy, that Commerce has become of very great importance and Art of very little. I say this will be generally admitted, but different persons will hold very different opinions not only as to whether this is well or ill, but even as to what it really means when we say that Commerce has become of supreme importance and that Art has sunk into an unimportant matter.

Allow me to give you my opinion of the meaning of it: which will lead me on to ask you to consider what remedies should be applied for curing the evils that exist in the relations between Art and Commerce. Now to speak plainly it seems to me that the supremacy of Commerce (as we understand the word) is an evil, and a very serious one; and I should call it an unmixed evil but for the strange continuity of life which runs through all historical events, and by means of which the very evils of such and such a period tend to abolish themselves. For to my mind it means this: that the world of modern civilisation in its haste to gain a very inequitably divided material prosperity has entirely suppressed popular Art; or in other words that the greater part of the people have no share in Art, which as things now are must be kept in the hands of a few rich or well-to-do people, who we may fairly say need it less and not more than the laborious workers. Nor is that all the evil, nor the worst of it; for the cause of this famine of Art is that whilst people work throughout the civilised world as laboriously as ever they did, they have lost, in losing an Art which was done by and for the people, the natural solace of their labour; a solace which they once had, and always should have; the opportunity of expressing their own thoughts to their fellows by means of that very labour, by means of that daily work which nature or long custom, a second nature, does indeed require of them, but without meaning that it should be an unrewarded and repulsive burden. But, through a strange blindness and error in the civilisation of these latter days, the world's work, almost all of it, the work some share of which should have been the helpful companion of every man, has become even such a burden, which every man, if he could, would shake off. I have said that people work no less laboriously than they ever did; but I should have said that they work more laboriously. The wonderful machines which in the hands of just and foreseeing men would have been used to minimise repulsive labour and to give pleasure, or in other words added life, to the human race, have been so used on the contrary that they have driven all men into mere frantic haste and hurry, thereby destroying pleasure, that is life, on all hands: they have, instead of lightening the labour of the workman, intensified it, and thereby added more weariness yet to the burden which the poor have to carry.

Nor can it be pleaded for the system of modern civilisation that the mere material or bodily gains of it balance the loss of pleasure which it has brought upon the world; for as I hinted before those gains have been so unfairly divided that the contrast between rich and poor has been fearfully intensified, so that in all civilised countries, but most of all in England, the terrible spectacle is exhibited of two peoples living street by street and door by door, people of the same blood, the same tongue, and at least nominally living under the same laws, but yet one civilised and the other uncivilised. All this I say is the result of the system that has trampled down Art, and exalted Commerce into a sacred religion; and it would seem is ready, with the ghastly stupidity which is its principal characteristic, to mock the Roman satirist for his noble warning by taking it in inverse meaning, and now bids us all for the sake of life to destroy the reasons for living.

And now in the teeth of this stupid tyranny I put forward a claim on behalf of labour enslaved by Commerce, which I know no thinking man can deny is reasonable, but which if acted on would involve such a change as would defeat Commerce; that is, would put Association instead of Competition, Social Order instead of Individualist Anarchy. Yet I have looked at this claim by the light of history and my own conscience, and it seems to me so looked at to be a most just claim, and that resistance to it means nothing short of a denial of the hope of civilisation. This then is the claim: *It is right and necessary that all men should have work to do which shall be worth doing, and be of itself pleasant to do; and which should be done under such conditions as would make it neither over-wearisome nor over-anxious.* Turn that claim about as I may, think of it as long as I can, I cannot find that it is an exorbitant claim; yet again I say if Society would or could admit it, the face of the world would be changed; discontent and strife and dishonesty would be ended. To feel that we were doing work useful to others and pleasant to ourselves, and that such work and its due reward could not fail us! What serious harm could happen to us then? And the price to be paid for so making the world happy is Revolution: Socialism instead of Laissez faire.

How can we of the middle classes help to bring such a state of things about: a state of things as nearly as possible the reverse of the present state of things? The reverse; no less than that. For first, **THE WORK MUST BE WORTH DOING**: think what a change that would make in the world! I tell you I feel dazed at the thought of the immensity of work which is undergone for the making of useless things. It would be an instructive day's work for any one of us who is strong enough to walk through two or three of the principal streets of London on a week-day, and take accurate note of everything in the shop windows which is embarrassing or superfluous to the daily life of a serious man. Nay, the most of these things no one, serious or unserious, wants at all;

only a foolish habit makes even the lightest-minded of us suppose that he wants them, and to many people even of those who buy them are obvious encumbrances to real work, thought, and pleasure. But I beg you to think of the enormous mass of men who are occupied with this miserable trumpery, from the engineers who have had to make the machines for making them, down to the hapless clerks who sit daylong year after year in the horrible dens wherein the wholesale exchange of them is transacted, and the shopmen who, not daring to call their sould their own, retail them amidst numberless insults which they must not resent, to the idle public which doesn't want them, but buys them to be bored by them and sick to death of them. I am talking of the merely useless things; but there are other matters not merely useless, but actively destructive and poisonous, which command a good price in the market; for instance, adulterated food and drink. Vast is the number of slaves whom competitive Commerce employs in turning out infamies such as these. But quite apart from them there is an enormous mass of labour which is just merely wasted; many thousands of men and women making Nothing with terrible and inhuman toil which deadens the soul and shortens mere animal life itself.

All these are the slaves of what is called luxury, which in the modern sense of the word comprises a mass of sham wealth, the invention of competitive Commerce, and enslaves not only the poor people who are compelled to work at its production, but also the foolish and not over happy people who buy it to harass themselves with its encumbrance. Now if we are to have popular Art, or indeed Art of any kind, we must at once and for all be done with this luxury; it is the supplanter, the changeling of Art; so much so that by those who know of nothing better it has even been taken for Art, the divine solace of human labour, the romance of each day's hard practice of the difficult art of living. But I say Art cannot live beside it, nor self-respect in any class of life. Effeminacy and brutality are its companions on the right hand and the left. This first of all, we of the well-to-do classes must get rid of if we are serious in desiring the new birth of Art: and if not, then corruption is digging a terrible pit of perdition for society, from which indeed the new birth may come, but surely from amidst of terror, violence, and misery. Indeed if it were but ridding ourselves, the well-to-do

Tremendous Sacrifice! 'This terrific satire on the sweating system was drawn by George Cruikshank more than fifty years ago, but there is reason to fear that at the present day it is still as well deserved as ever'. (Editor, 'The Picture Magazine', 1893).

people, of this mountain of rubbish, that would be something worth doing: things which everybody knows are of no use; the very capitalists know well that there is no genuine healthy demand for them, and they are compelled to foist them off on the public by stirring up a strange feverish desire for petty excitement, the outward token of which is known by the conventional name of fashion, a strange monster born of the vacancy of the lives of rich people, and the eagerness of competitive Commerce to make the most of the huge crowd of workmen whom it breeds as unregarded instruments for what is called the making of money.

Do not think it a little matter to resist this monster of folly; to think for yourselves what you yourselves really desire, will not only make men and women of you so far, but may also set you thinking of the due desires of other people, since you will soon find when you get to know a work of art, that slavish work is undesirable. And here furthermore is at least a little sign whereby to distinguish between a rag of fashion and a work of art: whereas the toys of fashion when the first gloss is worn off them do become obviously worthless even to the frivolous, a work of art, be it never so humble, is long lived; we never tire of it; as long as a scrap hangs together it is valuable and instructive to each new generation. All works of art in short have the property of becoming venerable amidst decay; and reason good, for from the first there was a soul in them, the thought of man, which will be visible in them so long as the body exists in which they were implanted.

And that last sentence brings me to considering the other side of the necessity for labour only occupying itself in making goods that are worth making. Hitherto we have been thinking of it only from the user's point of view; even so looked at it was surely important enough; yet from the other side, as to the producer, it is far more important still. For I say again that in buying these things

'Tis the lives of men you buy!

Will you from mere folly and thoughtlessness make yourselves partakers of the guilt of those who compel their fellow-men to labour uselessly? For when I said it was necessary for all things made to be worth making, I set up that claim chiefly on behalf of Labour; since the waste of making useless things grieves the workman doubly. As part of the public he is forced into buying them, and the more part of his miserable wages is squeezed out of him by a universal kind of truck system; as one of the producers he is forced into making them, and so into losing the very foundations of that pleasure in daily work which I claim as his birthright; he is compelled to labour joylessly at making the poison which the truck system compels him to buy. So that the huge mass of men who are compelled by folly and greed to make harmful and useless things are sacrificed to Society. I say that this would be terrible and unendurable even though they were sacrificed to the good of Society, if that were possible; but if they are sacrificed not for the welfare of Society but for its whims, to add to its degradation, what do luxury and fashion look like then? On one side ruinous and wearisome waste leading through corruption to corruption on to complete cynicism at last, and the disintegration of all Society; and on the other side implacable oppression destructive of all pleasure and hope in life, and leading — whitherward?

Here then is one thing for us of the middle classes to do before we can clear the ground for the new birth of Art, before we can clear our own consciences of the guilt of enslaving men by their labour. One thing; and if we could do it perhaps that one thing would be enough, and all other healthy changes would follow it: but can we do it? Can we escape from the corruption of Society which threatens us? Can the middle classes regenerate themselves? At first sight one would say that a body of people so powerful, who have built up the gigantic edifice of modern Commerce, whose science, invention, and energy have subdued the forces of nature to serve their everyday purposes, and who guide the organisation that keeps these natural powers in subjection in a way almost miraculous; at first sight one would say surely such a mighty mass of wealthy men could do anything they please. And yet I doubt it: their own creation, the Commerce they are so proud of, has become their master; and all we of the well-to-do classes, some of us with triumphant glee, some with dull satisfaction, and some with sadness of heart, are compelled to admit not that Commerce was made for man, but that man was made for Commerce.

Section O

Looking Forward

Advertising by photomontage: a modern medium. Postcard monument to 'Odol, The World's Dentifrice' before the Bank and Royal Exchange (1908). This anticipates the use of photomontage by artists a few years later.

SYSTEME NORMAL DU
DOCTEUR JAEGER
LA SANTÉ PAR LA LAINE

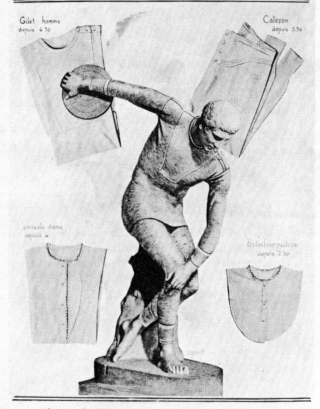

Turnabout. The utilitarian ornaments art. Advertisement of 1903 showing the famous Greek 'Discus-thrower' by Myron wearing a pair of genuine Jaegers. 'Imitated — but never duplicated' was the catch phrase used later when the Mona Lisa appeared in an advertisement for Rheingold's beer.

O 3 *A maze of wires on the roof of the telephone exchange in Lime Street, London, 1900.*

O 4 *Defects in wire photos due to telegraphic interference (1908). Curiously these aberrations seem to follow art. The transmission of linear images over telegraphic wire was known as early as 1851 but a means of reproducing pictures in half-tone was not practicable until Munich University scientist Korn introduced his method in 1903-6. Using Korn's device, the Daily Mirror inaugurated a Paris-London phototelegraphy service in November 1907. A new dimension was added to the technology of communication.*

Traffic in Fleet Street, 1905.

The Coming of the Automobile

Henri Fournier

O 6

The greatest change which I believe will be made in your cities by the perfect automobile will be in the wagon service. The old horse and wagon and horse and cart will have to go; the automobile is so much better, quicker, surer, cheaper. This will make a great difference, as it will just about abolish all stables throughout the city, and by clearing horses off the streets will at once render them much cleaner. . . .

In addition to this the new machines will greatly increase the wagon capacity of city streets, because they are so much shorter than a horse and wagon, and travel so much more swiftly. With the horse banished and complete auto service throughout the city the capacity of the streets would be at least quadrupled, which would do away with the blockades that are now so frequent on some of the narrow water front streets.

Then, of course, for conveyance to and from business and for coaching and pleasure riding the automobile is far superior to the old carriage, coach, or cab. It is not necessary that anyone should travel at the rate of 70 miles an hour. He need not race unless he so desires and the time and place are proper for racing. Twenty miles an hour is a good pace, although safer with the automobile than going 8 miles an hour behind a horse. And it is delightful to travel in an automobile going 20 miles an hour. The sensation is most exhilarating — like that of flying, as I imagine — and there are no ill effects.

The racing driver, Henri Fournier, in 'The Independent', New York, 12 December 1901.

Traffic in Fleet Street, 1924.

Louis Bleriot's cross-Channel flight, 25 July 1909. The event brilliantly dramatised Britain's new occassion with France andt the Entente Cordiale. But the flight cast an ominous shadow too. Britain could no longer feel an isolated and inaccessible island. The photograph is a fake, a montage made both to create and satisfy a public hunger for the image.

'OBSESSION: Scarcely has man invented something, than he busies himself with making his invention lethal. Now here is the military automobile, latest style — revolver style' (1910).

Part Four

Section P

Literature

Introduction

The material in this section has been chosen on a different principle than that governing the first three sections. There, a direct link existed between the selection of extracts and the requirements of the relevant correspondence material in the Humanities Foundation Course. Some of what follows has, of course, also been useful in that way, but as a whole, the section has a more general purpose. Industrialisation affected every aspect of Victorian society. To describe all the changes would be an enormous task. In effect, it would involve a comprehensive history of the period, and as the reader will already understand, the aim of this anthology has been only to illustrate selected aspects of the change. But it is at least possible to indicate something of its breadth and complexity by turning to the kind of record which literature can provide. The extracts in this section have been selected with that purpose in mind.

Most of them come from novels for the good reason that of all literary *genres* the novel is best adapted to the exploration of social change. Its use of narrative makes possible a long enough time-scale and a wide enough range of characters to create plausible facsimiles of social life; while its ability to attend closely to the personal fortunes of one or two characters brings the reader into sympathetic relationship with social events. Novels tell us two main things about social change. First, they usually contain a good deal of first-hand observation of its immediate effects. Like all observations, this will have its particular point of view, and as historians fairly insist, it is important to define the point of view, and where necessary, complement it from other sources — though it has to be added, that when one of the sources is a great novelist, deciding on relative authority is not a simple matter. Second, most novelists intend their work to influence the complex social process they are reporting. Novels involve assessment and interpretation as well as observation. This can take several forms: an explicit view of the issues; implicit raising of issues without the novelist adopting any definite attitude; or establishing the complexity of social events, of the tendency of human reality to resist abstract interpretation. In any of these ways, Victorian novels offer a record of the way industrialisation in its immediate and distant consequences impinged upon intelligent and articulate contemporaries. Extracts can only suggest an outline of this record, but it is to be hoped that the reader will find them interesting enough to lead him to some of the sources.

Some poems have also been included. Those by Thomas Hood and Tom Maguire illustrate two distinct phases in Victorian consciousness about industrialisation. The first belongs to the 1840s, when some of the human consequences began to impinge on the feelings of the educated middle class; the second to the 1890s, as part of the growth of British Socialism. Lastly, there are examples of the more complex writing of two Victorian poets, Alfred, Lord Tennyson and Matthew Arnold. Major social changes are felt in a variety of ways, and the most explicit responses to industrialisation are not for that reason more significant than others. Tennyson's 'Locksley Hall' has affinities with the social world observed by novelists, but its deeper interest derives from its attitude to the future. A similar note appears in 'Dover Beach', whose formal subject of religious doubt may seem little connected with industrialisation. But the connection lies in the new momentum for change, which industrialisation created.

The extracts have been supplied with titles and headnotes explaining the main point for illustration, and giving minimum information about the writer and the work in question. Suggestions for further reading in individual writers have also been added. One generally invaluable book may be mentioned here: Raymond Williams, 'Culture and Society 1780-1950' (1958). It contains separate sections relevant to extracts P 2, 4, 12, 15, 16; while for the general problem facing the artist at the beginning of the period, see pp. 30-48.

Liberal Doubts
Alfred, Lord Tennyson (1809–92)

'Black Tennyson, whose talents were / For an articulate despair': W. H. Auden's couplet about Tennyson may be one-sided but it is more perceptive than the view which most damaged his posthumous reputation, that he spoke only for the public complacencies of the high Victorian age. 'Locksley Hall' is not a poem of despair, but it expresses serious misgivings about the 'march of mind' of Victorian civilisation. First published in 1842, it is a dramatic monologue whose speaker begins by telling that as a young man he had loved and lost his cousin Amy who had jilted him for a member of the landed gentry. He attacks the social conventions which stifle true feeling, moving on to the reflections on the age printed below. Mainly optimistic and forward-looking, these also reveal a deep-seated revulsion from certain of its aspects. The interesting thing about the poem is that it dismisses rather than resolves this contradiction of feeling.

P 1

What is that which I should turn to, lighting upon days like these?
Every door is barr'd with gold, and opens but to golden keys.

Every gate is throng'd with suitors, all the markets overflow.
I have but an angry fancy: what is that which I should do?

I had been content to perish, falling on the foeman's ground,
When the ranks are roll'd in vapour, and the winds are laid with sound.

But the jingling of the guinea helps the hurt that Honour feels,
And the nations do but murmur, snarling at each other's heels.

Can I but relive in sadness? I will turn that earlier page.
Hide me from my deep emotion, O thou wondrous Mother-Age!

Make me feel the wild pulsation that I felt before the strife,
When I heard my days before me, and the tumult of my life;

Yearning for the large excitement that the coming years would yield,
Eager-hearted as a boy when first he leaves his father's field,

And at night along the dusky highway near and nearer drawn,
Sees in heaven the light of London flaring like a dreary dawn;

And his spirit leaps within him to be gone before him then,
Underneath the light he looks at, in among the throngs of men:

Men, my brothers, men the workers, ever reaping something new:
That which they have done but earnest of the things that they shall do:

For I dipt into the future, far as human eye could see,
Saw the Vision of the world, and all the wonder that would be;

Saw the heavens fill with commerce, argosies of magic sails,
Pilots of the purple twilight, dropping down with costly bales;

Heard the heavens fill with shouting, and there rain'd a ghastly dew
From the nations' airy navies grappling in the central blue;

Far along the world-wide whisper of the south-wind rushing warm,
With the standards of the peoples plunging thro' the thunder-storm;

Till the war-drum throbb'd no longer, and the battle-flags were furl'd
In the Parliament of man, the Federation of the world.

There the common sense of most shall hold a fretful realm in awe,
And the kindly earth shall slumber, lapt in universal law.

So I triumph'd ere my passion sweeping thro' me left me dry,
Left me with the palsied heart, and left me with the jaundiced eye;

Eye, to which all order festers, all things here are out of joint:
Science moves, but slowly slowly, creeping on from point to point:

Slowly comes a hungry people, as a lion creeping nigher,
Glares at one that nods and winks behind a slowly-dying fire.

Yet I doubt not thro' the ages one increasing purpose runs,
And the thoughts of men are widen'd with the process of the suns.

What is that to him that reaps not harvest of his youthful joys,
Tho' the deep heart of existence beat for ever like a boy's?

Knowledge comes, but wisdom lingers, and I linger on the shore,
And the individual withers, and the world is more and more.

Knowledge comes, but wisdom lingers, and he bears a laden breast,
Full of sad experience, moving toward the stillness of his rest.

Hark, my merry comrades call me, sounding on the bugle-horn,
They to whom my foolish passion were a target for their scorn:

Shall it not be scorn to me to harp on such a moulder'd string?
I am shamed thro' all my nature to have loved so slight a thing.

Weakness to be wroth with weakness! woman's pleasure, woman's
pain —
Nature made them blinder motions bounded in a shallower brain:

Woman is the lesser man, and all thy passions, match'd with mine,
Are as moonlight unto sunlight, and as water unto wine —

Here at least, where nature sickens, nothing. Ah, for some retreat
Deep in yonder shining Orient, where my life began to beat;

Where in wild Mahratta-battle fell my father evil-starr'd; —
I was left a trampled orphan, and a selfish uncle's ward.

Or to burst all links of habit — there to wander far away,
On from island unto island at the gateways of the day.

Larger constellations burning, mellow moons and happy skies,
Breadths of tropic shade and palms in cluster, knots of Paradise.

Never comes the trader, never floats an European flag,
Slides the bird o'er lustrous woodland, swings the trailer from the
      crag;

Droops the heavy-blossom'd bower, hangs the heavy-fruited tree —
Summer isles of Eden lying in dark-purple spheres of sea.

There methinks would be enjoyment more than in this march of mind,
In the steamship, in the railway, in the thoughts that shake mankind.

There the passions cramp'd no longer shall have scope and breathing
      space;
I will take some savage woman, she shall rear my dusky race.

Iron jointed, supple-sinew'd, they shall dive, and they shall run,
Catch the wild goat by the hair, and hurl their lances in the sun:

Whistle back the parrot's call, and leap the rainbows of the brooks,
Not with blinded eyesight poring over miserable books —

Fool, again the dream, the fancy! but I *know* my words are wild,
But I count the gray barbarian lower than the Christian child.

I, to herd with narrow foreheads, vacant of our glorious gains,
Like a beast with lower pleasures, like a beast with lower pains!

Mated with a squalid savage — what to me were sun or clime?
I the heir of all the ages, in the foremost files of time —

I that rather held it better men should perish one by one,
Than that earth should stand at gaze like Joshua's moon in Ajalon!

Not in vain the distance beacons. Forward, forward let us range,
Let the great world spin for ever down the ringing grooves of change.

Thro' the shadow of the globe we sweep into the younger day:
Better fifty years of Europe than a cycle of Cathay.

Mother-Age (for mine I knew not) help me as when life begun:
Rift the hills, and roll the waters, flash the lightings, weigh the Sun.

O, I see the crescent promise of my spirit hath not set.
Ancient founts of inspiration well thro' all my fancy yet.

Howsoever these things be, a long farewell to Locksley Hall!
Now for me the woods may wither, now for me the roof-tree fall.

Comes a vapour from the margin, blackening over heath and holt,
Cramming all the blast before it, in its breast a thunderbolt.

Let it fall on Locksley Hall, with rain or hail, or fire or snow;
For the mighty wind arises, roaring seaward, and I go.

See also H Introduction   'Locksley Hall', ll. 101-96

Further Reading

Alfred, Lord Tennyson, 'Locksley Hall: Sixty Years Afterwards'.
George MacBeth, 'The Penguin Book of Victorian Verse', 1969. pp.
    17-30.

Chartists
Mrs Gaskell (1810–65)

Mrs Elizabeth Gaskell was the wife of a Unitarian minister whose church was in Manchester. She married in 1832, and had an unrivalled opportunity for direct observation of the hardships of the working people during the formative years of industrial Manchester. 'Mary Barton' (1848) combines this knowledge with the limited criticisms of a liberally minded member of the middle class, convinced that more understanding and sympathy on both sides will be enough to remedy the social conflict between masters and men. She wrote in the preface, 'I know nothing of Political Economy or theories of trade.' She is not concerned to attack prevailing ideology. But her insight into the human problems which the onset of a trade depression caused for the working people accumulates a powerful argument in its own terms. In this extract, John Barton, the heroine's father, is about to take part in the Chartist demonstration of 1839, an event which the author sees more as a desperate reaction to the depression than to the growing awareness amongst the industrial working class that a common interest required common political effort. The mixture of confusion and shrewdness in the final dialogue has the authentic ring of popular politics.

P 2

For three years past, trade had been getting worse and worse, and the price of provisions higher and higher. This disparity between the amount of the earnings of the working classes, and the price of their food, occasioned in more cases than could well be imagined, disease and death. Whole families went through a gradual starvation. They only wanted a Dante to record their sufferings. And yet even his words would fall short of the awful truth; they could only present an outline of the tremendous facts of the destitution that surrounded thousands

Chartist Procession – Blackfriars Bridge, London 1848.

upon thousands in the terrible years 1839, 1840, and 1841. Even philanthropists who had studied the subject, were forced to own themselves perplexed in the endeavour to ascertain the real causes of the misery; the whole matter was of so complicated a nature that it became next to impossible to understand it thoroughly. It need excite no surprise then to learn that a bad feeling between working-men and the upper classes became very strong in this season of privation. The indigence and sufferings of the operatives induced a suspicion in the minds of many of them, that their legislators, their magistrates, their employers, and even the ministers of religion, were, in general, their oppressors and enemies; and were in league for their prostration and enthralment. The most deplorable and enduring evil that arose out of the period of commercial depression to which I refer, was this feeling of alienation between the different classes of society. It is so impossible to describe, or even faintly to picture, the state of distress which prevailed in the town at that time, that I will not attempt it; and yet I think again that surely, in a Christian land, it was not known even so feebly as words could tell it, or the more happy and fortunate would have thronged with their sympathy and their aid. In many instances the sufferers wept first, and then they cursed. Their vindictive feelings exhibited themselves in rabid politics. And when I hear, as I have heard, of the sufferings and privations of the poor, or provision shops where ha'porths of tea, sugar, butter, and even flour, were sold to accommodate the indigent, — of parents sitting in their clothes by the fire-side during the whole night for seven weeks together, in order that their only bed and bedding might be reserved for the use of their large family, — of others sleeping upon the cold hearth-stone for weeks in succession, without adequate means of providing themselves with food or fuel (and this in the depth of winter), — of others being compelled to fast for days together, uncheered by any hope of better fortune, living, moreover, or rather starving, in a crowded garret, or damp cellar, and gradually sinking under the pressure of want and despair into a premature grave; and when this has been confirmed by the evidence of their careworn looks, their excited feelings, and their desolate homes, — can I wonder that many of them, in such times of misery and destitution, spoke and acted with ferocious precipitation?

An idea was now springing up among the operatives, that originated with the Chartists, but which came at last to be cherished as a darling child by many and many a one. They could not believe that government knew of their misery: they rather chose to think it possible that men could voluntarily assume the office of legislators for a nation ignorant of its real state; as who should make domestic rules for the pretty behaviour of children without caring to know that these children had been kept for days without food. Besides, the starving multitudes had heard that the very existence of their distress had been denied in Parliament; and though they felt this strange and inexplicable, yet the idea that their misery had still to be revealed in all its depths, and that then some remedy would be found, soothed their aching hearts, and kept down their rising fury.

So a petition was framed, and signed by thousands in the bright spring days of 1839, imploring Parliament to hear witnesses who could testify to the unparalleled destitution of the manufacturing districts. Nottingham, Sheffield, Glasgow, Manchester, and many other towns were busy appointing delegates to convey this petition, who might speak, not merely of what they had seen and had heard, but from what they had borne and suffered. Life-worn, gaunt, anxious, hunger-stamped men, were those delegates.

One of them was John Barton. He would have been ashamed to own the flutter of spirits his appointment gave him. There was the childish delight of seeing London — that went a little way, and but a little way. There was the vain idea of speaking out his notions before so many grand folk — that went a little further; and last, there was the really pure gladness of heart arising from the idea that he was one of those chosen to be instruments in making known the distresses of the people, and consequently in procuring them some grand relief, by means of which they should never suffer want or care any more. He hoped largely, but vaguely, of the results of his expedition. An argosy of the precious hopes of many otherwise despairing creatures, was that petition to be heard concerning their sufferings.

The night before the morning on which the Manchester delegates were to leave for London, Barton might be said to hold a levée, so many neighbours came dropping in. Job Legh had early established himself and his pipe by John Barton's fire, not saying much, but puffing away, and imagining himself of use in adjusting the smoothing-irons that hung before the fire, ready for Mary when she should want them. As for Mary, her employment was the same as that of Beau Tibbs' wife, 'Just washing her father's two shirts,' in the pantry back-kitchen; for she was anxious about his appearance in London. (The coat had been redeemed, though the silk handkerchief was forfeited.) The door stood open, as usual, between the house-place and back-kitchen, so she gave her greeting to their friends as they entered.

'So, John, yo're bound for London, are yo?' said one.

'Ay, I suppose I mun go,' answered John, yielding to necessity as it were.

'Well, there's many a thing I'd like yo to speak on to the parliament people. Thou'lt not spare 'em, John, I hope. Tell 'em our minds; how we're thinking we've been clemmed long enough, and we donnot see whatten good they'n been doing, if they can't give us what we're all crying for sin' the day we were born.'

'Ay, ay! I'll tell 'em that, and much more to it, when it gets to my turn; but thou knows there's many will have their word afore me.'

'Well, thou'lt speak at last. Bless thee, lad, do ask 'em to make th' masters break th' machines. There's never been good times sin' spinning-jennies came up.'

'Machines is th' ruin of poor folk,' chimed in several voices.

'For my part,' said a shivering, half-clad man, who crept near the fire, as if ague-stricken, 'I would like thee to tell 'em to pass th' short-hours' bill. Flesh and blood gets wearied we' so much work; why should factory hands work so much longer nor other trades? Just ask 'em that, Barton, will ye?'

Barton was saved the necessity of answering, by the entrance of Mrs Davenport, the poor widow he had been so kind to; she looked half-fed, and eager, but was decently clad. In her hand she brought a little newspaper parcel, which she took to Mary, who opened it, and then called out, dangling a shirt collar from her soapy fingers:

'See, father, what a dandy you'll be in London! Mrs Davenport has brought you this; made new cut, all after the fashion. — Thank you for thinking on him.'

'Eh, Mary!' said Mrs Davenport, in a low voice. 'Whatten's all I can do, to what he's done for me and mine? But, Mary, sure I can help ye, for you'll be busy wi' this journey.'

'Just help me wring these out, and then I'll take 'em to th' mangle.'

So Mrs Davenport became a listener to the conversation; and after a while joined in.

'I'm sure, John Barton, if yo are taking messages to the parliament folk, yo'll not object to telling 'em what a sore trial it is, this law o' theirs, keeping childer fra' factory work, whether they be weakly or strong. There's our Ben; why, porridge seems to go no way wi' him, he eats so much; and I han gotten no money to send him t' school, as I would like; and there he is, rampaging about th' streets a' day, getting hungrier and hungrier, and picking up a' manner o' bad ways; and th' inspector won't let him in to work in th' factory, because he's not right age; though he's twice as strong as Sankey's little ritling* of a lad, as

* 'Ritling', probably a corruption of 'ricketling', a child that suffers from the rickets — a weakling.

works till he cries for his legs aching so, though he is right age, and better.'

'I've one plan I wish to tell John Barton,' said a pompous, careful-speaking man, 'and I should like him for to lay it afore the honourable house. My mother comed out o' Oxfordshire, and were under-laundry-maid in Sir Francis Dashwood's family; and when we were little ones, she'd tell us stories of their grandeur: and one thing she named were, that Sir Francis wore two shirts a day. Now he were all as one as a parliament man; and many on 'em, I han no doubt, are like extravagant. Just tell 'em, John, do, that they'd be doing th' Lancashire weavers a great kindness, if they'd ha' their shirts a' made o' calico; 'twould make trade brisk, that would, wi' the power o' shirts they wear.'

Job Legh now put in his word. Taking the pipe out of his mouth, and addressing the last speaker, he said:

'I'll tell ye what, Bill, and no offence mind ye; there's but hundreds of them parliament folk as wear so many shirts to their back; but there's thousands and thousands o' poor weavers as han only gotten one shirt i' th' world; ay, and don't know where t' get another when that rag's done, though they're turning out miles o' calico every day; and many o' mile o't is lying in warehouses, stopping up trade for want o' purchasers. Yo take my advice, John Barton, and ask parliament to set trade free, so as workmen can earn a decent wage, and buy their two, ay and three, shirts a year; that would make weaving brisk.'

He put his pipe in his mouth again, and redoubled his puffing to make up for lost time.

'I'm afeard, neighbours,' said John Barton, 'I've not much chance o' telling 'em all yo say; what I think on, is just speaking out about the distress, that they say is nought. When they hear o' children born on wet flags, without a rag t' cover 'em, or a bit o' food for th' mother; when they hear of folk lying down to die i' th' streets, or hiding their want i' some hole o' a cellar till death come to set 'em free; and when they hear o' all this plague, pestilence, and famine, they'll surely do somewhat wiser for us than we can guess at now. Howe'er, I han no objection, if so be there's an opening to speak up for what yo say; anyhow, I'll do my best, and yo see now, if better times don't come after Parliament knows all.'

Some shook their heads, but more looked cheery: and then one by one dropped off, leaving John and his daughter alone.

See also C 4, F 7, G 1, 5.   'Mary Barton', chap. 8.

Further Reading

Mrs Gaskell, 'North & South', 1850.
Arnold Kettle, 'The Early Victorian Social Problem Novel', in 'The Pelican Guide to English Literature', vi 1953, pp. 169-87.

Liberal Sympathy
Thomas Hood (1799–1845)

Thomas Hood was a successful literary journalist, mainly known for his humorous tales and verses. But he also wrote on more serious topics, and 'The Song of the Shirt' was a particularly effective expression of humane middle-class sympathies in clear and uncomplicated verse. It appeared anonymously in 'Punch' on 16 December 1843, prompted by an article about a woman who sewed trousers for 14 hours a day for a maximum wage of 7/-. The poem was widely reprinted, became the source of a play called 'The Sampstress', was translated into several European languages, recited at popular gatherings, read from pulpits, and printed on cotton handkerchiefs.

P 3

> With fingers weary and worn,
> > With eyelids heavy and red,
> A woman sat, in unwomanly rags,
> > Plying her needle and thread —
> > > Stitch! stitch! stitch!
> In poverty, hunger, and dirt,
> > And still with a voice of dolorous pitch
> She sang the 'Song of the Shirt.'

> 'Work! work! work!
> While the cock is crowing aloof!
> > And work — work — work,
> Till the stars shine through the roof!
> It's Oh! to be a slave
> > Along with the barbarous Turk,
> Where woman has never a soul to save,
> > If this is Christian work!

> 'Work — work — work
> Till the brain begins to swim;
> > Work — work — work
> Till the eyes are heavy and dim!

Seam, and gusset, and band,
    Band, and gusset, and seam,
Till over the buttons I fall asleep,
    And sew them on in a dream!

'Oh, Men, with Sisters dear!
    Oh, Men, with Mothers and Wives!
It is not linen you're wearing out,
    But human creatures' lives!
        Stitch — stitch — stitch,
    In poverty, hunger and dirt,
Sewing at once, with a double thread,
    A Shroud as well as a Shirt.

'But why do I talk of Death?
    That Phantom of grisly bone,
I hardly fear his terrible shape,
    It seems so like my own —
    It seems so like my own,
    Because of the fasts I keep;
Oh God! that bread should be so dear,
    And flesh and blood so cheap!

'Work — work — work!
    My labour never flags;
And what are its wages? A bed of straw,
    A crust of bread — and rags.
That shatter'd roof — and this naked floor —
    A table — a broken chair —
And a wall so blank, my shadow I thank
    For sometimes falling there!

'Work — work — work!
From weary chime to chime,
    Work — work — work —
As prisoners work for crime!
    Band, and gusset, and seam,
    Seam, and gusset, and band,
Till the heart is sick, and the brain benumb'd,
    As well as the weary hand.

'Work — work — work,
In the dull December light,
    And work — work — work,
When the weather is warm and bright —
While underneath the eaves
    The brooding swallows cling
As if to show me their sunny backs
    And twit me with the spring.

'Oh! but to breathe the breath
Of the cowslip and primrose sweet —
    With the sky above my head,
And the grass beneath my feet,
For only one short hour
    To feel as I used to feel,
Before I knew the woes of want
    And the walk that costs a meal!

'Oh! but for one short hour!
    A respite however brief!
No blessed leisure for Love or Hope,
    But only time for Grief!
A little weeping would ease my heart,
    But in their briny bed
My tears must stop, for every drop
    Hinders needle and thread!'

With fingers weary and worn,
    With eyelids heavy and red,
A woman sat in unwomanly rags,
    Plying her needle and thread —
      Stitch! stitch! stitch!
In poverty, hunger, and dirt,
And still with a voice of dolorous pitch, —
Would that its tone could reach the Rich! —
She sang this 'Song of the Shirt!'

See also F 2.

The Industrial Environment

Charles Dickens (1812–70)

Charles Dickens's concern for social injustice was never far from the centre of his work, but in the later part of his career, his attention shifted away from specific abuses like the scandal of Dotheboy's Hall in 'Nicholas Nickleby' (1839), or of Chancery procedures in 'Bleak House' (1853) towards a general indictment of the forces shaping Victorian society. 'Hard Times' (1854) and 'Our Mutual Friend' (1865) belong to this later phase. 'Hard Times' grew partly out of a visit Dickens made to Preston to report on a bitterly contested strike and lock-out of the cotton workers. Coketown is the 'fictional' result. Dickens links its oppressive physical environment with the ethos of the factory owners, Messrs Gradgrind and Bounderby, who — since 'fact' alone can be weighed, measured, bought and sold — deny the reality of every other human need. The comparison of the machines in the factory to 'melancholy mad elephants' is more than a verbal flourish. It suggests that their exhaustless energies are as misused as the lives of the workers by the social-economic system which set them in motion.

P 4

Coketown, to which Messrs Bounderby and Gradgrind now walked, was a triumph of fact; it had no greater taint of fancy in it than Mrs Gradgrind herself. Let us strike the keynote, Coketown, before pursuing our tune.

It was a town of red brick, or of brick that would have been red if the smoke and ashes had allowed it; but as matters stood it was a town of unnatural red and black like the painted face of a savage. It was a town of machinery and tall chimneys, out of which interminable serpents of smoke trailed themselves for ever and ever, and never got

Out-of-Work Mill-hands — Preston Moors, 1862.

uncoiled. It had a black canal in it, and a river that ran purple with ill-smelling dye, and vast piles of buildings full of windows where there was a rattling and a trembling all day long, and where the piston of the steam-engine worked monotonously up and down like the head of an elephant in a state of melancholy madness. It contained several large streets all very like one another, and many small streets still more like one another, inhabited by people equally like one another, who all went in and out at the same hours, with the same sound upon the same pavements, to do the same work, and to whom every day was the same as yesterday and to-morrow, and every year the counterpart of the last and the next.

These attributes of Coketown were in the main inseparable from the work by which it was sustained; against them were to be set off, comforts of life which found their way all over the world, and elegancies of life which made, we will not ask how much of the fine lady, who could scarcely bear to hear the place mentioned. The rest of its features were voluntary, and they were these.

You saw nothing in Coketown but what was severely workful. If the members of a religious persuasion built a chapel there — as the members of eighteen religious persuasions had done — they made it a pious warehouse of red brick, with sometimes (but this is only in highly ornamented examples) a bell in a birdcage on the top of it. The solitary exception was the New Church; a stuccoed edifice with a square steeple over the door, terminating in four short pinnacles like florid wooden legs. All the public inscriptions in the town were painted alike, in severe characters of black and white. The jail might have been the infirmary, the infirmary might have been the jail, the town-hall might have been either, or both, or anything else, for anything that appeared to the contrary in the graces of their construction. Fact, fact, fact, everywhere in the material aspect of the town; fact, fact, fact, everywhere in the immaterial. The M'Choakumchild school was all fact, and the school of design was all fact, and the relations between master and man were all fact, and everything was fact between the lying-in hospital and the cemetery, and what you couldn't state in figures, or show to be purchaseable in the cheapest market and saleable in the dearest, was not, and never should be, world without end, Amen. . . .

A sunny midsummer day. There was such a thing sometimes, even in Coketown.

Seen from a distance in such weather, Coketown lay shrouded in a haze of its own, which appeared impervious to the sun's rays. You only knew the town was there, because you knew there could have been no such sulky blotch upon the prospect without a town. A blur of soot and smoke, now confusedly tending this way, now that way, now aspiring to the vault of Heaven, now murkily creeping along the earth, as the wind rose and fell, or changed its quarter: a dense formless jumble, with sheets of cross light in it, that showed nothing but masses of darkness: — Coketown in the distance suggestive of itself, though not a brick of it could be seen.

The wonder was, it was there at all. It had been ruined so often, that it was amazing how it had borne so many shocks. Surely there never was such fragile china-ware as that of which the millers of Coketown were made. Handle them never so lightly and they fell to pieces with such ease that you might suspect them of having been flawed before. They were ruined, when they were required to send labouring children to school; they were ruined when inspectors were appointed to look into their works; they were ruined, when such inspectors considered it doubtful whether they were quite justified in chopping people up with their machinery; they were utterly undone, when it was hinted that perhaps they need not always make quite so much smoke. Besides Mr Bounderby's gold spoon which was generally received in Coketown, another prevalent fiction was very popular there. It took the form of a threat. Whenever a Coketowner felt he was ill-used — that is to say, whenever he was not left entirely alone, and it was proposed to hold him accountable for the consequences of any of his acts — he was sure to come out with the awful menace, that he would 'sooner pitch his property into the Atlantic.' This had terrified the Home Secretary within an inch of his life, on several occasions.

However, the Coketowners were so patriotic after all, that they never had pitched their property into the Atlantic yet, but, on the contrary, had been kind enough to take mighty good care of it. So there it was, in the haze yonder; and it increased and multiplied.

The streets were hot and dusty on the summer day, and the sun was so bright that it even shone through the heavy vapour drooping over Coketown, and could not be looked at steadily. Stokers emerged from low underground doorways into factory yards, and sat on steps, and posts, and palings, wiping their swarthy visages, and contemplating coals. The whole town seemed to be frying in oil. There was a stifling smell of hot oil everywhere. The steam-engines shone with it, the dresses of the Hands were soiled with it, the mills throughout their many stories oozed and trickled it. The atmosphere of those Fairy palaces was like the breath of the simoom: and their inhabitants, wasting with heat, toiled languidly in the desert. But no temperature made the melancholy mad elephants more mad or more sane. Their wearisome heads went up and down at the same rate, in hot weather and cold, wet weather and dry, fair weather and foul. The measured motion of their shadows on the walls, was the substitute Coketown had to show for the shadows of rustling woods; while, for the summer hum of insects, it could offer, all the year round, from the dawn of Monday to the night of Saturday, the whirr of shafts and wheels.

Drowsily they whirred all through this sunny day, making the passenger more sleepy and more hot as he passed the humming walls of the mills. Sun-blinds, and sprinklings of water, a little cooled the main streets and the shops; but the mills, and the courts and alleys, baked at a fierce heat. Down upon the river that was black and thick with dye, some Coketown boys who were at large — a rare sight there — rowed a crazy boat, which made a spumous track upon the water as it jogged along, while every dip of an oar stirred up vile smells. But the sun itself, however beneficent, generally, was less kind to Coketown than hard frost, and rarely looked intently into any of its closer regions without engendering more death than life.

See also A 1, B 3, C 5, H 2.   'Hard Times', book i, chap. 5;
                                                 book ii, chap. 1.

Further Reading

F. R. Leavis, 'The Great Tradition', 1949, pp. 227-47.

A Marriage Contract

Charles Dickens

'Money, money, money, and what money can make of life': so J. Hillis Miller defines the theme of Dickens's complex and elaborate novel 'Our Mutual Friend'. Its illusory promise invades the reality of all other experiences and the power of all other values. The satirical tone and presentation of events is intended to highlight the resulting unreality. The subject of this extract is a society marriage where each partner thinks the other has the money, an illusion fostered by Mr Veneering who arranges the match. Twemlow, the faded bachelor, is asked to give the bride away because of his genteel connections. 'The Analytical' is the butler.

P 5

There is excitement in the Veneering mansion. The mature young lady is going to be married (powder and all) to the mature young gentleman, and she is to be married from the Veneering house, and the Veneerings are to give the breakfast. The Analytical, who objects as a matter of principle to everything that occurs on the premises, necessarily objects to the match; but his consent has been dispensed with, and a spring van is delivering its load of greenhouse plants at the door, in order that to-morrow's feast may be crowned with flowers.

The mature young lady is a lady of property. The mature young gentleman is a gentleman of property. He invests his property. He goes, in a condescending amateurish way, into the City, attends meetings of Directors, and has to do with traffic in Shares. As is well known to the wise in their generation, traffic in Shares is the one thing to have to do with in this world. Have no antecedents, no established character, no cultivation, no ideas, no manners; have Shares. Have Shares enough to be on Boards of Direction in capital letters, oscillate on mysterious business between London and Paris, and be great. Where does he come from? Shares. Where is he going to? Shares. What are his tastes? Shares. Has he any principles? Shares. What squeezes him into Parliament? Shares. Perhaps he never of himself achieved success in anything, never originated anything, never produced anything! Sufficient answer to all: Shares. O mighty Shares! To set those blaring images so high, and to cause us smaller vermin, as under the influence of henbane or opium, to cry out night and day, 'Relieve us of our money, scatter it for us, buy us and sell us, ruin us, only we beseech ye take rank among the powers of the earth, and fatten on us!'

While the Loves and Graces have been preparing this torch for Hymen, which is to be kindled to-morrow, Mr Twemlow has suffered much in his mind. It would seem that both the mature young lady and the mature young gentleman must indubitably be Veneering's oldest friends. Wards of his, perhaps? Yet that can scarcely be, for they are older than himself. Veneering has been in their confidence throughout, and has done much to lure them to the altar. He has mentioned to Twemlow how he said to Mrs Veneering, 'Anastatia, this must be a match.' He has mentioned to Twemlow how he regards Sophronia Akershem (the mature young lady) in the light of a sister, and Alfred Lammle (the mature young gentleman) in the light of a brother. Twemlow has asked him whether he went to school as a junior with Alfred? He has answered, 'Not exactly.' Whether Sophronia was adopted by his mother? He has answered, 'Not precisely so.' Twemlow's hand has gone to his forehead with a lost air.

But, two or three weeks ago, Twemlow, sitting over his newspaper, and over his dry toast and weak tea, and over the stable-yard in Duke Street, St James's, received a highly-perfumed cocked-hat and monogram from Mrs Veneering, entreating her dearest Mr T., if not particularly engaged that day, to come like a charming soul and make a fourth at dinner with dear Mr Podsnap, for the discussion of an interesting family topic; the last three words doubly underlined and pointed with a note of admiration. And Twemlow, replying, 'Not engaged, and more than delighted,' goes, and this takes place:

'My dear Twemlow,' says Veneering, 'your ready response to

Anastatia's unceremonious invitation is truly kind, and like an old, old, friend. You know our dear friend Podsnap?'

Twemlow ought to know the dear friend Podsnap who covered him with so much confusion, and he says he does know him, and Podsnap reciprocates. Apparently, Podsnap has been so wrought upon in a short time, as to believe that he has been intimate in the house many, many, many years. In the friendliest manner he is making himself quite at home with his back to the fire, executing a statuette of the Colossus at Rhodes. Twemlow has before noticed in his feeble way how soon the Veneering guests become infected with the Veneering fiction. Not, however, that he has the least notion of its being his own case.

'Our friends, Alfred and Sophronia,' pursues Veneering the veiled prophet: 'our friends, Alfred and Sophronia, you will be glad to hear, my dear fellows, are going to be married. As my wife and I make it a family affair, the entire direction of which we take upon ourselves, of course our first step is to communicate the fact to our family friends.'

('Oh!' thinks Twemlow, with his eyes on Podsnap, 'then there are only two of us, and he's the other.')

'I did hope,' Veneering goes on, 'to have had Lady Tippins to meet you; but she is always in request, and is unfortunately engaged.'

(Oh!' thinks Twemlow, with his eyes wandering, 'then there are three of us, and *she's* the other.')

'Mortimer Lightwood,' resumes Veneering, 'whom you both know, is out of town; but he writes in his whimsical manner, that as we ask him to be bridegroom's best man when the ceremony takes place, he will not refuse, though he doesn't see what he has to do with it.'

('Oh!' thinks Twemlow, with his eyes rolling, 'then there are four of us, and *he's* the other.')

'Boots and Brewer,' observes Veneering, 'whom you also know, I have not asked to-day; but I reserve them for the occasion.'

('Then,' thinks Twemlow, with his eyes shut, 'there are si——' But here collapses and does not completely recover until dinner is over and the Analytical has been requested to withdraw.)

'We now come,' says Veneering, 'to the point, the real point, of our little family consultation. Sophronia, having lost both father and mother, has no one to give her away.'

'Give her away yourself,' says Podsnap.

'My dear Podsnap, no. For three reasons. Firstly, because I couldn't take so much upon myself when I have respected family friends to remember. Secondly, because I am not so vain as to think that I look the part. Thirdly, because Anastatia is a little superstitious on the subject and feels averse to my giving away anybody until baby is old enough to be married.'

'What would happen if he did?' Podsnap inquires of Mrs Veneering.

'My dear Mr Podsnap, it's very foolish, I know, but I have an instinctive presentiment that if Hamilton gave away anybody else first, he would never give away baby.' Thus Mrs Veneering, with her open hands pressed together, and each of her eight aquiline fingers looking so very like her one aquiline nose that the bran-new jewels on them seemed necessary for distinction's sake.

'But, my dear Podsnap,' quoth Veneering, 'there *is* a tried friend of our family who, I think and hope you will agree with me, Podsnap, is the friend on whom this agreeable duty almost naturally devolves. That friend,' saying the words as if the company were about a hundred and fifty in number, 'is now among us. That friend is Twemlow.'

'Certainly!' from Podsnap.

'That friend,' Veneering repeats with greater firmness, 'is our dear good Twemlow. And I cannot sufficiently express to you, my dear Podsnap, the pleasure I feel in having this opinion of mine and Anastatia's so readily confirmed by you, that other equally familiar and tried friend who stands in the proud position — I mean who proudly stands in the position — or I ought rather to say, who places Anastatia and myself in the proud position of himself standing in the simple position — of baby's godfather.' And, indeed, Veneering is much relieved in mind to find that Podsnap betrays no jealousy of Twemlow's elevation.

So, it has come to pass that the spring-van is strewing flowers on the rosy hours and on the staircase, and that Twemlow is surveying the ground on which he is to play his distinguished part to-morrow. He has already been to the church, and taken note of the various impediments in the aisle, under the auspices of an extremely dreary widow who opens the pews, and whose left hand appears to be in a state of acute rheumatism, but is in fact voluntarily doubled up to act as a money-box.

And now Veneering shoots out of the study wherein he is accustomed, when contemplative, to give his mind to the carving and gilding of the Pilgrims going to Canterbury, in order to show Twemlow the little flourish he has prepared for the trumpets of fashion, describing how that on the seventeenth instant, at St James's Church, the Reverend Blank Blank, assisted by the Reverend Dash Dash, united in the bonds of matrimony, Alfred Lammle, Esquire, of Sackville Street, Piccadilly, to Sophronia, only daughter of the late Horatio Akershem, Esquire, of Yorkshire. Also how the fair bride was married from the house of Hamilton Veneering, Esquire, of Stucconia, and was given away by Melvin Twemlow, Esquire, of Duke Street, St James's, second cousin to Lord Snigsworth, of Snigsworthy Park. While perusing which composition, Twemlow makes some opaque approach to perceiving that if the Reverend Blank Blank and the Reverend Dash Dash fail, after this introduction, to become enrolled in the list of Veneering's dearest and oldest friends, they will have none but themselves to thank for it.

After which, appears Sophronia (whom Twemlow has seen twice in his lifetime), to thank Twemlow for counterfeiting the late Horatio Akershem, Esquire, broadly of Yorkshire. And after her, appears Alfred (whom Twemlow has seen once in his lifetime), to do the same, and to make a pasty sort of glitter, as if he were constructed for candlelight only, and had been let out into daylight by some grand mistake. And after that, comes Mrs Veneering, in a pervadingly aquiline state of figure, and with transparent little knobs on her temper, like the little transparent knob on the bridge of her nose, 'Worn out by worry and excitement,' as she tells her dear Mr Twemlow, and reluctantly revived with curacoa by the Analytical. And after that, the bridesmaids begin to come by railroad from various parts of the country, and to come like adorable recruits enlisted by a sergeant not present; for, on arriving at the Veneering depot, they are in a barrack of strangers. . . .

Betimes next morning, that horrible old Lady Tippins (relicet of the late Sir Thomas Tippins, knighted in mistake for somebody else by His Majesty King George the Third, who, while performing the ceremony, was graciously pleased to observe 'What, what, what? Who, who, who? Why, why, why?') begins to be dyed and varnished for the interesting occasion. She has a reputation for giving smart accounts of things, and she must be at these people's early, my dear, to lose nothing of the fun. Whereabout in the bonnet and drapery announced by her name, any fragment of the real woman may be concealed, is perhaps known to her maid; but you could easily buy all you see of her, in Bond Street: or you might scalp her, and peel her, and scrape her, and make two Lady Tippinses out of her, and yet not penetrate to the genuine article. She has a large gold eye-glass, has Lady Tippins, to survey the proceedings with. If she had one in each eye, it might keep that other drooping lid up, and look more uniform. But perennial youth is in her artificial flowers, and her list of lovers is full. . . .

But, hark! A carriage at the gate, and Mortimer's man arrives, looking rather like a spurious Mephistopheles and an acknowledged member of that gentleman's family. Whom Lady Tippins, surveying through her eye-glass, considers a fine man, and quite a catch; and of whom Mortimer remarks, in the lowest spirits, as he approaches, 'I believe this is my fellow, confound him!' More carriages at the gate, and lo, the rest of the characters. Whom Lady Tippins, standing on a cushion, surveying through the eye-glass, thus checks off: 'Bride; five-and-forty if a day, thirty shillings a yard, veil fifteen pounds, pocket-handkerchief a present. Bridesmaids; kept down for fear of outshining bride, consequently not girls, twelve and sixpence a yard, Veneering's flowers, snub-nosed one rather pretty but too conscious of her stockings, bonnets three pound ten. Twemlow; blessed release for the dear man if she really was his daughter, nervous even under the pretence that she is, well he may be. Mrs Veneering; never saw such velvet, say two thousand pounds as she stands, absolute jeweller's window, father must have been a pawnbroker, or how could these people do it? Attendant unknowns; pokey.'

Ceremony performed, register signed, Lady Tippins escorted out of sacred edifice by Veneering, carriages rolling back to Stucconia, servants with favours and flowers, Veneering's house reached, drawing-rooms most magnificent. Here, the Podsnaps await the happy party; Mr Podsnap, with his hair-brushes made the most of; that imperial rocking-horse, Mrs Podsnap, majestically skittish. Here, too, are Boots and Brewer, and the two other Buffers; each Buffer with a flower in his button-hole, his hair curled, and his gloves buttoned on tight, apparently come prepared, if anything had happened to the bride-groom, to be married instantly. Here, too, the bride's aunt, and next relation; a widowed female of a Medusa sort, in a stony cap, glaring petrifaction at her fellow-creatures. Here, too, the bride's trustee; an oilcake-fed style of business-gentleman with mooney spectacles, and an object of much interest. Veneering launching himself upon this trustee as his oldest friend (which makes seven, Twemlow thought), and confidentially retiring with him into the conservatory, it is understood that Veneering is his co-trustee, and that they are arranging about the fortune. Buffers are even overheard to whisper Thir-ty Thou-sand Pou-nds! with a smack and a relish suggestive of the very finest oysters. Pokey unknowns, amazed to find how intimately they know Veneering, pluck up spirit, fold their arms, and begin to contradict him before breakfast. What time Mrs Veneering, carrying baby dressed as a brides-maid, flits about among the company, emitting flashes of many-coloured lightning from diamonds, emeralds, and rubies.

The Analytical, in course of time achieving what he feels to be due to himself in bringing to a dignified conclusion several quarrels he has on hand with the pastrycook's men, announces breakfast. Dining-room no less magnificent than drawing-room; tables superb; all the camels out, and all laden. Splendid cake, covered with Cupids, silver, and true-lovers' knots. Splendid bracelet, produced by Veneering before going down, and clasped upon the arm of bride. Yet nobody seems to think much more of the Veneerings than if they were a tolerable landlord and landlady doing the thing in the way of business at so much a head. The bride and bridegroom talk and laugh apart, as has always been their manner; and the Buffers work their way through the dishes with systematic perseverance; as has always been *their* manner; and the pokey unknowns are exceedingly benevolent to one another in invita-tions to take glasses of champagne; but Mrs Podsnap, arching her mane and rocking her grandest, has a far more deferential audience than Mrs Veneering; and Podsnap all but does the honours. . . .

Another objectionable circumstance is, that the pokey unknowns support each other in being unimpressible. They persist in not being frightened by the gold and silver camels, and they are banded together to defy the elaborately chased ice-pails. They even seem to unite in some vague utterance of the sentiment that the landlord and landlady will make a pretty good profit out of this, and they almost carry themselves like customers. Nor is there compensating influence in the adorable bridesmaids; for, having very little interest in the bride, and none at all in one another, those lovely beings become, each one on her own account, depreciatingly contemplative of the millinery present. While the bridegroom's man, exhausted, in the back of his chair, appears to be improving the occasion by penitentially contemplating all the wrong he has ever done; the difference between him and his friend Eugene being, that the latter, in the back of *his* chair, appears to be contemplating all the wrong he would like to do — particularly to the present company.

In which state of affairs, the usual ceremonies rather droop and flag, and the splendid cake when cut by the fair hand of the bride has but an indigestible appearance. However, all the things indispensable to be said are said, and all the things indispensable to be done are done (including Lady Tippins's yawning, falling asleep, and waking insensible), and there is hurried preparation for the nuptial journey to the Isle of Wight, and the outer air teems with brass bands and spectators. In full sight of whom, the malignant star of the Analytical has pre-ordained that pain and ridicule shall befall him. For he, standing on the doorsteps to grace the departure, is suddenly caught a most prodigious thump on the side of his head with a heavy shoe, which a Buffer in the hall, champagne-flushed and wild of aim, has borrowed on the spur of the moment from the pastrycook's porter, to cast after the departing pair as an auspicious omen.

So they all go up again into the gorgeous drawing-rooms — all of them flushed with breakfast, as having taken scarlatina sociably — and there the combined unknowns do malignant things with their legs to ottomans, and take as much as possible out of the splendid furniture. And so, Lady Tippins, quite undetermined whether to-day is the day before yesterday, or the day after to-morrow, or the week after next, fades away; and Mortimer Lightwood and Eugene fade away, and

Twemlow fades away, and the stony aunt goes away — she declines to fade, proving rock to the last — and even the unknowns are slowly strained off, and it is all over.

See also E 4, F 10, N 7.   'Our Mutual Friend', chap. 3.

Further Reading

Kettle, 'Our Mutual Friend', in 'Dickens and the Twentieth Century', 1962, ed. John Gross and Gabriel Pearson, pp. 213-25.

J. Hillis Miller, 'Our Mutual Friend', in 'Dickens: A Collection of Critical Essays', 1967, ed. Martin Price, pp. 169-77.

Agricultural Machinery

Thomas Hardy (1840–1928)

Thomas Hardy was brought up in Dorset, and his novels were largely based on his knowledge of a rural society, in many ways simpler than the main stream of Victorian life recorded by George Eliot and Charles Dickens. Yet like them, Hardy powerfully communicates the experience of social change. His major characters grapple with problems recognisably of their time, and in 'Tess of the d'Urbervilles' (1891) his heroine is the victim of several contemporary social influences: her father's meaningless claims to ancient family, her husband's conventional moral feelings, and the rigid Victorian view of marriage and sexuality. Though in the extract Tess is a farm-labourer, Hardy is concerned less with agricultural conditions than in emphasising her victim-state.

P 6

It is the threshing of the last wheat-rick at Flintcomb-Ash Farm. The dawn of the March morning is singularly inexpressive, and there is nothing to show where the eastern horizon lies. Against the twilight rises the trapezoidal top of the stack, which has stood forlornly here through the washing and bleaching of the wintry weather.

When Izz Huett and Tess arrived at the scene of operations only a rustling denoted that others had preceded them; to which, as the light increased, there were presently added the silhouettes of two men on the summit. They were busily 'unhaling' the rick, that is, stripping off the thatch before beginning to throw down the sheaves; and while this was in progress Izz and Tess, with the other women-workers, in their whitey-brown pinners, stood waiting and shivering, Farmer Groby having insisted upon their being on the spot thus early to get the job over if possible by the end of the day. Close under the eaves of the stack, and as yet barely visible, was the red tyrant that the women had come to serve — a timber-framed construction, with straps and wheels appertaining — the threshing-machine which, whilst it was going, kept up a despotic demand upon the endurance of their muscles and nerves.

A little way off there was another indistinct figure; this one black, with a sustained hiss that spoke of strength very much in reserve. The long chimney running up beside an ash-tree, and the warmth which radiated from the spot, explained without the necessity of much daylight that here was the engine which was to act as the *primum mobile* of this little world. By the engine stood a dark motionless being, a sooty and grimy embodiment of tallness, in a sort of trance, with a heap of coals by his side: it was the engine-man. The isolation of his manner and colour lent him the appearance of a creature from Tophet, who had strayed into the pellucid smokelessness of this region of yellow grain and pale soil, with which he had nothing in common, to amaze and to discompose its aborigines.

What he looked he felt. He was in the agricultural world, but not of it. He served fire and smoke; these denizens of the fields served vegetation, weather, frost, and sun. He travelled with his engine from farm to farm, from county to county, for as yet the steam threshing-machine was itinerant in this part of Wessex. He spoke in a strange northern accent; his thoughts being turned inwards upon himself, his eye on his iron charge, hardly perceiving the scenes around him, and caring for them not at all: holding only strictly necessary intercourse with the natives, as if some ancient doom compelled him to wander here against his will in the service of his Plutonic master. The long strap which ran from the driving-wheel of his engine to the red thresher under the rick was the sole tie-line between agriculture and him.

While they uncovered the sheaves he stood apathetic beside his portable repository of force, round whose hot blackness the morning air quivered. He had nothing to do with preparatory labour. His fire was waiting incandescent, his steam was at high pressure, in a few seconds he could make the long strap move at an invisible velocity. Beyond its extent the environment might be corn, straw, or chaos; it was all the same to him. If any of the autochthonous idlers asked him what he called himself, he replied shortly, 'an engineer.'

The rick was unhaled by full daylight; the men then took their places, the women mounted, and the work began. Farmer Groby — or, as they called him, 'he' — had arrived ere this, and by his orders Tess was placed on the platform of the machine, close to the man who fed it, her business being to untie every sheaf of corn handed on to her by Izz Huett, who stood next, but on the rick; so that the feeder could seize it and spread it over the revolving drum, which whisked out every grain in one moment.

They were soon in full progress, after a preparatory hitch or two, which rejoiced the hearts of those who hated machinery. The work sped on till breakfast-time, when the thresher was stopped for half an hour; and on starting again after the meal the whole supplementary strength of the farm was thrown into the labour of constructing the straw-rick, which began to grow beside the stack of corn. A hasty lunch was eaten as they stood, without leaving their positions, and then another couple of hours brought them near to dinner-time; the inexorable wheels continuing to spin, and the penetrating hum of the thresher to thrill to the very marrow all who were near the revolving wire-cage.

The old men on the rising straw-rick talked of the past days when they had been accustomed to thresh with flails on the oaken barn-floor; when everything, even to winnowing, was effected by hand-labour, which, to their thinking, though slow, produced better results. Those, too, on the corn-rick talked a little; but the perspiring ones at the machine, including Tess, could not lighten their duties by the exchange of many words. It was the ceaselessness of the work which tried her so severely, and began to make her wish that she had never come to Flintcomb-Ash. The women on the corn-rick — Marian, who was one of them, in particular — could stop to drink ale or cold tea from the flagon now and then, or to exchange a few gossiping remarks while they wiped their faces or cleared the fragments of straw and husk from their clothing; but for Tess there was no respite; for, as the drum never stopped, the man who fed it could not stop, and she, who had to supply the man with untied sheaves, could not stop either, unless Marian changed places with her, which she sometimes did for half an hour in spite of Groby's objection that she was too slow-handed for a feeder.

For some probably economical reason it was usually a woman who was chosen for this particular duty, and Groby gave as his motive in selecting Tess that she was one of those who best combined strength with quickness in untying, and both with staying power, and this may have been true. The hum of the thresher, which prevented speech, increased to a raving whenever the supply of corn fell short of the regular quantity. . . .

Dinner-time came, and the whirling ceased; whereupon Tess left her post, her knees trembling so wretchedly with the shaking of the machine that she could scarcely walk.

'You ought to het a quart o' drink into 'ee, as I've done,' said Marian. 'You wouldn't look so white then. Why, souls above us, your face is as if you'd been hagrode!'. . . .

In the afternoon the farmer made it known that the rick was to be finished at night, since there was a moon by which they could see to work, and the man with the engine was engaged for another farm on the morrow. Hence the twanging and humming and rustling proceeded with even less intermission than usual. . . .

Thus the afternoon dragged on. The wheat-rick shrank lower, and the straw-rick grew higher, and the corn-sacks were carted away. At six o'clock the wheat-rick was about shoulder-high from the ground. But the unthreshed sheaves remaining untouched seemed countless still, notwithstanding the enormous numbers that had been gulped down by the insatiable swallower, fed by the man and Tess, through whose two young hands the greater part of them had passed. And the immense stack of straw where in the morning there had been nothing, appeared as the *faeces* of the same buzzing red glutton. From the west sky a wrathful shine — all that wild March could afford in the way of sunset — had burst forth after the cloudy day, flooding the tired and sticky faces of the threshers, and dyeing them with a coppery light, as also the flapping garments of the women, which clung to them like dull flames.

A panting ache ran through the rick. The man who fed was weary, and Tess could see that the red nape of his neck was encrusted with dirt and husks. She still stood at her post, her flushed and perspiring face coated with the corn-dust, and her white bonnet embrowned by it. She was the only woman whose place was upon the machine so as to be shaken bodily by its spinning, and the decrease of the stack now separated her from Marian and Izz, and prevented their changing duties with her as they had done. The incessant quivering, in which every fibre of her frame participated, had thrown her into a stupefied reverie in which her arms worked on independently of her consciousness. She hardly knew where she was, and did not hear Izz Huett tell her from below that her hair was tumbling down.

By degrees the freshest among them began to grow cadaverous and saucer-eyed. Whenever Tess lifted her head she beheld always the great upgrown straw-stack, with the men in shirt-sleeves upon it, against the gray north sky; in front of it the long red elevator like a Jacob's ladder, on which a perpetual stream of threshed straw ascended, a yellow river running up-hill, and spouting out on the top of the rick.

See also C 5, 7.   'Tess of the d'Urbervilles', chap. 67-8.

Further Reading

'The Dorsetshire Labourer', in 'Hardy: Personal Writings', 1966, ed. Harold Urel, pp. 168-89.
Irving Howe, 'Thomas Hardy', 1967, pp. 109-32.

The Crisis in Belief

Matthew Arnold (1822-88)

A major strand in the social criticism of Matthew Arnold is the need to discover an ordering principle which would contain the thrust of individual self-interest encouraged by the new social forces, the 'doing as one likes' which he attacks in 'Culture and Anarchy' (1869). The loss of certainty in religious belief reveals a similar theme. With the ebbing of the 'Sea of Faith', the character of experience can only be symbolised in powerful images of disorder and conflict; and only in intimate personal relationships can the human soul look for protection and harmony. 'Dover Beach' was first published in 1867.

P 7   *Dover Beach*

The sea is calm tonight.
The tide is full, the moon lies fair
Upon the straits; on the French coast the light
Gleams and is gone; the cliffs of England stand,
Glimmering and vast, out in the tranquil bay.
Come to the window, sweet is the night air!
Only, from the long line of spray
Where the sea meets the moon-blanched land,
Listen! you hear the grating roar
Of pebbles which the waves suck back, and fling
At their return, up the high strand,
Begin, and cease, and then again begin,
With tremulous cadence slow, and bring
The eternal note of sadness in.

Sophocles long ago
Heard it on the Aegaean, and it brought
Into his mind the turbid ebb and flow
Of human misery; we
Find also in the sound a thought,
Hearing it by this distant northern sea.
The Sea of Faith
Was once, too, at the full, and round earth's shore
Lay like the folds of a bright girdle furled;
But now I only hear
Its melancholy, long, withdrawing roar,
Retreating, to the breath
Of the night-wind, down the vast edges drear
And naked shingles of the world.

Ah, love, let us be true
To one another! for the world, which seems
To lie before us like a land of dreams,
So various, so beautiful, so new,
Hath really neither joy, nor love, nor light,
Nor certitude, nor peace, nor help for pain;
And-we are here as on a darkling plain
Swept with confused alarms of struggle and flight,
Where ignorant armies clash by night.

See also J 4, H 7.

Further Reading
Basil Willey, 'Nineteenth Century Studies', 1949, pp. 263-83.

Clerical Work

Mark Rutherford (1831–1913)

William Hale White, son of a Bedford shopkeeper, was brought up in the spiritually arid faith of the Calvinistic Independent Chapel. He recounted his progress towards a more satisfactory belief in the fictional version of his life published under the pseudonym Mark Rutherford, as 'Autobiography' (1881) and 'The Deliverance' (1885). Basil Willey has described him as representative of 'the Puritan who, emancipated by Wordsworth, Carlyle, (and) German biblical criticism . . . has rejected orthodox Christianity and ventured on the lonely quest for God'. One stage of this quest prompts Rutherford and a like-minded journalist M'Kay to befriend some of London's near-derelicts, materially needy and even more deeply deprived by the age's spiritual barrenness. In the following extract Rutherford tells the story of one of the group.

P 8

Another friend, and the last whom I shall name, was a young man named Clark. He was lame, and had been so from childhood. His father was a tradesman, working hard from early morning till late at night, and burdened with a number of children. The boy Richard, shut out from the companionship of his fellows, had a great love of books. When he left school his father did not know what to do with him — in fact there was only one occupation open to him, and that was clerical work of one kind or another. At last he got a place in a house in Fleet Street, which did a large business in those days in sending newspapers into the country. His whole occupation all day long was to write addresses, and for this he received twenty-five shillings a week, his hours being from nine o'clock till seven. The office in which he sat was crowded, and in order to squeeze the staff into the smallest space, rent being dear, a gallery had been run round the wall about four feet from the ceiling. This was provided with desks and gas lamps, and up there Clark sat, artificial light being necessary four days out of five. He came straight from the town in which his father lived to Fleet Street, and once settled in it there seemed no chance of change for the better. He knew what his father's struggles were; he could not go back to him, and he had not the energy to attempt to lift himself. It is very doubtful too whether he could have succeeded in achieving any improvement, whatever his energy might have been. He had got lodgings in Newcastle Street, and to these he returned in the evening, remaining there alone with his little library, and seldom moving out of doors. He was unhealthy constitutionally, and his habits contributed to make him more so. Everything which he saw which was good seemed only to sharpen the contrast between himself and his lot, and his reading was a curse to him rather than a blessing. I sometimes wished that he had never inherited any love whatever for what is usually considered to be the Best and that he had been endowed with an organisation coarse and commonplace, like that of his colleagues. If he went into company which suited him, or read anything which interested him, it seemed as if the ten hours of the gallery in Fleet Street had been made thereby only the more insupportable, and his habitual mood was one of despondency, so that his fellow clerks who knew his tastes not unnaturally asked what was the use of them if they only made him wretched; and they were more than ever convinced that in their amusements lay true happiness. Habit, which is the saviour of most of us, the opiate which dulls the otherwise unbearable miseries of life, only served to make Clark more sensitive. The monotony of that perpetual address-copying was terrible. He has told me with a kind of shame what an effect it had upon him — that sometimes for days he would feed upon the prospect of the most childish trifle because it would break in some slight degree the uniformity of his toil. For example, he would sometimes change from quill to steel pens and back again, and he found himself actually looking forward with a kind of joy — merely because of the variation — to the day on which he had fixed to go back to the quill after using steel. He would determine, two or three days beforehand, to get up earlier, and to walk to Fleet Street by way of Great Queen Street and Lincoln's Inn Fields, and upon this he would subsist till the day came. He could make no longer excursions because of his lameness. All this may sound very much like simple silliness to most people, but those who have not been bound to a wheel do not know what thoughts come into the head of the strongest man who is extended on it. Clark sat side by side in his gallery with other young men of rather a degraded type, and the confinement bred in them a filthy grossness with which they tormented him. They excited in him loathsome images, from which he could not free himself either by day or night. He was peculiarly weak in his inability to cast off impressions, or to get rid of mental pictures when once formed, and his distress at being haunted by these hateful, disgusting thoughts was pitiable. They were in fact almost more than thoughts, they were transportations out of himself — real visions. It would have been his salvation if he could have been a carpenter or a bricklayer, in country air, but this could not be.

See also M 3, N 3.   'The Deliverance', chap. 5.

Further Reading

Mark Rutherford, 'The Revolution in Tanner's Lane', 1887.
Basil Willey, 'More Nineteenth Century Studies', 1956, pp. 186-247.

Socialist Polemic

Tom Maguire (1865–94)

With the development of British Socialism in the 1880s, a number of writers began to contribute satirical and polemical poems to Socialist periodicals and journals. Tom Maguire was active in William Morris's Socialist League, and later founder-member of the Independent Labour Party. 'Depression in Duckland', published in 1892, is an Aesop-like tale satirising capitalist economics.

P 9 *Depression in Duckland*

A silly, self-sufficient goose
Laid golden eggs for an old duck's use;
And the old duck lived on the golden eggs,
While the goose ate worms and marsh-bank dregs.
But the duck had title deeds to show
That the marsh-bank dregs and the worms below
Were his sole, exclusive propertee,
On which the goose might fatten free;
To yield a regular egg supply
Was the one condition he bound her by.

So the goose had plenty of worms and dregs,
And the duck had plenty of golden eggs;
And the duck waxed fat and round and sleek,
While the goose waned wiry, worn and meek.
But on Sunday mornings the goose would hie
Regularly to the pond close by,
Where the duck would hold a service of prayer

For the good of the goose attending there,
And the sinful goose cried 'Alas!' and 'Alack!'
Whenever she heard the good duck quack.

For the duck would speak of the wicked ways
Of geese beginning and ending their days
A thriftless, shiftless, lazy lot,
Who didn't thank god for the worms they got.
He exhorted the goose to labour and lay
An extra golden egg per day,
To enable him to spread the light
Of his teachings and law in the lands of night,
For heathen turkeys and heathen 'chucks'
Might all be geese, though they couldn't be ducks.

So the simple goose laid eggs galore,
And the artful duck still called for more,
Till at length so great was the egg supply,
That the duck complained of their quality.
'Supply' exceeding her sister 'Demand'
The duck brought things to a sudden stand,
Declared a stop to the laying of eggs,
The killing of worms or the drinking of dregs;
Saying out to the goose, 'You must now make shift,
As I shall do, on the savings of thrift.'

'Alas!' the goose cried out in her woe,
'May I lay for myself?' but the duck said 'No!'
'Then oh!' she exclaimed in wild dismay,
'May I drink the dregs?' but the duck said 'Nay!
The dregs are mine, and mine are the worms,
And did you not agree to my terms?'
'But,' argued the goose, 'I have changed your dregs,
By labour and skill into golden eggs!
What is the remedy for my lack?'
The duck's laconic reply was 'Quack!'

See also H 4, 12.

Bringing Civilisation to Africa

Joseph Conrad (1857–1924)

Joseph Conrad, the son of a minor Polish landowner, left Poland in 1873, eventually joining the British Merchant Marine as a deck-hand and working his way up to ship's captain, before settling to the life of a writer in 1894. 'The Heart of Darkness' (1902) was based on his own experience of commanding a river steamer in 1889 in the Belgian Congo. Mainly concerned with the impact of a primitive culture on the European mind, it reveals the brutal side of European commercial expansion into Africa. In this extract the narrator describes his journey along the African coast and upriver to the chief trading station of the colonial power.

P 10

'I left in a French steamer, and she called in every blamed port they have out there, for, as far as I could see, the sole purpose of landing soldiers and custom-house officers. I watched the coast. Watching a coast as it slips by the ship is like thinking about an enigma. There it is before you — smiling, frowning, inviting, grand, mean, insipid, or savage, and always mute with an air of whispering, come and find out. This one was almost featureless, as if still in the making, with an aspect of monotonous grimness. The edge of a colossal jungle, so dark-green as to be almost black, fringed with white surf, ran straight, like a ruled line, far, far away along a blue sea whose glitter was blurred by a creeping mist. The sun was fierce, the land seemed to glisten and drip with steam. Here and there grayish-whitish specks showed up clustered inside the white surf, with a flag flying above them perhaps. Settlements some centuries old, and still no bigger than pin-heads on the untouched expanse of their background. We pounded along, stopped, landed soldiers; went on, landed custom-house clerks to levy toll in what looked like a God-forsaken wilderness, with a tin shed and a flag-pole lost in it; landed more soldiers — to take care of the custom-house clerks, presumably. Some, I heard, got drowned in the surf; but whether they did or not, nobody seemed particularly to care. They were just flung out there and on we went. Every day the coast looked the same as though we had not moved: but we passed various places — trading places — with names like Gran' Bassam., Little Popo; names that seemed to belong to some sordid farce acted in front of a sinister back-cloth. The idleness of a passenger, my isolation amongst all these men with whom I had no point of contact, the oily and languid sea, the uniform sombreness of the coast, seemed to keep me away from the truth of things, within the toil of a mournful and senseless delusion. The voice of the surf heard now and then was a positive pleasure, like the speech of a brother. It was something natural, that had its reason, that had a meaning. Now and then a boat from the shore gave one a momentary contact with reality. It was paddled by black fellows. You could see from afar the white of their eyeballs glistening. They shouted, sang; their bodies streamed with perspiration; they had faces like grotesque masks — these chaps; but they had bone, muscle, a wild vitality, an intense energy of movement, that was as natural and true as the surf along their coast. They wanted no excuse for being there. They were a great comfort to look at. For a time I would feel I belonged still to a world of straightforward facts; but the feeling would not last long. Something would turn up to scare it away. Once, I remember, we came upon a man-of-war anchored off the coast. There wasn't even a shed there, and she was shelling the bush. It appears the French had one of their wars going on thereabouts. Her ensign dropped limp like a rag; the muzzles of the long six-inch guns stuck out all over the low hull; the greasy, slimy swell swung her up lazily and let her down. swaying her thin masts. In the empty immensity of earth, sky, and water, there she was, incomprehensible, firing into a continent. Pop, would go one of the six-inch guns; a small flame would dart and vanish, a little white smoke would disappear, a tiny projectile would give a feeble screech — and nothing happened. Nothing could happen. There was a touch of insanity in the proceeding, a sense of lugubrious drollery in the sight;

and it was not dissipated by somebody on board assuring me earnestly there was a camp of natives — he called them enemies! — hidden out of sight somewhere.

'We gave her her letters (I heard the men in that lonely ship were dying of fever at the rate of three a-day) and went on. . . .

'At last we opened a reach. A rocky cliff appeared, mounds of turned-up earth by the shore, houses on a hill, others with iron roofs, amongst a waste of excavations, or hanging to the declivity. A continuous noise of the rapids above hovered over this scene of inhabited devastation. A lot of people, mostly black and naked, moved about like ants. A jetty projected into the river. A blinding sunlight drowned all this at times in a sudden recrudescence of glare. "There's your Company's station," said the Swede, pointing to three wooden barrack-like structures on the rocky slope. "I will send your things up. Four boxes did you say? So. Farewell."

'I came upon a boiler wallowing in the grass, then found a path leading up the hill. It turned aside for the boulders, and also for an undersized railway-truck lying there on its back with its wheels in the air. One was off. The thing looked as dead as the carcass of some animal. I came upon more pieces of decaying machinery, a stack of rusty rails. To the left a clump of trees made a shady spot, where dark things seemed to stir feebly. I blinked, the path was steep. A horn tooted to the right, and I saw the black people run. A heavy and dull detonation shook the ground, a puff of smoke came out of the cliff, and that was all. No change appeared on the face of the rock. They were building a railway. The cliff was not in the way or anything; but this objectless blasting was all the work going on.

'A slight clinking behind me made me turn my head. Six black men advanced in a file, toiling up the path. They walked erect and slow, balancing small baskets full of earth on their heads, and the clink kept time with their footsteps. Black rags were wound round their loins, and the short ends behind waggled to and fro like tails. I could see every rib, the joints of their limbs were like knots in a rope; each had an iron collar on his neck, and all were connected together with a chain whose bights swung between them, rhythmically clinking. Another report from the cliff made me think suddenly of that ship of war I had seen firing into a continent. It was the same kind of ominous voice; but these men could by no stretch of imagination be called enemies. They were called criminals, and the outraged law, like the bursting shells, had come to them, an insoluble mystery from the sea. All their meagre breasts panted together, the violently dilated nostrils quivered, the eyes stared stonily up-hill. They passed me within six inches, without a glance, with that complete, deathlike indifference of unhappy savages. Behind this raw matter one of the reclaimed, the product of the new forces at work, strolled despondently, carrying a rifle by its middle. He had a uniform jacket with one button off, and seeing a white man on the path hoisted his weapon to his shoulder with alacrity. This was simple prudence, white men being so much alike at a distance that he could not tell who I might be. He was speedily reassured, and with a large, white, rascally grin, and a glance at his charge, seemed to take me into partnership in his exalted trust. After all, I also was a part of the great cause of these high and just proceedings.

'Instead of going up, I turned and descended to the left. My idea was to let that chain-gang get out of sight before I climbed the hill. You know I am not particularly tender; I've had to strike and to fend off. I've had to resist and to attack sometimes — that's only one way of resisting — without counting the exact cost, according to the demands of such sort of life as I had blundered into. I've seen the devil of violence, and the devil of greed, and the devil of hot desire; but, by all the stars! these were strong, lusty, red-eyed devils, that swayed and drove men — men, I tell you. But as I stood on this hillside, I foresaw that in the blinding sunshine of that land I would become acquainted with a flabby, pretending, weak-eyed devil of a rapacious and pitiless folly. How insidious he could be, too, I was only to find out several months later and a thousand miles farther. For a moment I stood appalled, as though by a warning. Finally I descended the hill, obliquely, towards the trees I had seen.

'I avoided a vast artificial hole somebody had been digging on the slope, the purpose of which I found it impossible to divine. It wasn't a quarry or a sandpit, anyhow. It was just a hole. It might have been connected with the philanthropic desire of giving the criminals something to do. I don't know. Then I nearly fell into a very narrow ravine, almost no more than a scar in the hillside. I discovered that a lot of imported drainage-pipes for the settlement had been tumbled in there. There wasn't one that was not broken. It was a wanton smash-up. At last I got under the trees. My purpose was to stroll into the shade for a moment; but no sooner within than it seemed to me I had stepped into the gloomy circle of some Inferno. The rapids were near, and an uninterrupted, uniform, headlong, rushing noise filled the mournful stillness of the grove, where not a breath stirred, not a leaf moved, with a mysterious sound — as though the tearing pace of the launched earth had suddenly become audible.

'Black shapes crouched, lay, sat between the trees leaning against the trunks, clinging to the earth, half coming out, half effaced within the dim light, in all the attitudes of pain, abandonment, and despair. Another mine on the cliff went off, followed by a slight shudder of the soil under my feet. The work was going on. The work! And this was the place where some of the helpers had withdrawn to die.

'They were dying slowly — it was very clear. They were not enemies, they were not criminals, they were nothing earthly now, — nothing but black shadows of disease and starvation, lying confusedly in the greenish gloom. Brought from all the recesses of the coast in all the legality of time contracts, lost in uncongenial surroundings, fed on unfamiliar food, they sickened, became inefficient, and were then allowed to crawl away and rest. These moribund shapes were free as air — and nearly as thin. I began to distinguish the gleam of the eyes under the trees. Then, glancing down, I saw a face near my hand. The black bones reclined at full length with one shoulder against the tree, and slowly the eyelids rose and the sunken eyes looked up at me, enormous and vacant, a kind of blind, white flicker in the depths of the orbs, which died out slowly. The man seemed young — almost a boy — but you know with them it's hard to tell. I found nothing else to do but to offer him one of my good Swede's ship's biscuits I had in my pocket. The fingers closed slowly on it and held — there was no other movement and no other glance. He had tied a bit of white worsted round his neck — Why? Where did he get it? Was it a badge — an ornament — a charm — a propitiatory act? Was there any idea at all connected with it? It looked startling round his black neck, this bit of white thread from beyond the seas.

'Near the same tree two more bundles of acute angles sat with their legs drawn up. One, with his chin propped on his knees, stared at nothing, in an intolerable and appalling manner: his brother phantom rested its forehead, as if overcome with a great weariness; and all about others were scattered in every pose of contorted collapse, as in some picture of a massacre or a pestilence. While I stood horror-struck, one of these creatures rose to his hands and knees, and went off on all-fours towards the river to drink. He lapped out of his hand, then sat up in the sunlight, crossing his shins in front of him, and after a time let his woolly head fall on his breastbone.

'I didn't want any more loitering in the shade, and I made haste towards the station. When near the buildings I met a white man, in such an unexpected elegance of get-up that in the first moment I took him for a sort of vision. I saw a high starched collar, white cuffs, a light alpaca jacket, snowy trousers, a clean necktie, and varnished boots. No hat. Hair parted, brushed, oiled, under a green-lined parasol held in a big white hand. He was amazing, and had a penholder behind his ear.

'I shook hands with this miracle, and I learned he was the Company's chief accountant, and that all the book-keeping was done at this station. He had come out for a moment, he said, "to get a breath of fresh air." The expression sounded wonderfully odd, with its suggestion of sedentary desk-life. I wouldn't have mentioned the fellow to you at all, only it was from his lips that I first heard the name of the man who is so indissolubly connected with the memories of that time. Moreover, I respected the fellow. Yes; I respected his collars, his vast cuffs, his brushed hair. His appearance was certainly that of a hairdresser's dummy; but in the great demoralization of the land he kept up his appearance. That's backbone. His starched collars and got-up shirt-fronts were achievements of character. He had been out nearly three years; and, later, I could not help asking him how he managed to sport such linen. He had just the faintest blush, and said modestly, "I've been teaching one of the native women about the station. It was difficult. She had a distaste for the work." Thus this man had verily accomplished something. And he was devoted to his books, which were in apple-pie order.

'Everything else in the station was in a muddle, — heads, things, buildings. Strings of dusty niggers with splay feet arrived and departed; a stream of manufactured goods, rubbishy cottons, beads, and brass-wire set into the depths of darkness, and in return came a precious trickle of ivory.'

See also H 8.   'The Heart of Darkness', chap. 1.

Further Reading

Douglas Hewitt, 'Conrad: A Re-assessment', 1969, chap. 2.
Ian Watt, 'Joseph Conrad: Alienation and Commitment', in 'The English Mind', 1964, ed. Hugh Sykes Davies and George Watson, pp. 257-78.

The Role of Advertising

H. G. Wells (1866–1946)

H. G. Wells grew up in Bromley, Kent, son of an unsuccessful shop-owner. Largely by his own efforts, he managed to get a university education, graduating B.Sc. from London University. He achieved his first success as a writer with his scientific romances of the 1890s. 'Tono-Bungay' (1909) is his most ambitious attempt at a social novel. Its 'scene' is the world of company finance, a dramatic example of the socially chaotic effects of capitalism. Tono-Bungay was a patent medicine which with skilful advertising and selling made the fortune of its inventor, George Ponderevo. In this extract his nephew, self-educated in science, and influenced by Socialist thinking, describes the early advertising campaigns which launched Tono-Bungay.

P 11

You know, from first to last, I saw the business with my eyes open, I saw its ethical and moral values quite clearly. Never for a moment do I remember myself faltering from my persuasion that the sale of Tono-Bungay was a thoroughly dishonest proceeding. The stuff was, I perceived, a mischievous trash, slightly stimulating, aromatic, and attractive, likely to become a bad habit and train people in the habitual use of stronger tonics, and insidiously dangerous to people with defective kidneys. It would cost about sevenpence the large bottle to make, including bottling, and we were to sell it at half a crown plus the cost of the patent medicine stamp. A thing that I will confess deterred me from the outset far more than the sense of dishonesty in this affair, was the supreme silliness of the whole concern. I still clung to the idea that the world of men was or should be a sane and just organisation, and the idea that I should set myself gravely, just at the fine springtime of my life, to developing a monstrous bottling and packing warehouse, bottling rubbish for the consumption of foolish, credulous, and depressed people, had in it a touch of insanity. My early beliefs still clung to me. I felt assured that somewhere there must be a hitch in the fine prospect of ease and wealth under such conditions; that somewhere, a little overgrown, perhaps, but still traceable, lay a neglected, wasted path of use and honour for me.

My inclination to refuse the whole thing increased rather than diminished at first as I went along the Embankment. In my uncle's presence there had been a sort of glamour that had prevented an outright refusal. It was a revival of affection for him I felt in his presence I think, in part, and in part an instinctive feeling that I must consider him as my host. But much more was it a curious persuasion he had the knack of inspiring — a persuasion not so much of his integrity and capacity as of the reciprocal and yielding foolishness of the world. One felt that he was silly and wild, but in some way silly and wild after the fashion of the universe. After all, one must live somehow. I astonished him and myself by temporising.

'No,' said I, 'I'll think it over!'

And as I went along the Embankment, the first effect was all against my uncle. He shrank — for a little while he continued to shrink — in perspective until he was only a very small shabby little man in a dirty back street, sending off a few hundred bottles of rubbish to foolish buyers. The great buildings on the right of us, the Inns and the School Board place — as it was then — Somerset House, the big hotels, the great bridges, Westminster's outlines ahead, had an effect of grey largeness that reduced him to the proportions of a busy blackbeetle in a crack in the floor.

And then my eye caught the advertisements on the south side of 'Sorber's Food,' of 'Cracknell's Ferric Wine,' very bright and prosperous signs, illuminated at night, and I realised how astonishingly they looked at home there, how evidently part they were in the whole thing.

I saw a man come charging out of Palace Yard — the policeman touched his helmet to him — with a hat and a bearing astonishingly like my uncle's. After all — didn't Cracknell himself sit in the House?

Tono-Bungay shouted at me from a hoarding near Adelphi Terrace, I saw it afar off near Carfax Street, it cried out again upon me in Kensington High Street and burst into a perfect clamour, six or seven times I saw it, as I drew near my diggings. It certainly had an air of being something more than a dream.

Yes, I thought it over — thoroughly enough. . . . Trade rules the world. Wealth rather than trade! The thing was true, and true too was my uncle's proposition that the quickest way to get wealth is to sell the cheapest thing possible in the dearest bottle. He was frightfully right after all. *Pecunia non olet* — a Roman emperor said that. Perhaps my great heroes in Plutarch were no more than such men, fine now only because they are distant; perhaps after all this Socialism to which I had been drawn was only a foolish dream, only the more foolish because all its promises were conditionally true. Morris and these others played with it wittingly; it gave a zest, a touch of substance to their aesthetic pleasures. Never would there be good faith enough to bring such things about. They knew it; every one, except a few fools, knew it. As I crossed the corner of St James's Park wrapped in thought, I dodged back just in time to escape a prancing pair of greys. A stout, common-looking woman, very magnificently dressed, regarded me from the carriage with a scornful eye. 'No doubt,' thought I, 'a pill-vendor's wife.' . . .

So I made my peace with my uncle and we set out upon this bright enterprise of selling slightly injurious rubbish at one-and-three-halfpence and two-and-nine a bottle, including the Government stamp. We made Tono-Bungay hum!. . . .

It was my uncle's genius that did it. No doubt he needed me — I was, I will admit, his indispensable right hand; but his was the brain to conceive. He wrote every advertisement; some of them even he sketched. You must remember that those were the days before the *Times* took to enterprise and the vociferous hawking of that antiquated *Encyclopaedia*. That alluring, button-holing, let-me-just-tell-you-quite-soberly-something-you-ought-to-know style of newspaper advertisement, with every now and then a convulsive jump of some attractive phrase into capitals, was then almost a novelty. 'Many people who are MODERATELY well think they are QUITE well,' was one of his early efforts. The jerks in capitals were, 'DO NOT NEED DRUGS OR MEDICINE,' and 'SIMPLY A PROPER REGIMEN TO GET YOU IN TONE.' One was warned against the chemist or druggist who pushed 'much advertised nostrums' on one's attention. That trash did more harm than good. The thing needed was regimen — and Tono-Bungay!

Very early, too, was that bright little quarter column, at least it was usually a quarter column, in the evening papers: 'HILARITY — TONO-BUNGAY. Like Mountain Air in the Veins.' The penetrating trio of questions: 'Are you bored with your Business? Are you bored with your Dinner? Are you bored with your Wife?' — that, too, was in our Gower Street days. Both these we had in our first campaign when we worked London south, central, and west; and then, too, we had our first poster — the HEALTH, BEAUTY, AND STRENGTH one. That was his design; I happen still to have got by me the first sketch he made for it. I have reproduced it here with one or two others to enable the reader to understand the mental quality that initiated these familiar ornaments of London. (The second one is about eighteen months later, the germ of the well-known 'Fog' poster; the third was designed for an influenza epidemic, but never issued. . . .

My special and distinctive duty was to give Tono-Bungay substance and an outward and visible bottle, to translate my uncle's great imaginings into the creation of case after case of labelled bottles of nonsense, and the punctual discharge of them by railway, road, and steamer towards their ultimate goal in the Great Stomach of the People. By all modern standards the business was, as my uncle would say, 'absolutely *bona fide*.' We sold our stuff and got the money, and spent the money honestly in lies and clamour to sell more stuff. Section by section we spread it over the whole of the British Isles; first working the middle-class London suburbs, then the outer suburbs, then the home counties, then going (with new bills and a more pious style of 'ad') into Wales, a great field always for a new patent-medicine, and then into Lancashire. My uncle had in his inner office a big map of England, and as we took up fresh sections of the local press and our consignments invaded new areas, flags for advertisements and pink underlines for orders showed our progress.

'The romance of modern commerce, George!' my uncle would say, rubbing his hands together and drawing in the air through his teeth. 'The romance of modern commerce, eh? Conquest. Province by province. Like sogers.'

We subjugated England and Wales; we rolled over the Cheviots with a special adaptation containing eleven per cent of absolute alcohol: 'Tono-Bungay. Thistle Brand.' We also had the Fog poster adapted to a kilted Briton in a misty Highland scene.

Under the shadow of our great leading line we were presently taking subsidiary specialities into action; 'Tono-Bungay Hair Stimulant' was our first supplement. Then came 'Concentrated Tono-Bungay' for the eyes. That didn't go, but we had a considerable success with the Hair Stimulant. We broached the subject, I remember, in a little catechism beginning: 'Why does the hair fall out? Because the follicles are fagged. What are the follicles? . . .' So it went on to the climax that the Hair Stimulant contained all 'The essential principles of that most reviving tonic, Tono-Bungay, together with an emollient and nutritious oil derived from crude Neat's Foot Oil by a process of refinement, separation, and deodorisation. . . . It will be manifest to any one of scientific attainments that in Neat's Foot Oil derived from the hoofs and horns of beasts, we must necessarily have a *natural* skin and hair lubricant.'

And we also did admirable things with our next subsidiaries, 'Tono-Bungay Lozenges,' and 'Tono-Bungay Chocolate'. These we urged upon the public for their extraordinary nutritive and recuperative value in cases of fatigue and strain. We gave them posters and illustrated advertisements showing climbers hanging from marvellously vertical cliffs, cyclist champions upon the track, mounted messengers engaged in Aix-to-Ghent rides, soldiers lying out in action under a hot sun. 'You can GO for twenty-four hours,' we declared, 'on Tono-Bungay Chocolate.' We didn't say whether you could return on the same commodity. We also showed a dreadfully barristerish barrister, wig, side-whiskers, teeth, a horribly life-like portrait of all existing barristers, talking at a table, and beneath, this legend: 'A Four Hours' Speech on Tono-Bungay Lozenges, and as fresh as when he began.' That brought in regiments of school-teachers, revivalist ministers, politicians and the like. I really do believe there was an element of 'kick' in the strychnine in these lozenges, especially in those made according to our earlier formula. For we altered all our formulae — invariably weakening them enormously as sales got ahead. . . .

My uncle's last addition to the Tono-Bungay group was the Tono-

Bungay Mouthwash. The reader has probably read a hundred times that inspiring inquiry of his, 'You are Young Yet, but are you Sure Nothing has Aged your Gums?'

See also N 6.   'Tono-Bungay', chaps. 2, 3.

Further Reading

H. G. Wells, 'Kipps', 1905; 'Experiment in Autobiography', 1934, chaps. 3, 5, 9.

Power and Morality

George Bernard Shaw (1856–1950)

'Not that we want no aristocracy,' wrote Carlyle, 'but that we want a *new* one.' George Bernard Shaw was a Socialist, but he shared Carlyle's pessimism about democracy, creating in 'Major Barbara' (1905) a dramatic parable on the theme that industrialisation had released social forces which only a new aristocracy could put to creative use. Andrew Undershaft, owner of an armaments firm, represents the material power of modern industry. He is married to Lady Britomart, a member of the English governing class which has failed to come to terms with the new force. His daughter Barbara, thinking that only religion can save men, is a Major in the Salvation Army till her father convinces her that its influence finally depends on the charity of the rich. The extract comes from the play's last act, after Undershaft has shown his model factory to his family, arguing that morality depends upon power. Adolphus Cusins, once a Professor of Greek, now about to inherit Undershaft's power and marry his daughter, represents the humanist intellectual accepting full social and political responsibility, and creating the new aristocracy.

P 12

Barbara (*hypnotized*): Before I joined the Salvation Army, I was in my own power; and the consequence was that I never knew what to do with myself. When I joined it, I had not time enough for all the things I had to do.

Undershaft (*approvingly*): Just so. And why was that, do you suppose?

Barbara: Yesterday I should have said, because I was in the power of God. (*She resumes her self-possession, withdrawing her hands from his with a power equal to his own.*) But you came and shewed me

Heavy Artillery — Alexandria 1882.

that I was in the Power of Bodger and Undershaft. Today I feel —
oh! how can I put it into words? Sarah: do you remember the
earthquake at Cannes, when we were little children? — how little the
surprise of the first shock mattered compared to the dread and
horror of waiting for the second? That is how I feel in this place
today. I stood on the rock I thought eternal; and without a word of
warning it reeled and crumbled under me. I was safe with an infinite
wisdom watching me, an army marching to Salvation with me; and
in a moment, at a stroke of your pen in a cheque book, I stood
alone; and the heavens were empty. That was the first shock of the
earthquake: I am waiting for the second.

Undershaft: Come, come, my daughter! dont make too much of your
little tinpot tragedy. What do we do here when we spend years of

work and thought and thousands of pounds of solid cash on a new gun or an aerial battleship that turns out just a hairsbreadth wrong after all? Scrap it. Scrap it without wasting another hour or another pound on it. Well, you have made for yourself something that you call a morality or a religion or what not. It doesnt fit the facts. Well, scrap it. Scrap it and get one that does fit. That is what is wrong with the world at present. It scraps its obsolete steam engines and dynamos; but it wont scrap its old prejudices and its old moralities and its old religions and its old political constitutions. Whats the result? In machinery it does very well; but in morals and religion and politics it is working at a loss that brings it nearer bankruptcy every year. Dont persist in that folly. If your old religion broke down yesterday, get a newer and a better one for tomorrow.

Barbara: Oh how gladly I would take a better one to my soul! But you offer me a worse one. (*Turning on him with sudden vehemence*) Justify yourself: shew me some light through the darkness of this dreadful place, with its beautifully clean workshops, and respectable workmen, and model homes.

Undershaft: Cleanliness and respectability do not need justification, Barbara: they justify themselves. I see no darkness here, no dreadfulness. In your Salvation shelter I saw poverty, misery, cold and hunger. You gave them bread and treacle and dreams of heaven, I give from thirty shillings a week to twelve thousand a year. They find their own dreams; but I look after the drainage.

Barbara: And their souls?

Undershaft: I save their souls just as I saved yours.

Barbara (*revolted*): You saved my soul! What do you mean?

Undershaft: I fed you and clothed you and housed you. I took care that you should have money enough to live handsomely — more than enough; so that you could be wasteful, careless, generous. That saved your soul from the seven deadly sins.

Barbara (*bewildered*): The seven deadly sins!

Undershaft: Yes, the deadly seven. (*Counting on his fingers*) Food, clothing, firing, rent, taxes, respectability and children. Nothing can lift those seven millstones from Man's neck but money; and the spirit cannot soar until the millstones are lifted. I lifted them from your spirit. I enabled Barbara to become Major Barbara; and I saved her from the crime of poverty.

Cusins: Do you call poverty a crime?

Undershaft: The worst of crimes. All the other crimes are virtues beside it: all the other dishonors are chivalry itself by comparison. Poverty blights whole cities; spreads horrible pestilences; strikes dead the very souls of all who come within sight, sound, or smell of it. What you call crime is nothing: a murder here and a theft there, a blow now and a curse then: what do they matter? they are only the accidents and illnesses of life: there are not fifty genuine professional criminals in London. But there are millions of poor people, abject people, dirty people, ill fed, ill clothed people. They poison us morally and physically: they kill the happiness of society: they force us to do away with our own liberties and to organize unnatural cruelties for fear they should rise against us and drag us down into their abyss. Only fools fear crime: we all fear poverty. Pah! (turning on Barbara) you talk of your half-saved ruffian in West Ham: you accuse me of dragging his soul back to perdition. Well, bring him to me here; and I will drag his soul back again to salvation for you. Not by words and dreams; but by thirtyeight shillings a week, a sound house in a handsome street, and a permanent job. In three weeks he will have a fancy waistcoat; in three months a tall hat and a chapel sitting; before the end of the year he will shake hands with a duchess at a Primrose League meeting, and join the Conservative Party.

Barbara: And will he be the better for that?

Undershaft: You know he will. Dont be a hypocrite, Barbara. He will be better fed, better housed, better clothed, better behaved; and his children will be pounds heavier and bigger. That will be better than an American cloth mattress in a shelter, chopping firewood, eating bread and treacle, and being forced to kneel down from time to time to thank heaven for it: knee drill, I think you call it. It is cheap work converting starving men with a Bible in one hand and a slice of bread in the other. I will undertake to convert West Ham to Mahometanism on the same terms. Try your hand on my men: their souls are hungry because their bodies are full.

Barbara: And leave the east end to starve?

Undershaft (*his energetic tone dropping into one of bitter and brooding remembrance*): I was an east ender. I moralised and starved until one day I swore that I would be a full-fed free man at all costs; that nothing should stop me except a bullet, neither reason nor morals nor the lives of other men. I said 'Thou shalt starve ere I starve'; and with that word I became free and great. I was a dangerous man until I had my will: now I am a useful, beneficent, kindly person. That is the history of most self-made millionaires, I fancy. When it is the history of every Englishman we shall have an England worth living in.

Lady Britomart: Stop making speeches, Andrew. This is not the place for them.

Undershaft (*punctured*): My dear: I have no other means of conveying my ideas.

Lady Britomart: Your ideas are nonsense. You got on because you were selfish and unscrupulous.

Undershaft: Not at all. I had the strongest scruples about poverty and starvation. Your moralists are quite unscrupulous about both: they make virtues of them. I had rather be a thief than a pauper. I had rather be a murderer than a slave. I dont want to be either; but if you force the alternative on me, then, by Heaven, I'll choose the braver and more moral one. I hate poverty and slavery worse than any other crimes whatsoever. And let me tell you this. Poverty and slavery have stood up for centuries to your sermons and leading articles: they will not stand up to my machine guns. Dont preach at them: dont reason with them. Kill them.

Barbara: Killing. Is that your remedy for everything?

Undershaft: It is the final test of conviction, the only lever strong enough to overturn a social system, the only way of saying Must. Let six hundred and seventy fools loose in the streets; and three policemen can scatter them. But huddle them together in a certain house in Westminster; and let them go through certain ceremonies and call themselves certain names until at last they get the courage to kill; and your six hundred and seventy fools become a government. Your pious mob fills up ballot papers and imagines it is governing its masters; but the ballot paper that really governs is the paper that has a bullet wrapped up in it.

Cusins: That is perhaps why, like most intelligent people, I never vote.

Undershaft: Vote! Bah! When you vote, you only change the names of the cabinet. When you shoot, you pull down governments, inaugurate new epochs, abolish old orders and set up new. Is that historically true, Mr Learned Man, or is it not?

Cusins: It is historically true. I loathe having to admit it. I repudiate your sentiments. I abhor your nature. I defy you in every possible way. Still, it is true. But it ought not to be true.

Undershaft: Ought! ought! ought! ought! ought! Are you going to spend your life saying ought, like the rest of our moralists? Turn your oughts into shalls, man. Come and make explosives with me. Whatever can blow men up can blow society up. The history of the world is the history of those who had courage enough to embrace this truth. Have you the courage to embrace it, Barbara?

Lady Britomart: Barbara: I positively forbid you to listen to your father's abominable wickedness. And you, Adolphus, ought to know better than to go about saying that wrong things are true. What does it matter whether they are true if they are wrong?

Undershaft: What does it matter whether they are wrong if they are true? . . .

Barbara and Cusins, left alone together, look at one another silently.

Cusins: Barbara: I am going to accept this offer.

Barbara: I thought you would.

Cusins: You understand, dont you, that I had to decide without consulting you. If I had thrown the burden of the choice on you, you would sooner or later have despised me for it.

Barbara: Yes: I did not want you to sell your soul for me any more than for this inheritance.

Cusins: It is not the sale of my soul that troubles me: I have sold it too often to care about that. I have sold it for a professorship. I have sold it for an income. I have sold it to escape being imprisoned for refusing to pay taxes for hangmen's ropes and unjust wars and things that I abhor. What is all human conduct but the daily and hourly sale of our souls for trifles? What I am now selling it for is neither money nor position nor comfort, but for reality and for power.

Barbara: You know that you will have no power, and that he has none.

Cusins: I know. It is not for myself alone. I want to make power for the world.

Barbara: I want to make power for the world too; but it must be spiritual power.

Cusins: I think all power is spiritual: these cannons will not go off by themselves. I have tried to make spiritual power by teaching Greek. But the world can never be really touched by a dead language and a dead civilization. The people must have power; and the people cannot have Greek. Now the power that is made here can be wielded by all men.

Barbara: Power to burn women's houses down and kill their sons and tear their husbands to pieces.

Cusins: You cannot have power for good without having power for evil too. Even mother's milk nourishes murderers as well as heroes. This power which only tears men's bodies to pieces has never been so horribly abused as the intellectual power, the imaginative power, the poetic, religious power that can enslave men's souls. As a teacher of Greek I gave the intellectual man weapons against the common man. I now want to give the common man weapons against the intellectual man. I love the common people. I want to arm them against the lawyers, the doctors, the priests, the literary men, the professors, the artists, and the politicians, who, once in authority, are more disastrous and tyrannical than all the fools, rascals, and impostors. I want a power simple enough for common men to use, yet strong enough to force the intellectual oligarchy to use its genius for the general good.

Barbara: Is there no higher power than that (*pointing to the shell*)?

Cusins: Yes; but that power can destroy the higher powers just as a tiger can destroy a man: therefore Man must master that power first. I admitted this when the Turks and Greeks were last at war. My best pupil went out to fight for Hellas. My parting gift to him was not a copy of Plato's Republic, but a revolver and a hundred Undershaft cartridges. The blood of every Turk he shot — if he shot any — is on my head as well as on Undershaft's. That act committed me to this place for ever. Your father's challenge has beaten me. Dare I make war on war? I must. I will.

See also A 1, D 2, H 12.   'Major Barbara', Act 3.

Further Reading

George Bernard Shaw, 'Heartbreak House', 1915.
Edmund Wilson, 'Bernard Shaw at Eighty', in 'The Triple Thinkers', 1938.
Louis Crompton, 'Shaw's Challenge to Liberalism', in 'Shaw, A Collection of Critical Essays', 1965, ed. R. B. Kaufman.

Money and the Pursuit of Culture

E. M. Forster (1879–1970)

As a novelist, E. M. Forster belongs to 'the fag-end of Victorian Liberalism', accurately sensing the major changes brought about by industrialisation, but too deeply influenced by the world it was replacing to feel comfortable in the twentieth century. Something of this conflict appears in 'Howards End' (1910). It concerns two representative Edwardian families, the cultivated, liberal-minded Schlegels, living on investment income; the energetic, philistine Wilcoxes, active in business with imperialist connections; and a character victimised in different ways by both Schlegels and Wilcoxes, Leonard Bast, an insurance clerk struggling to educate himself in the approved Victorian manner. Forster's concern here is to point the connection between the Victorian cultural ideal and the possession of an adequate income.

P 13

The boy, Leonard Bast, stood at the extreme verge of gentility. He was not in the abyss, but he could see it, and at times people whom he knew had dropped in, and counted no more. He knew that he was poor, and would admit it: he would have died sooner than confess any inferiority to the rich. This may be splendid of him. But he was inferior to most rich people, there is not the least doubt of it. He was not as courteous as the average rich man, nor as intelligent, nor as healthy, nor as lovable. His mind and his body had been alike underfed, because he was poor; and because he was modern they were always craving better food. Had he lived some centuries ago, in the brightly coloured civilisations of the past, he would have had a definite status, his rank and his income would have corresponded. But in his day the angel of

Democracy had arisen, enshadowing the classes with leathern wings, and proclaiming, 'All men are equal — all men, that is to say, who possess umbrellas,' and so he was obliged to assert gentility, lest he slipped into the abyss where nothing counts, and the statements of Democracy are inaudible.

As he walked away from Wickham Place, his first care was to prove that he was as good as the Miss Schlegels. Obscurely wounded in his pride, he tried to wound them in return. They were probably not ladies. Would real ladies have asked him to tea? They were certainly ill-natured and cold. At each step his feeling of superiority increased. Would a real lady have talked about stealing an umbrella? Perhaps they were thieves after all, and if he had gone into the house they would have clapped a chloroformed handkerchief over his face. He walked on complacently as far as the Houses of Parliament. There an empty stomach asserted itself, and told him that he was a fool.

'Evening, Mr Bast.'

'Evening, Mr Dealtry.'

'Nice evening.'

'Evening.'

Mr Dealtry, a fellow clerk, passed on, and Leonard stood wondering whether he would take the tram as far as a penny would take him, or whether he would walk. He decided to walk — it is no good giving in, and he had spent money enough at Queen's Hall — and he walked over Westminster Bridge, in front of St Thomas's Hospital, and through the immense tunnel that passes under the South-Western main line at Vauxhall. In the tunnel he paused and listened to the roar of the trains. A sharp pain darted through his head, and he was conscious of the exact form of his eye sockets. He pushed on for another mile, and did not slacken speed until he stood at the entrance of a road called Camelia Road, which was at present his home.

Here he stopped again, and glanced suspiciously to right and left, like a rabbit that is going to bolt into its hole. A block of flats, constructed with extreme cheapness, towered on either hand. Farther down the road two more blocks were being built, and beyond these an old house was being demolished to accommodate another pair. It was the kind of scene that may be observed all over London, whatever the locality — bricks and mortar rising and falling with the restlessness of the water in a fountain, as the city receives more and more men upon her soil. Camelia Road would soon stand out like a fortress, and command, for a little, an extensive view. Only for a little. Plans were out for the erection of flats in Magnolia Road also. And again a few years, and all the flats in either road might be pulled down, and new buildings, of a vastness at present unimaginable, might arise where they had fallen. . . .

Then Leonard entered Block B of the flats, and turned, not upstairs, but down, into what is known to house agents as a semi-basement, and to other men as a cellar. He opened the door, and cried 'Hullo!' with the pseudo-geniality of the Cockney. There was no reply. 'Hullo!' he repeated. The sitting-room was empty, though the electric light had been left burning. A look of relief came over his face, and he flung himself into the armchair.

The sitting-room contained, besides the armchair, two other chairs, a piano, a three-legged table, and a cosy corner. Of the walls, one was occupied by the window, the other by a draped mantelshelf bristling with Cupids. Opposite the window was the door, and beside the door a bookcase, while over the piano there extended one of the masterpieces of Maud Goodman. It was an amorous and not unpleasant little hole when the curtains were drawn, and the lights turned on, and the gas-stove unlit. But it struck that shallow makeshift note that is so often heard in the modern dwelling-place. It had been too easily gained, and could be relinquished too easily.

As Leonard was kicking off his boots he jarred the three-legged table, and a photograph frame, honourably poised upon it, slid sideways, fell off into the fireplace, and smashed. He swore in a colourless sort of way, and picked the photograph up. It represented a young lady called Jacky, and had been taken at the time when young ladies called Jacky were often photographed with their mouths open. Teeth of dazzling whiteness extended along either of Jacky's jaws, and positively weighed her head sideways, so large were they and so numerous. Take my word for it, that smile was simply stunning, and it is only you and I who will be fastidious, and complain that true joy begins in the eyes, and that the eyes of Jacky did not accord with her smile, but were anxious and hungry.

Leonard tried to pull out the fragments of glass, and cut his fingers and swore again. A drop of blood fell on the frame, another followed, spilling over on to the exposed photograph. He swore more vigorously, and dashed into the kitchen, where he bathed his hands. The kitchen was the same size as the sitting-room: through it was a bedroom. This completed his home. He was renting the flat furnished: of all the objects that encumbered it none were his own except the photograph frame, the Cupids, and the books.

'Damn, damn, damnation!' he murmured, together with such other words as he had learnt from older men. Then he raised his hand to his forehead and said, 'Oh, damn it all ——' which meant something different. He pulled himself together. He drank a little tea, black and silent, that still survived upon an upper shelf. He swallowed some dusty crumbs of a cake. Then he went back to the sitting-room, settled himself anew, and began to read a volume of Ruskin.

'Seven miles to the north of Venice ——'

How perfectly the famous chapter opens! How supreme its command of admonition and of poetry! The rich man is speaking to us from his gondola.

'Seven miles to the north of Venice the banks of sand which nearer the city rise little above low-water mark attain by degrees a higher level, and knit themselves at last into fields of salt morass, raised here and there into shapeless mounds, and intercepted by narrow creeks of sea.'

Leonard was trying to form his style on Ruskin: he understood him to be the greatest master of English Prose. He read forward steadily, occasionally making a few notes.

'Let us consider a little each of these characters in succession, and first (for of the shafts enough has been said already), what is very peculiar to this church — its luminousness.'

Was there anything to be learnt from this fine sentence? Could he adapt it to the needs of daily life? Could he introduce it, with modifications, when he next wrote a letter to his brother, the lay-reader? For example —

'Let us consider a little each of these characters in succession, and first (for of the absence of ventilation enough has been said already), what is very peculiar to this flat — its obscurity.'

Something told him that the modifications would not do; and that something, had he known it, was the spirit of English Prose. 'My flat is dark as well as stuffy.' Those were the words for him.

And the voice in the gondola rolled on, piping melodiously of Effort and Self-Sacrifice, full of high purpose, full of beauty, full even of sympathy and the love of men, yet somehow eluding all that was actual and insistent in Leonard's life. For it was the voice of one who had never been dirty or hungry, and had not guessed successfully what dirt and hunger are.

Leonard listened to it with reverence. He felt that he was being done good to, and that if he kept on with Ruskin, and the Queen's Hall Concerts, and some pictures by Watts, he would one day push his head out of the grey waters and see the universe. He believed in sudden conversion, a belief which may be right, but which is peculiarly attractive to a half-baked mind. It is the basis of much popular religion: in the domain of business it dominates the Stock Exchange, and becomes that 'bit of luck' by which all successes and failures are explained. 'If only I had a bit of luck, the whole thing would come straight. . . . He's got a most magnificent place down at Streatham and a 20 h.p. Fiat, but then, mind you, he's had luck. . . . I'm sorry the wife's so late, but she never has any luck over catching trains.' Leonard was superior to these people; he did believe in effort and in a steady preparation for the change that he desired. But of a heritage that may expand gradually, he had no conception: he hoped to come to Culture suddenly, much as the Revivalist hopes to come to Jesus. Those Miss Schlegels had come to it; they had done the trick; their hands were upon the ropes, once and for all. And meanwhile, his flat was dark, as well as stuffy.

See also H 7, 11, M 3.   'Howards End', chap. 6.

Further Reading

E. M. Forster, 'Two Cheers for Democracy', 1938, pp. 55-60, 67-76, 273-4.

Frederick C. Crews, 'The Perils of Humanism', 1962, pp. 105-23.

Technology and the Future

H. G. Wells

H. G. Wells's most original single contribution to literature was the scientific romance, progenitor of modern science fiction, which explores the social and moral consequences of swift technological change, in itself a long-term result of the industrial revolution. 'The War of the Worlds' (1898) is one of his most successful stories in this vein. The extract takes up at the point when the invading Martians have begun their advance on London from the south-west, releasing for the first time the full power of their superior weapons. The theme of the fear of invasion by creatures with a more powerful technology may be said to symbolise a major cultural response to the machine, the recognition that man has radically changed his relationship with his natural environment, and that in so doing he faces as many dangers as benefits.

P 14

'It's bows and arrows against the lightning, anyhow,' said the artillery-man. 'They 'aven't seen that fire-beam yet.'

The officers who were not actively engaged stood and stared over the tree-tops south-westward, and the men digging would stop every now and again to stare in the same direction.

Byfleet was in a tumult, people packing, and a score of hussars, some of them dismounted, some on horseback, were hunting them about. Three or four black Government wagons, with crosses in white circles, and an old omnibus, among other vehicles, were being loaded in the village street. There were scores of people, most of them sufficiently Sabbatical to have assumed their best clothes. The soldiers were having the greatest difficulty in making them realize the gravity of their position. We saw one shrivelled old fellow with a huge box and a score or more of flower-pots containing orchids, angrily expostulating with the corporal who would leave them behind. I stopped and gripped his arm.

'Do you know what's over there?' I said, pointing at the pine-tops that hid the Martians.

'Eh?' said he, turning. 'I was explainin' these is vallyble.'

'Death!' I shouted. 'Death is coming! Death!' and, leaving him to digest that if he could, I hurried on after the artilleryman. At the corner I looked back. The soldier had left him, and he was still standing by his box with the pots of orchids on the lid of it, and staring vaguely over the trees.

No one in Weybridge could tell us where the headquarters were established; the whole place was in such confusion as I had never seen in any town before. Carts, carriages everywhere, the most astonishing miscellany of conveyances and horseflesh. The respectable inhabitants of the place, men in golf and boating costumes, wives prettily dressed, were packing, riverside loafers, energetically helping, children excited, and, for the most part, highly delighted at this astonishing variation of their Sunday experiences. In the midst of it all the worthy vicar was very pluckily holding an early celebration, and his bell was jangling out above the excitement.

I and the artilleryman, seated on the step of the drinking-fountain, made a very passable meal upon what we had brought with us. Patrols of soldiers – here no longer hussars, but grenadiers in white – were warning people to move now or to take refuge in their cellars as soon as the firing began. We saw as we crossed the railway bridge that a growing crowd of people had assembled in and about the railway station, and the swarming platform was piled with boxes and packages. The ordinary traffic had been stopped, I believe, in order to allow of the passage of troops and guns to Chertsey, and I had heard since that a savage struggle occurred for places in the special trains that were put on at a later hour.

We remained at Weybridge until midday, and at that hour we found ourselves at the place near Shepperton Lock where the Wey and Thames join. Part of the time we spent helping two old women to pack a little cart. The Wey has a treble mouth, and at this point boats are to be hired, and there was a ferry across the river. On the Shepperton side was an inn, with a lawn, and beyond that the tower of Shepperton Church — it has been replaced by a spire — rose above the trees.

Here we found an excited and noisy crowd of fugitives. As yet the flight had not grown to a panic, but there were already far more people than all the boats going to and fro could enable to cross. People came panting along under heavy burdens; one husband and wife were even carrying a small out-house door between them, with some of their household goods piled thereon. One man told us he meant to try to get away from Shepperton Station.

There was a lot of shouting, and one man was even jesting. The idea people seemed to have here was that the Martians were simply formidable human beings, who might attack and sack the town, to be certainly destroyed in the end. Every now and then people would glance nervously across the Wey, at the meadows towards Chertsey, but everthing over there was still.

Across the Thames, except just where the boats landed, everything was quiet, in vivid contrast with the Surrey side. The people who landed there from the boats went tramping off down the lane. The big ferry-boat had just made a journey. Three or four soldiers stood on the lawn of the inn, staring and jesting at the fugitives, without offering to help. The inn was closed, as it was now within prohibited hours.

'What's that!' cried a boatman, and 'Shut up, you fool!' said a man near me to a yelping dog. Then the sound came again, this time from the direction of Chertsey, a muffled thud — the sound of a gun.

The fighting was beginning. Almost immediately unseen batteries across the river to our right, unseen because of the trees, took up the chorus, firing heavily one after the other. A woman screamed. Everyone stood arrested by the sudden stir of battle, near us and yet invisible to us. Nothing was to be seen save flat meadows, cows feeding uncon-cernedly for the most part, and silvery pollard willows motionless in the warm sunlight.

'The sojers 'll stop 'em,' said a woman beside me doubtfully. A haziness rose over the tree-top.

Then suddenly we saw a rush of smoke far away up the river, a puff of smoke that jerked up into the air, and hung, and forthwith the ground heaved underfoot and a heavy explosion shook the air, smashing two or three windows in the houses near, and leaving us astonished.

'Here they are!' shouted a man in a blue jersey. 'Yonder! D'yer see them? Yonder!'

Quickly, one after the other, one, two, three, four of the armoured Martians appeared, far away over the little trees, across the flat meadows that stretch towards Chertsey, and striding hurredly towards the river. Little cowled figures they seemed at first, going with a rolling motion and as fast as flying birds.

Then, advancing obliquely towards us, came a fifth. Their armoured bodies glittered in the sun, as they swept swiftly forward upon the guns, growing rapidly larger as they drew nearer. One on the extreme left, the remotest, that is, flourished a huge case high in the air, and the ghostly terrible Heat-Ray I had already seen on Friday night smote towards Chertsey, and struck the town.

At sight of these strange, swift, and terrible creatures, the crowd along by the water's edge seemed to me to be for a moment horror-struck. There was no screaming or shouting, but a silence. Then a hoarse murmur and a movement of feet — a splashing from the water. A man, too frightened to drop the portmanteau he carried on his shoulder, swung round and sent me staggering with a blow from the corner of his burden. A woman thrust at me with her hand and rushed past me. I turned, too, with the rush of the people, but I was not too terrified for thought. The terrible Heat-Ray was in my mind. To get under water! That was it!.

'Get under water!' I shouted unheeded.

I faced about again, and rushed towards the approaching Martian — rushed right down the gravelly beach and headlong into the water. Others did the same. A boatload of people putting back came leaping out as I rushed past. The stones under my feet were muddy and slippery, and the river was so low that I ran perhaps twenty feet scarcely waist-deep. Then, as the Martian towered overhead scarcely a couple of hundred yards away. I flung myself forward under the surface. The splashes of the people in the boats leaping into the river sounded like thunder-claps in my ears. People were landing hastily on both sides of the river.

But the Martian machine took no more notice for the moment of the people running this way and that than a man would of the confusion of ants in a nest against which his foot has kicked. When, half suffocated, I raised my head above water the Martian's hood pointed at the batteries that were still firing across the river, and as it advanced it swung loose what must have been the generator of the Heat-Ray.

In another moment it was on the bank, and in a stride wading half-way across. The knees of its foremost legs bent at the farther bank, and in another moment it had raised itself to its full height again, close to the village of Shepperton. Forthwith the six guns, which, unknown to anyone on the right bank, had been hidden behind the outskirts of that village, fired simultaneously. The sudden near concussions, the last close upon the first, made my heart jump. The monster was already raising the case generating the Heat-Ray, as the first shell burst six yards above the hood.

I gave a cry of astonishment. I saw and thought nothing of the other four Martian monsters: my attention was riveted upon the nearer incident. Simultaneously two other shells burst in the air near the body as the hood twisted round in time to receive, but not in time to dodge, the fourth shell.

The shell burst clean in the face of the thing. The hood bulged, flashed, was whirled off in a dozen tattered fragments of glittering metal.

'Hit!' shouted I, with something between a scream and a cheer.

I heard answering shouts from the people in the water about me. I could have leapt out of the water with that momentary exultation.

The decapitated colossus reeled like a drunken giant; but it did not fall over. It recovered its balance by a miracle, and, no longer heeding its steps, and with the camera that fired the Heat-Ray now rigidly upheld, it reeled swiftly upon Shepperton. The living intelligence, the Martian within the hood, was slain and splashed to the four winds of heaven, and the thing was now but a mere intricate device of metal whirling to destruction. It drove along in a straight line, incapable of guidance. It struck the tower of Shepperton Church, smashing it down as the impact of a battering-ram might have done, swerved aside, blundered on, and collapsed with a tremendous impact into the river out of my sight.

A violent explosion shook the air, and a spout of water, steam, mud, and shattered metal, shot far up into the sky. As the camera of the Heat-Ray hit the water, the latter had incontinently flashed into steam. In another moment a huge wave, like a muddy tidal bore, but almost scaldingly hot, came sweeping round the bend up-stream. I saw people struggling shorewards, and heard their screaming and shouting faintly above the seething and roar of the Martian's collapse.

For the moment I heeded nothing of the heat, forgot the patent need of self-preservation. I splashed through the tumultuous water, pushing aside a man in black to do so, until I could see round the bend. Half a dozen deserted boats pitched aimlessly upon the confusion of the waves. The fallen Martian came into sight down-stream, lying across the river, and for the most part submerged.

Thick clouds of steam were pouring off the wreckage, and through the tumultuously whirling wisps I could see, intermittently and vaguely, the gigantic limbs churning the water and flinging a splash and spray of mud and froth into the air. The tentacles swayed and struck like living arms, and, save for the helpless purposelessness of these movements, it was as if some wounded thing struggled for life amidst the waves. Enormous quantities of a ruddy brown fluid were spurting up in noisy jets out of the machine.

My attention was diverted from this sight by a furious yelling, like that of the thing called a siren in our manufacturing towns. A man, knee-deep near the towing-path, shouted inaudibly to me and pointed. Looking back, I saw the other Martians advancing with gigantic strides down the river-bank from the direction of Chertsey. The Shepperton guns spoke this time unavailingly.

At that I ducked at once under water, and, holding my breath until movement was an agony, blundered painfully along under the surface as long as I could. The water was in a tumult about me, and rapidly growing hotter.

When for a moment I raised my head to take breath, and throw the hair and water from my eyes, the steam was rising in a whirling white fog that at first hid the Martians altogether. The noise was deafening. Then I saw them dimly, colossal figures of grey, magnified by the mist.

They had passed by me, and two were stooping over the frothing tumultuous ruins of their comrade.

The third and fourth stood beside him in the water, one perhaps 200 yards from me, the other towards Laleham. The generators of the Heat-Rays waved high, and the hissing beams smote down this way and that.

The air was full of sound, a deafening and confusing conflict of noises, the clangorous din of the Martians, the crash of falling houses, the thud of trees, fences, sheds, flashing into flame, and the crackling and roaring of fire. Dense black smoke was leaping up to mingle with the steam from the river, and as the Heat-Ray went to and fro over Weybridge, its impact was marked by flashes of incandescent white, that gave place at once to a smoky dance of lurid flames. The nearer houses still stood intact, awaiting their fate, shadowy, faint and pallid in the steam, with the fire behind them going to and fro.

For a moment, perhaps, I stood there, breast-high in the almost boiling water, dumbfounded at my position; hopeless of escape. Through the reek I could see the people who had been with me in the river scrambling out of the water through the reeds, like little frogs hurrying through grass from the advance of a man, or running to and fro in utter dismay on the towing-path.

Then suddenly the white flashes of the Heat-Ray came leaping towards me. The houses caved in as they dissolved at its touch, and darted out flames; the trees changed to fire with a roar. It flickered up and down the towing-path, licking off the people who ran this way and that, and came down to the water's edge not fifty yards from where I stood. It swept across the river to Shepperton, and the water in its track rose in a boiling wheal crested with steam. I turned shoreward.

In another moment the huge wave, well-nigh at the boiling-point, had rushed upon me. I screamed aloud, and scalded, half-blinded, agonized, I staggered through the leaping, hissing water towards the shore. Had my foot stumbled, it would have been the end. I fell helplessly, in full sight of the Martians, upon the broad, bare gravelly spit that runs down to mark the angle of the Wey and Thames. I expected nothing but death.

I have a dim memory of the foot of a Martian coming down within a score of yards of my head, driving straight into the loose gravel, whirling it this way and that, and lifting again; of a long suspense, and then of the four carrying the debris of their comrade between them, now clear, and then presently faint, through a veil of smoke, receding interminably, as it seemed to me, across a vast space of river and meadow. And then, very slowly, I realised that by a miracle I had escaped.

See also M 4, N Introduction.   'The War of the Worlds', chap. 12.

Further Reading

H. G. Wells, 'The Time Machine', 1895; 'The Island of Dr Moreau', 1896.
Bernard Bergonzi, 'The Early H. G. Wells', 1961, pp. 123-39.

The Social Machine

D. H. Lawrence (1885–1930)

D. H. Lawrence, son of a Nottinghamshire miner, with a more immediate experience of industrialisation than many nineteenth-century commentators, developed an individual criticism of its effects. 'The industrial problem', he wrote in 1929, 'arises from the base forcing of all human energy into a competition of mere acquisition.' He attacked what he felt to be the invasion of the human psyche at a deep level by impoverished and cramping conceptions of a desirable human life, and he explores these issues particularly in 'The Rainbow' (1915), and 'Women in Love' (1921). The first extract is a brief illustration of this kind of analysis. Lawrence also had a definite, though idiosyncratic, sense of history. He wrote for the future, hoping that his work would help to sustain the quality of life he most valued: openness and sensitivity of feeling. In the second extract, his description of the Italian peasants illustrates something of this quality. It also voices the positive attractiveness of the new world, characterised by money and change, for those whose pattern of life had been changeless for centuries. Both extracts are from 'Twilight in Italy' (1915), an account of Lawrence's travels and sojourn in north Italy in 1912-14 when he had begun work on 'The Rainbow'.

P 15

Lucerne and its lake were as irritating as ever — like the wrapper round milk chocolate. I could not sleep even one night there: I took the steamer down the lake, to the very last station. There I found a good German inn, and was happy.

There was a tall thin young man, whose face was red and inflamed from the sun. I thought he was a German tourist. He had just come in;

and he was eating bread and milk. He and I were alone in the eating-room. He was looking at an illustrated paper.

'Does the steamer stop here all night?' I asked him in German, hearing the boat bustling and blowing her steam on the water outside, and glancing round at her lights, red and white, in the pitch darkness.

He only shook his head over his bread and milk, and did not lift his face.

'Are you English, then?' I said.

No one but an Englishman would have hidden his face in a bowl of milk, and have shaken his red ears in such painful confusion.

'Yes,' he said, 'I am.'

And I started almost out of my skin at the unexpected London accent. It was as if one suddenly found oneself in the Tube.

'So am I,' I said, 'Where have you come from?'

Then he began, like a general explaining his plans, to tell me. He had walked round over the Furka Pass, had been on foot four or five days. He had walked tremendously. Knowing no German, and nothing of the mountains, he had set off alone on this tour: he had a fortnight's holiday. So he had come over the Rhône Glacier across the Furka and down from Andermatt to the Lake. On this last day he had walked about thirty mountain miles.

'But weren't you tired?' I said, aghast.

He was. Under the inflamed redness of his sun-and-wind-and-snow-burned face he was sick with fatigue. He had done over a hundred miles in the last four days.

'Did you enjoy it?' I asked.

'Oh yes. I wanted to do it all.' He wanted to do it, and he *had* done it. But God knows what he wanted to do it for. He had now one day at Lucerne, one day at Interlaken and Berne, then London.

I was sorry for him in my soul, he was so cruelly tired, so perishingly victorious.

'Why did you do so much?' I said, 'Why did you come on foot all down the valley when you could have taken the train? Was it worth it?'

'I think so,' he said.

Yet he was sick with fatigue and over-exhaustion. His eyes were quite dark, sightless: he seemed to have lost the power of seeing, to be virtually blind. He hung his head forward when he had to write a post card, as if he felt his way. But he turned his post card so that I should not see to whom it was addressed; not that I was interested; only I noticed his little, cautious, English movement of privacy.

'What time will you be going on?' I asked.

'When is the first steamer?' he said, and he turned out a guide-book with a time-table. He would leave at about seven.

'But why so early?' I said to him.

He must be in Lucerne at a certain hour, and at Interlaken in the evening.

'I suppose you will rest when you get to London?' I said.

He looked at me quickly, reservedly.

I was drinking beer: I asked him wouldn't he have something. He thought a moment, then said he would have another glass of hot milk. The landlord came —'And bread?' he asked.

The Englishman refused. He could not eat, really. Also he was poor; he had to husband his money. The landlord brought the milk and asked me, when would the gentleman want to go away. So I made arrangements between the landlord and the stranger. But the Englishman was slightly uncomfortable at my intervention. He did not like me to know what he would have for breakfast.

I could feel so well the machine that had him in its grip. He slaved for a year, mechanically, in London, riding in the Tube, working in the office. Then for a fortnight he was let free. So he rushed to Switzerland, with a tour planned out, and with just enough money to see him through, and to buy presents at Interlaken: bits of the edelweiss pottery: I could see him going home with them.

So he arrived, and with amazing, pathetic courage set forth on foot in a strange land, to face strange landlords, with no language but English at his command, and his purse definitely limited. Yet he wanted to go among the mountains, to cross a glacier. So he had walked on and on, like one possessed, ever forward. His name might have been Excelsior, indeed.

But then, when he reached his Furka, only to walk along the ridge and to descend on the same side! My God, it was killing to the soul. And here he was, down again from the mountains, beginning his journey home again: steamer and train and steamer and train and Tube, till he was back in the machine.

It hadn't let him go, and he knew it. Hence his cruel self-torture of fatigue, his cruel exercise of courage. He who hung his head in his milk in torment when I asked him a question in German, what courage had he not needed to take this his very first trip out of England, alone, on foot!

His eyes were dark and deep with unfathomable courage. Yet he was going back in the morning. He was going back. All he had courage for was to go back. He would go back, though he died by inches. Why not? It was killing him, it was like living loaded with irons. But he had the courage to submit, to die that way, since it was the way allotted to him.

The way he sank on the table in exhaustion, drinking his milk, his will, nevertheless, so perfect and unblemished, triumphant, though his body was broken and in anguish, was almost too much to bear. My heart was wrung for my countryman, wrung till it bled.

I could not bear to understand my countryman, a man who worked for his living, as I had worked, as nearly all my countrymen work. He would not give in. On his holiday he would walk, to fulfil his purpose, walk on; no matter how cruel the effort were, he would not rest, he would not relinquish his purpose nor abate his will, not by one jot or tittle. His body must pay whatever his will demanded, though it were torture.

It all seemed to me so foolish. I was almost in tears. He went to bed. I walked by the dark lake, and talked to the girl in the inn. She was a pleasant girl: it was a pleasant inn, a homely place. One could be happy there.

In the morning it was sunny, the lake was blue. By night I should be nearly at the crest of my journey. I was glad.

The Englishman had gone. I looked for his name in the book. It was written in a fair, clerkly hand. He lived at Streatham. Suddenly I hated him. The dogged fool, to keep his nose on the grindstone like that. What was all his courage but the very tip-top of cowardice? What a vile nature — almost Sadish, proud, like the infamous Red Indians, of being able to stand torture.

The landlord came to talk to me. He was fat and comfortable and too respectful. But I had to tell him all the Englishman had done, in the way of a holiday, just to shame his own fat, ponderous, inn-keeper's luxuriousness that was too gross. Then all I got out of his enormous comfortableness was:

'Yes, that's a *very* long step to take.'

'Twilight in Italy', pp. 154-8.

P 16

It was when Marco was a baby that Paolo had gone to America. They were poor on San Gaudenzio. There were the few olive trees, the grapes, and the fruit; there was the one cow. But these scarcely made a living. Neither was Maria content with the real peasant's lot any more, polenta at midday and vegetable soup in the evening, and no way out, nothing to look forward to, no future, only this eternal present. She had been in service, and had eaten bread and drunk coffee, and known the flux and variable chance of life. She had departed from the old static conception. She knew what one might be, given a certain chance. The fixture was the thing she militated against. So Paolo went to America, to California, into the gold-mines.

Maria wanted the future, the endless possibility of life on earth. She wanted her sons to be freer, to achieve a new plane of living. The peasant's life was a slave's life, she said, railing against the poverty and the drudgery. And it was quite true, Paolo and Giovanni worked twelve and fourteen hours a day at heavy laborious work that would have broken an Englishman. And there was nothing at the end of it. Yet Paolo was even happy so. This was the truth to him.

It was the mother who wanted things different. It was she who railed and railed against the miserable life of the peasants. When we were going to throw to the fowls a dry broken penny roll of white bread, Maria said, with anger and shame and resentment in her voice: 'Give it to Marco, he will eat it. It isn't too dry for him.'

White bread was a treat for them even now, when everybody eats bread. And Maria Fiori hated it, that bread should be a treat to her children, when it was the meanest food of all the rest of the world. She was in opposition to this order. She did not want her sons to be peasants, fixed and static as posts driven in the earth. She wanted them to be in the great flux of life in the midst of all possibilities. So she at length sent Paolo to America to the gold-mines. Meanwhile, she covered the wall of her parlour with picture postcards, to bring the outer world of cities and industries into her house.

Paolo was entirely remote from Maria's world. He had not yet even grasped the fact of money, not thoroughly. He reckoned in land and olive trees. So he had the old fatalistic attitude to his circumstances, even to his food. The earth was the Lord's and the fulness thereof; also the leanness thereof. Paolo could only do his part and leave the rest. If he ate in plenty, having oil and wine and sausage in the house, and plenty of maize-meal, he was glad with the Lord. If he ate meagrely, of poor polenta, that was fate, it was the skies that ruled these things, and no man ruled the skies. He took his fate as it fell from the skies.

Maria was exorbitant about money. She would charge us all she could for what we had and for what was done for us.

Yet she was not mean in her soul. In her soul she was in a state of anger because of her own closeness. It was a violation of her strong animal nature. Yet her mind had wakened to the value of money. She knew she could alter her position, the position of her children, by virtue of money. She knew it was only money that made the difference between master and servant. And this was all the difference she would acknowledge. So she ruled her life according to money. Her supreme passion was to be mistress rather than servant, her supreme aspiration for her children was that in the end they might be masters and not servants.

Paolo was untouched by all this. For him there was some divinity about a master which even America had not destroyed. If we came in for supper whilst the family was still at table he would have the children at once take their plates to the wall, he would have Maria at once set the table for us, though their own meal were never finished. And this was not servility, it was the dignity of a religious conception. Paolo regarded us as belonging to the Signoria, those who are elect, near to God. And this was part of his religious service. His life was a ritual. It was very beautiful, but it made me unhappy, the purity of his spirit was so sacred and the actual facts seemed such a sacrilege to it. Maria was nearer to the actual truth when she said that money was the only distinction. But Paolo had hold of an eternal truth, where hers was temporal. Only Paolo misapplied this eternal truth. He should not have given Giovanni the inferior status and a fat, mean Italian tradesman the superior. That was false, a real falsity. Maria knew it and hated it. But Paolo could not distinguish between the accident of riches and the aristocracy of the spirit. So Maria rejected him altogether, and went to the other extreme. We were all human beings like herself; naked, there was no distinction between us, no higher nor lower. But we were possessed of more money than she. And she had to steer her course between these two conceptions. The money alone made the real distinction, the separation; the being, the life made the common level.

Paolo had the curious peasant's avarice also, but it was not meanness. It was a sort of religious conservation of his own power, his own self. Fortunately he could leave all business transactions on our account to Maria, so that his relation with us was purely ritualistic. He would have given me anything, trusting implicitly that I would fulfil my own nature as Signore, one of those more godlike, nearer the light of perfection than himself, a peasant. It was pure bliss to him to bring us the first-fruit of the garden, it was like laying it on an altar.

And his fulfilment was in a fine, subtle, exquisite relationship, not of manners, but subtle interappreciation. He worshipped a finer understanding and a subtler tact. A further fineness and dignity and freedom in bearing was to him an approach towards the divine, so he loved men best of all, they fulfilled his soul. A woman was always a woman, and sex was a low level whereon he did not esteem himself. But a man, a doer, the instrument of God, he was really godlike. . . .

Giovanni was patiently labouring to learn a little English. Paolo knew only four or five words, the chief of which were 'a'right', 'boss', 'bread', and 'day'. The youth had these by heart, and was studying a little more. He was very graceful and lovable, but he found it difficult to learn. A confused light, like hot tears, would come into his eyes when he had again forgotten the phrase. But he carried the paper about with him, and he made steady progress.

He would go to America, he also. Not for anything would he stay in San Gaudenzio. His dream was to be gone. He would come back. The world was not San Gaudenzio to Giovanni.

The old order, the order of Paolo and of Pietro di Paoli, the aristocratic order of the supreme God, God the Father, the Lord, was passing away from the beautiful little territory. The household no longer receives its food, oil and wine and maize, from out of the earth in the motion of fate. The earth is annulled, and money takes its place. The landowner, who is the lieutenant of God and of Fate, like Abraham, he, too, is annulled. There is now the order of the rich, which supersedes the order of the Signoria.

It is passing away from Italy as it has passed from England. The peasant is passing away, the workman is taking his place. The stability is gone. Paolo is a ghost, Maria is the living body. And the new order means sorrow for the Italian more even than it has meant for us. But he will have the new order.

San Gaudenzio is already becoming a thing of the past. Below the house, where the land drops in sharp slips to the sheer cliff's edge, over which it is Maria's constant fear that Felicina will tumble, there are the deserted lemon gardens of the little territory, snug down below. They are invisible till one descends by tiny paths, sheer down into them. And there they stand, the pillars and walls erect, but a dead emptiness prevailing, lemon trees all dead, gone, a few vines in their place. It is only twenty years since the lemon trees finally perished of a disease and were not renewed. But the deserted terrace, shut between great walls, descending in their openness full to the south, to the lake and the mountain opposite, seem more terrible than Pompeii in their silence and utter seclusion. The grape hyacinths flower in the cracks, the lizards run, this strange place hangs suspended and forgotten, forgotten for ever, its erect pillars utterly meaningless.

I used to sit and write in the great loft of the lemon-house, high up, far, far from the ground, the open front giving across the lake and the mountain snow opposite, flush with twilight. The old matting and boards, the old disused implements of lemon culture made shadows in the deserted place. Then there would come the call from the back, away above: '*Venga, venga mangiare.*'

We ate in the kitchen, where the olive and laurel wood burned in the open fireplace. It was always soup in the evening. Then we played games or cards, all playing; or there was singing, with the accordion, and sometimes a rough mountain peasant with a guitar.

But it is all passing away. Giovanni is in America, unless he has come back to the War. He will not want to live in San Gaudenzio when he is a man, he says. He and Marco will not spend their lives wringing a little oil and wine out of the rocky soil, even if they are not killed in the fighting which is going on at the end of the lake. In my loft by the lemon-houses now I should hear the guns. And Giovanni kissed me with a kind of supplication when I went on to the steamer, as if he were beseeching for a soul. His eyes were bright and clear and lit up with courage. He will make a good fight for the new soul he wants — that is, if they do not kill him in this War.

See also A 1.   'Twilight in Italy', pp. 94-6, 101-2.

Further Reading

D. H. Lawrence, 'Odour of Chrysanthemums', 'Goose Fair', 'Fanny and Annie', in 'Collected Tales'; 'Nottingham and the Mining Countryside', in 'Selected Essays', Penguin, 1950.

Notes on the Editors

CHRISTOPHER HARVIE is Lecturer in History at the Open University. He was born in Motherwell in 1944 and holds a degree from Edinburgh University where he was subsequently engaged in postgraduate research and tutoring before joining the staff of the Open University in 1969. His main research interest is in the movement to reform English universities in the mid-nineteenth century, and in the politics of contemporary university intelligentsia.

GRAHAM MARTIN is Reader in Literature at the Open University. He was born in Glasgow in 1927. After gaining a B.Sc. in biochemistry at the University of St Andrews, he studied for a B.A. in English Literature and Language at Jesus College, Oxford. His postgraduate work in English Literature was done at Merton College. Mr Martin has held lectureships at Leeds University and Bedford College, London. He has been a part-time tutor in Literature for the University of Oxford Extramural Delegacy. His interests focus on Romantic poetry and twentieth-century English literature.

AARON SCHARF is Professor of Fine Arts at the Open University. He was born in the United States in 1922. After gaining a B.A. at the University of California in painting and anthropology, he studied for a Ph.D. at the Courtauld Institute of Art, London. Professor Scharf was Head of the Department of History of Art and Complementary Studies, St Martin's School of Art, from 1961 to 1969. His special field of interest is in the history of art and photography in the nineteenth and twentieth centuries.

Index

References to illustrations and their captions are shown in italic type.